The wind will not stop. Gusts of sand swirl before me, stinging my face. But there is still too much to see and marvel at, the world very much alive in the bright light and wind, exultant with the fever of spring, the delight of morning. Strolling on, it seems to me that the strangeness and wonder of existence are emphasized here, in the desert, by the comparative sparsity of the flora and fauna: life not crowded upon life as in other places but scattered abroad in spareness and simplicity, with a generous gift of space for each herb and bush and tree, each stem of grass, so that the living organism stands out bold and brave and vivid against the lifeless sand and barren rock. The extreme clarity of the desert light is equaled by the extreme individuation of desert life-forms. Love flowers best in openness and freedom.

Since its first publication in 1968, DESERT SOLITAIRE has steadily attracted a legion of fierce advocates. It reaches them with the directness of its theme—there is a happiness a man can encounter that is unique when he is a part of the land, especially the desert.

DESERT SOLITAIRE

A SEASON IN THE WILDERNESS

EDWARD ABBEY

BALLANTINE BOOKS · NEW YORK

Library of Congress Catalog Card Number: 67-26166

ISBN 0-345-27866-6

This edition published by arrangement with McGraw-Hill Book Company

Manufactured in the United States of America

First Ballantine Books Edition: September 1971
Ninth Printing: April 1981

Cover photograph by Eliot Porter

for Josh and Aaron

CONTENTS

AUTHOR'S INTRODUCTION

ABOUT TEN years ago I took a job as a seasonal park ranger in a place called Arches National Monument near the little town of Moab in southeast Utah. Why I went there no longer matters; what I found there is the subject of this book.

My job began on the first of April and ended on the last day of September. I liked the work and the canyon country and returned the following year for a second season. I would have returned the third year too and each year thereafter but unfortunately for me the Arches, a primitive place when I first went there, was developed and improved so well that I had to leave. But after a number of years I returned anyway, traveling full circle, and stayed for a third season. In this way I was better able to appreciate the changes which had been made during my absence.

Those were all good times, especially the first two seasons when the tourist business was poor and the time passed extremely slowly, as time should pass, with the days lingering and long, spacious and free as the summers of childhood. There was time enough for once to do nothing, or next to nothing, and most of the substance of this book is drawn, sometimes direct and unchanged, from the pages of the journals I kept and filled through the undivided, seamless days of those marvelous summers. The remainder of the book consists of digressions and excursions into ideas and places that border in varied ways upon that central season in the canyonlands.

This is not primarily a book about the desert. In recording my impressions of the natural scene I have striven above all for accuracy, since I believe that there is a kind of poetry, even a kind of truth, in simple fact. But the desert is a vast world, an oceanic world, as deep in its way and complex and various as the sea. Language makes a mighty loose net with which to go fishing for simple facts, when facts are infinite. If a man knew enough he could write a whole book about the juniper tree. Not juniper trees in general but that one particular juniper tree which grows from a ledge of naked sandstone near the old entrance to Arches National Monument. What I have tried to do then is something a bit different. Since you cannot get the desert into a book any more than a fisherman can haul up the sea with his nets, I have tried to create a world of words in which the desert figures more as medium than as material. Not imitation but evocation has been the goal.

Aside from this modest pretension the book is fairly plain and straight. Certain faults will be obvious to the general reader, of course, and for these I wish to apologize. I quite agree that much of the book will seem coarse, rude, bad-tempered, violently prejudiced, unconstructive—even frankly antisocial in its point of view. Serious critics, serious librarians, serious associate professors of English will if they read this work dislike it intensely; at least I hope so. To others I can only say that if the book has virtues they cannot be disentangled from the faults; that there is a way of being wrong which is also sometimes necessarily right.

It will be objected that the book deals too much with mere appearances, with the surface of things, and fails to engage and reveal the patterns of unifying relationships which form the true underlying reality of existence. Here I must confess that I know nothing whatever about true underlying reality, having never met any. There are many people who say they have, I know, but they've been luckier than I.

For my own part I am pleased enough with surfaces —in fact they alone seem to me to be of much importance. Such things for example as the grasp of a child's hand in your own, the flavor of an apple, the embrace of friend or lover, the silk of a girl's thigh, the sunlight on rock and leaves, the feel of music, the bark of a tree, the abrasion of granite and sand, the plunge of clear water into a pool, the face of the wind—what else is there? What else do we need?

Regrettably I have found it unavoidable to write some harsh words about my seasonal employer the National Park Service, Department of the Interior, United States Government. Even the Government itself has not entirely escaped censure. I wish to point out therefore that the Park Service has labored under severe pressure from powerful forces for many decades and that under the circumstances and so far it has done its work rather well. As governmental agencies go the Park Service is a good one, far superior to most. This I attribute not to the administrators of the Park Service—like administrators everywhere they are distinguished chiefly by their ineffable mediocrity —but to the actual working rangers in the field, the majority of whom are capable, honest, dedicated men. Preeminent among those I have known personally is Mr. Bates Wilson of Moab, Utah, who might justly be considered the founder of Canyonlands National Park. He cannot be held responsible for any of the opinions expressed herein, but he is responsible for much of what understanding I have of a country we both love.

A note on names. All of the persons and places men-

tioned in this book are or were real. However for the sake
of their privacy I have invented fictitious names for some
of the people I once knew in the Moab area and in a
couple of cases relocated them in space and time. Those
who read this will, I hope, understand and forgive me;
the others will not mind.

Finally a word of caution:

Do not jump into your automobile next June and rush
out to the Canyon country hoping to see some of that
which I have attempted to evoke in these pages. In the
first place you can't see *anything* from a car; you've got
to get out of the goddamned contraption and walk, better
yet crawl, on hands and knees, over the sandstone and
through the thornbush and cactus. When traces of blood
begin to mark your trail you'll see something, maybe.
Probably not. In the second place most of what I write
about in this book is already gone or going under fast. This
is not a travel guide but an elegy. A memorial. You're
holding a tombstone in your hands. A bloody rock. Don't
drop it on your foot—throw it at something big and glassy.
What do you have to lose?

> E. A.
> April 1967
> Nelson's Marine Bar
> Hoboken

Give me silence, water, hope
Give me struggle, iron, volcanoes
                              —Neruda

DESERT SOLITAIRE

THE FIRST MORNING

THIS IS the most beautiful place on earth.

There are many such places. Every man, every woman, carries in heart and mind the image of the ideal place, the right place, the one true home, known or unknown, actual or visionary. A houseboat in Kashmir, a view down Atlantic Avenue in Brooklyn, a gray gothic farmhouse two stories high at the end of a red dog road in the Allegheny Mountains, a cabin on the shore of a blue lake in spruce and fir country, a greasy alley near the Hoboken waterfront, or even, possibly, for those of a less demanding sensibility, the world to be seen from a comfortable apartment high in the tender, velvety smog of Manhattan, Chicago, Paris, Tokyo, Rio or Rome—there's no limit to the human capacity for the homing sentiment. Theologians, sky pilots, astronauts have even felt the appeal of home calling to them from up above, in the cold black outback of intersteller space.

1

For myself I'll take Moab, Utah. I don't mean the town itself, of course, but the country which surrounds it—the canyonlands. The slickrock desert. The red dust and the burnt cliffs and the lonely sky—all that which lies beyond the end of the roads.

The choice became apparent to me this morning when I stepped out of a Park Service housetrailer—my caravan— to watch for the first time in my life the sun come up over the hoodoo stone of Arches National Monument.

I wasn't able to see much of it last night. After driving all day from Albuquerque—450 miles—I reached Moab after dark in cold, windy, clouded weather. At park headquarters north of town I met the superintendent and the chief ranger, the only permanent employees, ex- cept for one maintenance man, in this particular unit of America's national park system. After coffee they gave me a key to the housetrailer and directions on how to reach it; I am required to live and work not at headquarters but at this one-man station some twenty miles back in the in- terior, on my own. The way I wanted it, naturally, or I'd never have asked for the job.

Leaving the headquarters area and the lights of Moab, I drove twelve miles farther north on the highway until I came to a dirt road on the right, where a small wooden sign pointed the way: Arches National Monument Eight Miles. I left the pavement, turned east into the howling wilderness. Wind roaring out of the northwest, black clouds across the stars—all I could see were clumps of brush and scattered junipers along the roadside. Then another modest signboard:

WARNING: QUICKSAND
DO NOT CROSS WASH
WHEN WATER IS RUNNING

The wash looked perfectly dry in my headlights. I drove down, across, up the other side and on into the night. Glimpses of weird humps of pale rock on either side, like petrified elephants, dinosaurs, stone-age hobgoblins. Now and then something alive scurried across the road: kangaroo mice, a jackrabbit, an animal that looked like a cross between a raccoon and a squirrel—the ringtail cat. Farther on a pair of mule deer started from the brush and bounded obliquely through the beams of my lights, raising puffs of dust which the wind, moving faster than my pickup truck, caught and carried ahead of me out of sight into the dark. The road, narrow and rocky, twisted sharply left and right, dipped in and out of tight ravines, climbing by degrees toward a summit which I would see only in the light of the coming day.

Snow was swirling through the air when I crossed the unfenced line and passed the boundary marker of the park. A quarter-mile beyond I found the ranger station— a wide place in the road, an informational display under a lean-to shelter, and fifty yards away the little tin government housetrailer where I would be living for the next six months.

A cold night, a cold wind, the snow falling like confetti. In the lights of the truck I unlocked the housetrailer, got out bedroll and baggage and moved in. By flashlight I found the bed, unrolled my sleeping bag, pulled off my boots and crawled in and went to sleep at once. The last I knew was the shaking of the trailer in the wind and the sound, from inside, of hungry mice scampering around with the good news that their long lean lonesome winter was over—their friend and provider had finally arrived.

This morning I awake before sunrise, stick my head out of the sack, peer through a frosty window at a scene dim and vague with flowing mists, dark fantastic shapes looming beyond. An unlikely landscape.

I get up, moving about in long underwear and socks, stooping carefully under the low ceiling and the lower doorways of the housetrailer, a machine for living built so efficiently and compactly there's hardly room for a man to breathe. An iron lung it is, with windows and venetian blinds.

The mice are silent, watching me from their hiding places, but the wind is still blowing and outside the ground is covered with snow. Cold as a tomb, a jail, a cave; I lie down on the dusty floor, on the cold linoleum sprinkled with mouse turds, and light the pilot on the butane heater. Once this thing gets going the place warms up fast, in a dense unhealthy way, with a layer of heat under the ceiling where my head is and nothing but frigid air from the knees down. But we've got all the indispensable conveniences: gas cookstove, gas refrigerator, hot water heater, sink with running water (if the pipes aren't frozen), storage cabinets and shelves, everything within arm's reach of everything else. The gas comes from two steel bottles in a shed outside; the water comes by gravity flow from a tank buried in a hill close by. Quite luxurious for the wilds. There's even a shower stall and a flush toilet with a dead rat in the bowl. Pretty soft. My poor mother raised five children without any of these luxuries and might be doing without them yet if it hadn't been for Hitler, war and general prosperity.

Time to get dressed, get out and have a look at the lay of the land, fix a breakfast. I try to pull on my boots but they're stiff as iron from the cold. I light a burner on the stove and hold the boots upside down above the flame until they are malleable enough to force my feet into. I put on a coat and step outside. In the center of the world, God's navel, Abbey's country, the red wasteland.

The sun is not yet in sight but signs of the advent are plain to see. Lavender clouds sail like a fleet of ships across the pale green dawn; each cloud, planed flat on the wind, has a base of fiery gold. Southeast, twenty miles by line of sight, stand the peaks of the Sierra La Sal, twelve to thirteen thousand feet above sea level, all covered with snow and rosy in the morning sunlight. The air is dry and clear as well as cold; the last fogbanks left over from last night's storm are scudding away like ghosts, fading into nothing before the wind and the sunrise.

The view is open and perfect in all directions except to the west where the ground rises and the skyline is only a few hundred yards away. Looking toward the mountains I can see the dark gorge of the Colorado River five or six miles away, carved through the sandstone mesa, though nothing of the river itself down inside the gorge. Southward, on the far side of the river, lies the Moab valley between thousand-foot walls of rock, with the town of Moab somewhere on the valley floor, too small to be seen from here. Beyond the Moab valley is more canyon and tableland stretching away to the Blue Mountains fifty miles south. On the north and northwest I see the Roan Cliffs and the Book Cliffs, the two-level face of the Uinta Plateau. Along the foot of those cliffs, maybe thirty miles off, invisible from where I stand, runs U.S. 6–50, a major east-west artery of commerce, traffic and rubbish, and the main line of the Denver–Rio Grande Railroad. To the east, under the spreading sunrise, are more mesas, more canyons, league on league of red cliff and arid tablelands, extending through purple haze over the bulging curve of the planet to the ranges of Colorado—a sea of desert.

Within this vast perimeter, in the middle ground and foreground of the picture, a rather personal demesne, are the 33,000 acres of Arches National Monument of which I am now sole inhabitant, usufructuary, observer and custodian.

What are the Arches? From my place in front of the housetrailer I can see several of the hundred or more of them which have been discovered in the park. These are natural arches, holes in the rock, windows in stone, no two alike, as varied in form as in dimension. They range in size from holes just big enough to walk through to openings large enough to contain the dome of the Capitol building in Washington, D.C. Some resemble jug handles or flying buttresses, others natural bridges but with this technical distinction: a natural bridge spans a watercourse—a natural arch does not. The arches were formed through hundreds of thousands of years by the weathering of the huge sandstone walls, or fins, in which they are found. Not the work of a cosmic hand, nor sculptured by sand-bearing winds, as many people prefer to believe, the arches came into being and continue to come into being through the modest wedging action of rain-water, melting snow, frost, and ice, aided by gravity. In color they shade from off-white through buff, pink, brown and red, tones which also change with the time of day and the moods of the light, the weather, the sky.

Standing there, gaping at this monstrous and inhuman spectacle of rock and cloud and sky and space, I feel a ridiculous greed and possessiveness come over me. I want to know it all, possess it all, embrace the entire scene intimately, deeply, totally, as a man desires a beautiful woman. An insane wish? Perhaps not—at least there's nothing else, no one human, to dispute possession with me.

The snow-covered ground glimmers with a dull blue light, reflecting the sky and the approaching sunrise. Leading away from me the narrow dirt road, an alluring and primitive track into nowhere, meanders down the slope and toward the heart of the labyrinth of naked stone. Near the first group of arches, looming over a bend in the road, is a balanced rock about fifty feet high, mounted on a pedestal of equal height; it looks like a head from Easter Island, a stone god or a petrified ogre.

Like a god, like an ogre? The personification of the natural is exactly the tendency I wish to suppress in myself, to eliminate for good. I am here not only to evade for a while the clamor and filth and confusion of the cultural apparatus but also to confront, immediately and directly if it's possible, the bare bones of existence, the elemental and fundamental, the bedrock which sustains us. I want to be able to look at and into a juniper tree, a piece of quartz, a vulture, a spider, and see it as it is in itself, devoid of all humanly ascribed qualities, anti-Kantian, even the categories of scientific description. To meet God or Medusa face to face, even if it means risking everything human in myself. I dream of a hard and brutal mysticism in which the naked self merges with a non-human world and yet somehow survives still intact, individual, separate. Paradox and bedrock.

Well—the sun will be up in a few minutes and I haven't

even begun to make coffee. I take more baggage from my pickup, the grub box and cooking gear, go back in the trailer and start breakfast. Simply breathing, in a place like this, arouses the appetite. The orange juice is frozen, the milk slushy with ice. Still chilly enough inside the trailer to turn my breath to vapor. When the first rays of the sun strike the cliffs I fill a mug with steaming coffee and sit in the doorway facing the sunrise, hungry for the warmth.

Suddenly it comes, the flaming globe, blazing on the pinnacles and minarets and balanced rocks, on the canyon walls and through the windows in the sandstone fins. We greet each other, sun and I, across the black void of ninety-three million miles. The snow glitters between us, acres of diamonds almost painful to look at. Within an hour all the snow exposed to the sunlight will be gone and the rock will be damp and steaming. Within minutes, even as I watch, melting snow begins to drip from the branches of a juniper nearby; drops of water streak slowly down the side of the trailerhouse.

I am not alone after all. Three ravens are wheeling near the balanced rock, squawking at each other and at the dawn. I'm sure they're as delighted by the return of the sun as I am and I wish I knew the language. I'd sooner exchange ideas with the birds on earth than learn to carry on intergalactic communications with some obscure race of humanoids on a satellite planet from the world of Betelgeuse. First things first. The ravens cry out in husky voices, blue-black wings flapping against the golden sky. Over my shoulder comes the sizzle and smell of frying bacon.

That's the way it was this morning.

SOLITAIRE

STILL THE first day, All Fools' Day, here at the Center. Merle McRae and Floyd Bence—the superintendent and the chief ranger—appear at noon, bringing me five hundred gallons of water in a tank truck and a Park Service pickup truck outfitted with shortwave radio, fire tools, climbing rope, shovel, tow chain, first aid kit, stretcher, axe, etc.; the pickup and its equipment they will leave with me. I am to use it in patrolling the roads within the park, for assisting tourists in trouble, and for hauling firewood to and garbage from the campgrounds. Once a week I may drive the government vehicle to headquarters and Moab for fuel and supplies.

We fill the water tank buried in the slope above the housetrailer and have lunch together in the sunshine, sitting at a wooden picnic table near my doorway. Merle the super, the boss, is a slender, graceful man of about fifty years, with a fine, grave, expressive face toughened though not hardened by a life spent mostly out-of-doors. He was born and raised on a small ranch in New Mexico, went to the University of Virginia, and has made his living as a cattle rancher, dude rancher, CCC supervisor (during the Great Depression) and, since 1940, as a ranger in the National Park Service. He gives me an impression of tenderness, generosity and imperturbable good humor, but also complains, gently, of the hypothetical ulcer he expects to acquire from his years of struggle with administrative paper work. Married, he has three children; the oldest boy attends the University of Utah.

Floyd Bence is a tall powerful man around thirty years old, an archeologist by training, married, with two children. Because of his interests and academic background he should be working at some place like Mesa Verde or Chaco Canyon, poking about in dusty ruins, but is happy enough with his present situation so long as he is free to spend at least part of his time outside the office; the two things he dreads most, as a Park Service career man, are promotion to a responsible high-salaried administrative position, and a transfer back East to one of the cannonball parks like Appomattox or Gettysburg or Ticonderoga. Like myself he'd rather go hungry in the West than flourish and fatten in the Siberian East. A violent prejudice, doomed to disappointment. But at the moment, in the sparkling air and brilliant sunlight of the Utah desert, bad news seems far away.

"Well, Ranger Abbey," says Merle, "how do you like it out here in the middle of nowhere?"

I said it was okay by me.

They smile. "Kind of lonesome?" Floyd asks.

I said it was all right.

After lunch we get into the cab of the government pickup, all three of us, and tour the park. Arches National Monument remains at this time what the Park Service calls an undeveloped area, although to me it appears quite adequately developed. The roads, branching out, lead to within easy walking distance of most of the princi-

pal arches, none more than two miles beyond the end
of a road. The roads are not paved, true, but are easily
passable to any automobile except during or immediately
after a rainstorm. The trails are well marked, easy to
follow; you'd have to make an effort to get lost. There are
three small camp grounds, each with tables, fireplaces,
garbage cans and pit toilets. (Bring your own water.) We
even supply the firewood, in the form of pinyon pine logs
and old fence posts of cedar, which it will be my task to
find and haul to the campgrounds.

We drive the dirt roads and walk out some of the
trails. Everything is lovely and wild, with a virginal sweet-
ness. The arches themselves, strange, impressive, grotesque, form but a small and inessential part of the general
beauty of this country. When we think of rock we usually
think of stones, broken rock, buried under soil and plant
life, but here all is exposed and naked, dominated by the
monolithic formations of sandstone which stand above
the surface of the ground and extend for miles, sometimes
level, sometimes tilted or warped by pressures from below,
carved by erosion and weathering into an intricate maze
of glens, grottoes, fissures, passageways, and deep narrow
canyons.

At first look it all seems like a geologic chaos, but there
is method at work here, method of a fanatic order and
perseverance: each groove in the rock leads to a natural
channel of some kind, every channel to a ditch and gulch
and ravine, each larger waterway to a canyon bottom or
broad wash leading in turn to the Colorado River and
the sea.

As predicted, the snowfall has disappeared by this time
and all watercourses in the park are dry except for the
one spring-fed perennial stream known as Salt Creek, a
glassy flow inches deep that trickles over shoals of quicksand and between mud flats covered with white crusts of
alkali. Though it looks potable the water is too saline for
human consumption; horses and cattle can drink it but
not men. Or so I am informed by Merle and Floyd. I
choose to test their belief by experiment. Squatting on the

shore of the stream, I dip my cupped hands into the water and sample a little. Pretty bad, neither potable nor palatable. Perhaps, I suggest, a man could learn to drink this water by taking only a little each day, gradually increasing the dosage . . . ?

"You try that," says Merle.

"Yeah," Floyd says, "give us a report at the end of the summer."

Late this afternoon we return to the housetrailer. Floyd lends me a park ranger shirt which he says he doesn't need anymore and which I am to wear in lieu of a uniform, so as to give me an official sort of aspect when meeting the tourists. Then there's this silver badge I'm supposed to pin to the shirt. The badge gives me the authority to arrest malefactors and evildoers, Floyd explains. Or anyone at all, for that matter.

I place both Floyd and Merle under arrest at once, urging them to stay and have supper with me. I've got a big pot of pinto beans simmering on the stove. But they won't stay, they have promises to keep and must leave, and soon they're driving off in the watertruck over the rocky road to the highway and Moab. Climbing the rise behind the housetrailer I watch them go, the truck visible for a mile or so before the road winds deeper into the complex of sand dunes, corraded monoliths and hogback ridges to the west.

Beyond the highway, about ten miles away, rise the talus slopes and vertical red walls of Dead Horse Mesa, a flat-topped uninhabited island in the sky which extends for thirty miles north and south between the convergent canyons of the Green and Colorado rivers. Public domain. Above the mesa the sun hangs behind streaks and streamers of wind-whipped clouds. More storms coming.

But for the time being, around my place at least, the air is untroubled, and I become aware for the first time today of the immense silence in which I am lost. Not a silence so much as a great stillness—for there are a few sounds: the creak of some bird in a juniper tree, an eddy of wind which passes and fades like a sigh, the ticking of the watch on my wrist—slight noises which break the sensation of absolute silence but at the same time exaggerate my sense of the surrounding, overwhelming peace. A suspension of time, a continuous present. If I look at the small device strapped to my wrist the numbers, even the sweeping second hand, seem meaningless, almost ridiculous. No travelers, no campers, no wanderers have come to this part of the desert today and for a few moments I feel and realize that I am very much alone.

There is nothing to do but return to the trailer, open a can of beer, eat my supper.

Afterwards I put on hat and coat and go outside again, sit on the table, and watch the sky and the desert dissolve slowly into the mystery under the chemistry of twilight. We need a fire. I range around the trailer, pick up some dead sticks from under the junipers and build a little squaw fire, for company.

Dark clouds sailing overhead across the fields of the stars. Stars which are usually bold and close, with an icy glitter in their light—glints of blue, emerald, gold. Out there, spread before me to the south, east, and north, the arches and cliffs and pinnacles and balanced rocks of sandstone (now entrusted to my care) have lost the rosy glow of sunset and become soft, intangible, in unnamed unnameable shades of violet, colors that seem to radiate from—not overlay—their surfaces.

A yellow planet floats on the west, brightest object in the sky. Venus. I listen closely for the call of an owl, a dove, a nighthawk, but can hear only the crackle of my fire, a breath of wind.

The fire. The odor of burning juniper is the sweetest fragrance on the face of the earth, in my honest judgment; I doubt if all the smoking censers of Dante's paradise could equal it. One breath of juniper smoke, like the perfume of sagebrush after rain, evokes in magical catalysis, like certain music, the space and light and clarity and piercing strangeness of the American West. Long may it burn.

The little fire wavers, flickers, begins to die. I break

another branch of juniper over my knee and add the fragments to the heap of coals. A wisp of bluish smoke goes up and the wood, arid as the rock from which it came, blossoms out in fire.

> Go thou my incense upward from this hearth
> And ask the gods to pardon this clear flame.

I wait and watch, guarding the desert, the arches, the sand and barren rock, the isolated junipers and scattered clumps of sage surrounding me in stillness and simplicity under the starlight.

Again the fire begins to fail. Letting it die, I take my walking stick and go for a stroll down the road into the thickening darkness. I have a flashlight with me but will not use it unless I hear some sign of animal life worthy of investigation. The flashlight, or electrical torch as the English call it, is a useful instrument in certain situations but I can see the road well enough without it. Better, in fact.

There's another disadvantage to the use of the flashlight: like many other mechanical gadgets it tends to separate a man from the world around him. If I switch it on my eyes adapt to it and I can see only the small pool of light which it makes in front of me; I am isolated. Leaving the flashlight in my pocket where it belongs, I remain a part of the environment I walk through and my vision though limited has no sharp or definite boundary.

This peculiar limitation of the machine becomes doubly apparent when I return to the housetrailer. I've decided to write a letter (to myself) before going to bed, and rather than use a candle for light I'm going to crank up the old generator. The generator is a small four-cylinder gasoline engine mounted on a wooden block not far from the trailer. Much too close, I'd say. I open the switch, adjust the choke, engage the crank and heave it around. The engine sputters, gasps, catches fire, gains momentum, winds up into a roar, valves popping, rockers thumping, pistons hissing up and down inside their oiled jackets.

Fine: power surges into the wiring, the light bulbs inside the trailer begin to glow, brighten, becoming incandescent. The lights are so bright I can't see a thing and have to shade my eyes as I stumble toward the open door of the trailer. Nor can I hear anything but the clatter of the generator. I am shut off from the natural world and sealed up, encapsulated, in a box of artificial light and tyrannical noise.

Once inside the trailer my senses adjust to the new situation and soon enough, writing the letter, I lose awareness of the lights and the whine of the motor. But I have cut myself off completely from the greater world which surrounds the man-made shell. The desert and the night are pushed back—I can no longer participate in them or observe; I have exchanged a great and unbounded world for a small, comparatively meager one. By choice, certainly; the exchange is temporarily convenient and can be reversed whenever I wish.

Finishing the letter I go outside and close the switch on the generator. The light bulbs dim and disappear, the furious gnashing of pistons whimpers to a halt. Standing by the inert and helpless engine, I hear its last vibrations die like ripples on a pool somewhere far out on the tranquil sea of desert, somewhere beyond Delicate Arch, beyond the Yellow Cat badlands, beyond the shadow line.

I wait. Now the night flows back, the mighty stillness embraces and includes me; I can see the stars again and the world of starlight. I am twenty miles or more from the nearest fellow human, but instead of loneliness I feel loveliness. Loveliness and a quiet exultation.

THE SERPENTS
OF PARADISE

THE APRIL mornings are bright, clear and calm. Not until the afternoon does the wind begin to blow, raising dust and sand in funnelshaped twisters that spin across the desert briefly, like dancers, and then collapse—whirlwinds from which issue no voice or word except the forlorn moan of the elements under stress. After the reconnoitering dust-devils comes the real, the serious wind, the voice of the desert rising to a demented howl and blotting out sky and sun behind yellow clouds of dust, sand, confusion, embattled birds, last year's scrub-oak leaves, pollen, the husks of locusts, bark of juniper. . . .

Time of the red eye, the sore and bloody nostril, the sand-pitted windshield, if one is foolish enough to drive his car into such a storm. Time to sit indoors and continue that letter which is never finished—while the fine dust forms neat little windrows under the edge of the door and on the windowsills. Yet the springtime winds are as much a part of the canyon country as the silence and the glamorous distances; you learn, after a number of years, to love them also.

The mornings therefore, as I started to say and meant to say, are all the sweeter in the knowledge of what the afternoon is likely to bring. Before beginning the morning chores I like to sit on the sill of my doorway, bare feet planted on the bare ground and a mug of hot coffee in hand, facing the sunrise. The air is gelid, not far above freezing, but the butane heater inside the trailer keeps my back warm, the rising sun warms the front, and the coffee warms the interior.

Perhaps this is the loveliest hour of the day, though it's hard to choose. Much depends on the season. In midsummer the sweetest hour begins át sundown, after the awful heat of the afternoon. But now, in April, we'll take the opposite, that hour beginning with the sunrise. The birds, returning from wherever they go in winter, seem inclined to agree. The pinyon jays are whirling in garrulous, gregarious flocks from one stunted tree to the next and back again, erratic exuberant games without any apparent practical function. A few big ravens hang around and croak harsh clanking statements of smug satisfaction from the rimrock, lifting their greasy wings now and then to probe for lice. I can hear but seldom see the canyon wrens singing their distinctive song from somewhere up on the cliffs: a flutelike descent—never ascent—of the whole-tone scale. Staking out new nesting claims, I understand. Also invisible but invariably present at some indefinable distance are the mourning doves whose plaintive call suggests irresistibly a kind of seeking-out, the attempt by separated souls to restore a lost communion:

Hello ... they seem to cry, *who* ... *are* ... *you?*

And the reply from a different quarter. *Hello* ... (pause) *where* ... *are* ... *you?*

No doubt this line of analogy must be rejected. It's foolish and unfair to impute to the doves, with serious concerns of their own, an interest in questions more appropriate to their human kin. Yet their song, if not a mating call or a warning, must be what it sounds like, a brooding meditation on space, on solitude. The game.

Other birds, silent, which I have not yet learned to identify, are also lurking in the vicinity, watching me. What the ornithologist terms l.g.b.'s—little gray birds—they flit about from point to point on noiseless wings, their origins obscure.

As mentioned before, I share the housetrailer with a number of mice. I don't know how many but apparently only a few, perhaps a single family. They don't disturb me and are welcome to my crumbs and leavings. Where they came from, how they got into the trailer, how they survived before my arrival (for the trailer had been locked up for six months), these are puzzling matters I am not prepared to resolve. My only reservation concerning the mice is that they do attract rattlesnakes.

I'm sitting on my doorstep early one morning, facing the sun as usual, drinking coffee, when I happen to look down and see almost between my bare feet, only a couple of inches to the rear of my heels, the very thing I had in mind. No mistaking that wedgelike head, that tip of horny segmented tail peeping out of the coils. He's under the doorstep and in the shade where the ground and air remain very cold. In his sluggish condition he's not likely to strike unless I rouse him by some careless move of my own.

There's a revolver inside the trailer, a huge British Webley .45, loaded, but it's out of reach. Even if I had it in my hands I'd hesitate to blast a fellow creature at such close range, shooting between my own legs at a living target flat on solid rock thirty inches away. It would be like murder; and where would I set my coffee? My cherrywood walking stick leans against the trailerhouse wall only a few feet away but I'm afraid that in leaning over for it I might stir up the rattler or spill some hot coffee on his scales.

Other considerations come to mind. Arches National

Monument is meant to be among other things a sanctuary for wildlife—for all forms of wildlife. It is my duty as a park ranger to protect, preserve and defend all living things within the park boundaries, making no exceptions. Even if this were not the case I have personal convictions to uphold. Ideals, you might say. I prefer not to kill animals. I'm a humanist; I'd rather kill a *man* than a snake.

What to do. I drink some more coffee and study the dormant reptile at my heels. It is not after all the mighty diamondback, *Crotalus atrox*, I'm confronted with but a smaller species known locally as the horny rattler or more precisely as the Faded Midget. An insulting name for a rattlesnake, which may explain the Faded Midget's alleged bad temper. But the name is apt: he is small and dusty-looking, with a little knob above each eye—the horns. His bite though temporarily disabling would not likely kill a full-grown man in normal health. Even so I don't really want him around. Am I to be compelled to put on boots or shoes every time I wish to step outside? The scorpions, tarantulas, centipedes, and black widows are nuisance enough.

I finish my coffee, lean back and swing my feet up and inside the doorway of the trailer. At once there is a buzzing sound from below and the rattler lifts his head from his coils, eyes brightening, and extends his narrow black tongue to test the air.

After thawing out my boots over the gas flame I pull them on and come back to the doorway. My visitor is still waiting beneath the doorstep, basking in the sun, fully alert. The trailerhouse has two doors. I leave by the other and get a long-handled spade out of the bed of the government pickup. With this tool I scoop the snake into the open. He strikes; I can hear the click of the fangs against steel, see the strain of venom. He wants to stand and fight, but I am patient; I insist on herding him well away from the trailer. On guard, head aloft—that evil slit-eyed weaving head shaped like the ace of spades—tail whirring, the rattler slithers sideways, retreating slowly before me until he reaches the shelter of a sandstone slab. He backs under it.

You better stay there, cousin, I warn him; if I catch you around the trailer again I'll chop your head off.

A week later he comes back. If not him, his twin brother. I spot him one morning under the trailer near the kitchen drain, waiting for a mouse. I have to keep my promise.

This won't do. If there are midget rattlers in the area there may be diamondbacks too—five, six or seven feet long, thick as a man's wrist, dangerous. I don't want *them* camping under my home. It looks as though I'll have to trap the mice.

However, before being forced to take that step I am lucky enough to capture a gopher snake. Burning garbage one morning at the park dump, I see a long slender yellow-brown snake emerge from a mound of old tin cans and plastic picnic plates and take off down the sandy bed of a gulch. There is a burlap sack in the cab of the truck which I carry when plucking Kleenex flowers from the brush and cactus along the road; I grab that and my stick, run after the snake and corner it beneath the exposed roots of a bush. Making sure it's a gopher snake and not something less useful, I open the neck of the sack and with a great deal of coaxing and prodding get the snake into it. The gopher snake, *Drymarchon corais couperi*, or bull snake, has a reputation as the enemy of rattlesnakes, destroying or driving them away whenever encountered.

Hoping to domesticate this sleek, handsome and docile reptile, I release him inside the trailerhouse and keep him there for several days. Should I attempt to feed him? I decide against it—let him eat mice. What little water he may need can also be extracted from the flesh of his prey.

The gopher snake and I get along nicely. During the day he curls up like a cat in the warm corner behind the heater and at night he goes about his business. The mice, singularly quiet for a change, make themselves scarce. The snake is passive, apparently contented, and makes no resistance when I pick him up with my hands and drape him over an arm or around my neck. When I take him outside into the wind and sunshine his favorite place seems to be inside my shirt, where he wraps himself around my waist and rests on my belt. In this position he sometimes sticks his head out between shirt buttons for a survey of the weather, astonishing and delighting any tourists who may happen to be with me at the time. The scales of a snake are dry and smooth, quite pleasant to the touch. Being a cold-blooded creature, of course, he takes his temperature from that of the immediate environment —in this case my body.

We are compatible. From my point of view, friends. After a week of close association I turn him loose on the warm sandstone at my doorstep and leave for patrol of the park. At noon when I return he is gone. I search everywhere beneath, nearby and inside the trailerhouse, but my companion has disappeared. Has he left the area entirely or is he hiding somewhere close by? At any rate I am troubled no more by rattlesnakes under the door.

The snake story is not yet ended.

In the middle of May, about a month after the gopher snake's disappearance, in the evening of a very hot day, with all the rosy desert cooling like a griddle with the fire turned off, he reappears. This time with a mate.

I'm in the stifling heat of the trailer opening a can of beer, barefooted, about to go outside and relax after a hard day watching cloud formations. I happen to glance out the little window near the refrigerator and see two gopher snakes on my verandah engaged in what seems to be a kind of ritual dance. Like a living caduceus they wind and unwind about each other in undulant, graceful, perpetual motion, moving slowly across a dome of sandstone. Invisible but tangible as music is the passion which joins them—sexual? combative? both? A shameless *voyeur*, I stare at the lovers, and then to get a closer view run outside and around the trailer to the back. There I get down on hands and knees and creep toward the dancing snakes, not wanting to frighten or disturb them. I crawl to within six feet of them and stop, flat on my belly, watching from the snake's-eye level. Obsessed with their ballet, the serpents seem unaware of my presence.

The two gopher snakes are nearly identical in length and coloring; I cannot be certain that either is actually my former household pet. I cannot even be sure that they are male and female, though their performance resembles so strongly a *pas de deux* by formal lovers. They intertwine and separate, glide side by side in perfect congruence, turn like mirror images of each other and glide back again, wind and unwind again. This is the basic pattern but there is a variation: at regular intervals the snakes elevate their heads, facing one another, as high as they can go, as if each is trying to outreach or overawe the other. Their heads and bodies rise, higher and higher, than topple together and the rite goes on.

I crawl after them, determined to see the whole thing. Suddenly and simultaneously they discover me, prone on my belly a few feet away. The dance stops. After a moment's pause the two snakes come straight toward me, still in flawless unison, straight toward my face, the forked tongues flickering, their intense wild yellow eyes staring directly into my eyes. For an instant I am paralyzed by wonder; then, stung by a fear too ancient and powerful to overcome I scramble back, rising to my knees. The snakes veer and turn and race away from me in parallel motion, their lean elegant bodies making a soft hissing noise as they slide over the sand and stone. I follow them for a short distance, still plagued by curiosity, before remembering my place and the requirements of common courtesy. For godsake let them go in peace, I tell myself. Wish them luck and (if lovers) innumerable offspring, a life of happily ever after. Not for their sake alone but for your own.

In the long hot days and cool evenings to come I will not see the gopher snakes again. Nevertheless I will feel their presence watching over me like totemic deities, keeping the rattlesnakes far back in the brush where I like them best, cropping off the surplus mouse population, maintaining useful connections with the primeval. Sympathy, mutual aid, symbiosis, continuity.

How can I descend to such anthropomorphism? Easily —but is it, in this case entirely false? Perhaps not. I am

not attributing human motives to my snake and bird
acquaintances. I recognize that when and where they serve
purposes of mine they do so for beautifully selfish reasons of their own. Which is exactly the way it should be.
I suggest, however, that it's a foolish, simple-minded
rationalism which denies any form of emotion to all animals but man and his dog. This is no more justified than
the Moslems are in denying souls to women. It seems to
me possible, even probable, that many of the nonhuman
undomesticated animals experience emotions unknown to
us. What do the coyotes mean when they yodel at the
moon? What are the dolphins trying so patiently to
tell us? Precisely what did those two enraptured gopher
snakes have in mind when they came gliding toward my
eyes over the naked sandstone? If I had been as capable
of trust as I am susceptible to fear I might have learned
something new or some truth so very old we have all forgotten it.

They do not sweat and whine about their condition,
They do not lie awake in the dark and weep for their
    sins. . . .

All men are brothers, we like to say, half-wishing sometimes in secret it were not true. But perhaps it is true.
And is the evolutionary line from protozoan to Spinoza
any less certain? That also may be true. We are obliged,
therefore, to spread the news, painful and bitter though it
may be for some to hear, that all living things on earth
are kindred.

CLIFFROSE AND BAYONETS

MAY DAY.

A crimson sunrise streaked with gold flares out beyond Balanced Rock, beyond the arches and windows, beyond Grand Mesa in Colorado. Dawn winds are driving streamers of snow off the peaks of the Sierra La Sal and old man Tukuhnikivats, mightiest of mountains in the land of Moab, will soon be stripped bare to the granite if this wind doesn't stop. Blue scarves of snow flying in the wind twenty miles away—you wouldn't want to be up there now, as they say out here, 13,000 feet above the sea, with only your spurs on.

In honor of the occasion I tack a scarlet bandanna to the ridgepole of the ramada, where my Chinese windbells also hang, jingling and jangling in the breeze. The red rag flutters brightly over the bells—poetry and revolution before breakfast. Afterwards I hoist the Stars and

Stripes to the top of the flagpole up at the entrance station. Impartial and neutralist, taking no chances, I wish good fortune to both sides, good swill for all. Or conversely, depending on my mood of the moment, damn both houses and *pox vobiscum*. Swinish politics, our ball and chain.

The gopher snake has deserted me, taking with him most of my mice, and the government trailerhouse is a lonely place this morning. Leaving the coffee to percolate slowly over the lowest possible flame, I take my cherry-wood and go for a walk before breakfast. The wind blows sand in my teeth but also brings the scent of flowering cliffrose and a hint of mountain snow, more than adequate compensation.

Time to inspect the garden. I refer to the garden which lies all around me, extending from here to the mountains, from here to the Book Cliffs, from here to Roberts' Roost and Land's End—an area about the size of the Negev and, excepting me and the huddled Moabites, uninhabited.

Inventory. Great big yellow mule-ear sunflowers are blooming along the dirt road, where the drainage from the road provides an extra margin of water, a slight but significant difference. Growing among the sunflowers and scattered more thinly over the rest of the desert are the others: yellow borage, Indian paintbrush, scarlet penstemon, skyrocket gilia, prickly pear, hedgehog cactus, purple locoweed, the coral-red globemallow, dockweed, sand verbena. Loveliest of all, however, gay and sweet as a pretty girl, with a fragrance like that of orange blossoms, is the cliffrose, *Cowania stansburiana*, also known—by the anesthetic—as buckbrush or quinine bush.

The cliffrose is a sturdy shrub with gnarled trunk and twisting branches, growing sometimes to twice a man's height. When not in bloom it might not catch your eye; but after the winter snows and a trace of rain in the spring it comes on suddenly and gloriously like a swan, like a maiden, and the shaggy limbs go out of sight behind dense clusters of flowers creamy white or pale yellow, like wild roses, each with its five perfect petals and a golden center.

There's a cliffrose standing near the shed behind the trailer, shaking in the wind, a dazzling mass of blossoms, and another coming up out of solid sandstone beside the ramada, ten feet tall and clothed in a fire of flowers. If Housman were here he'd alter those lines to

> Loveliest of shrubs the cliffrose now
> Is hung with bloom along the bough . . .

The word "shrub" presents a challenge, at least to such verse as this; but poetry is nothing if not exact. The poets lie too much, said Jeffers. Exactly. We insist on precision around here, though it bend the poesy a little out of shape.

The cliffrose is practical as well as pretty. Concealed by the flowers at this time are the leaves, small, tough, wax-coated, bitter on the tongue—thus the name quinine bush—but popular just the same among the deer as browse when nothing better is available—buckbrush. The Indians too, a practical people, once used the bark of this plant for sandals, mats and rope, and the Hopi medicine man is said, even today, to mash and cook the leaves as an emetic for his patients.

Because of its clouds of flowers the cliffrose is the showiest plant in the canyon country, but the most beautiful individual flower, most people would agree, is that of the cacti: the prickly pear, the hedgehog, the fishhook. Merely opinion, of course. But the various cactus flowers have earned the distinction claimed for them on the basis of their large size, their delicacy, their brilliance, and their transcience—they bloom, many of them, for one day only in each year. Is that a fair criterion of beauty? I don't know. For myself I hold no preference among flowers, so long as they are wild, free, spontaneous. (Bricks to all greenhouses! Black thumb and cutworm to the potted plant!)

The cactus flowers are all much alike, varying only in

color within and among the different species. The prickly pear, for example, produces a flower that may be violet, saffron, or red. It is cup-shaped, filled with golden stamens that respond with sensitive, one might almost say sensual, tenderness to the entrance of a bee. This flower is indeed irresistibly attractive to insects; I have yet to look into one and not find a honeybee or bumblebee wallowing drunkenly inside, powdered with pollen, glutting itself on what must be a marvelous nectar. You can't get them out of there—they won't go home. I've done my best to annoy them, poking and prodding with a stem of grass, but a bee in a cactus bloom will not be provoked; it stays until the flower wilts. Until closing time.

The true distinction of these flowers, I feel, is found in the contrast between the blossom and the plant which produces it. The cactus of the high desert is a small, grubby, obscure and humble vegetable associated with cattle dung and overgrazing, interesting only when you tangle with it in the wrong way. Yet from this nest of thorns, this snare of hooks and fiery spines, is born once each year a splendid flower. It is unpluckable and except to an insect almost unapproachable, yet soft, lovely, sweet, desirable, exemplifying better than the rose among thorns the unity of opposites.

Stepping carefully around the straggling prickly pear I come after a few paces over bare sandstone to a plant whose defensive weaponry makes the cactus seem relatively benign. This one is formed of a cluster of bayonetlike leaves pointing up and outward, each stiff green blade tipped with a point as intense and penetrating as a needle. Out of the core of this untouchable dagger's-nest rises a slender stalk, waist-high, gracefully curved, which supports a heavy cluster of bell-shaped, cream-colored, wax-coated, exquisitely perfumed flowers. This plant, not a cactus but a member of the lily family, is a type of yucca called Spanish bayonet.

Despite its fierce defenses, or perhaps because of them, the yucca is as beautiful as it is strange, perfect in its place wherever that place may be—on the Dagger Flats of

Big Bend, the high grasslands of southern New Mexico, the rim and interior of Grand Canyon or here in the Arches country, growing wide-spaced and solitaire from the red sands of Utah.

The yucca is bizarre not only in appearance but in its mode of reproduction. The flowers are pollinated not by bees or hummingbirds but exclusively by a moth of the genus *Pronuba* with which the yucca, aided by a liberal allowance of time, has worked out a symbiotic relationship beneficial and necessary to both. The moth lays its eggs at the proper time in the ovary of the yucca flower where the larvae, as they develop, feed on the growing seeds, eating enough of them to reach maturity but leaving enough in the pod to allow the plant, assisted by the desert winds, to sow next year's yucca crop. In return for this nursery care the moth performs an essential service for the yucca: in the process of entering the flower the moth—almost accidentally it might seem to us—transfers the flower's pollen from anther to pistil, thus accomplishing pollination. No more; but it is sufficient.

The wind will not stop. Gusts of sand swirl before me, stinging my face. But there is still too much to see and marvel at, the world very much alive in the bright light and wind, exultant with the fever of spring, the delight of morning. Strolling on, it seems to me that the strangeness and wonder of existence are emphasized here, in the desert, by the comparative sparsity of the flora and fauna: life not crowded upon life as in other places but scattered abroad in spareness and simplicity, with a generous gift of space for each herb and bush and tree, each stem of grass, so that the living organism stands out bold and brave and vivid against the lifeless sand and barren rock. The extreme clarity of the desert light is equaled by the extreme individuation of desert life-forms. Love flowers best in openness and freedom.

Patterns in the sand, tracks of tiger lizards, birds, kangaroo rats, beetles. Circles and semicircles on the red dune where the wind whips the compliant stems of the wild ricegrass back and forth, halfway around and back again. On the crest of the dune is a curving cornice from which flies a constant spray of fine sand. Crescent-shaped, the dune shelters on its leeward side a growth of sunflowers and scarlet penstemon. I lie on my belly on the edge of the dune, back to the wind, and study the world of the flowers from ground level, as a snake might see it. From below the flowers of the penstemon look like flying pennants; the sunflowers shake and creak from thick green hairy stalks that look, from a snake's viewpoint, like the trunks of trees.

I get up and start back to the trailer. A smell of burning coffee on the wind. On the way I pass a large anthill, the domed city of the harvester ants. Omnivorous red devils with a vicious bite, they have denuded the ground surrounding their hill, destroying everything green and living within a radius of ten feet. I cannot resist the impulse to shove my walking stick into the bowels of their hive and rowel things up. Don't actually care for ants. Neurotic little pismires. Compared to ants the hairy scorpion is a beast of charm, dignity and tenderness.

My favorite juniper stands before me glittering shaggily in the sunrise, ragged roots clutching at the rock on which it feeds, rough dark boughs bedecked with a rash, with a shower of turquoise-colored berries. A female, this ancient grandmother of a tree may be three hundred years old; growing very slowly, the juniper seldom attains a height greater than fifteen or twenty feet even in favorable locations. My juniper, though still fruitful and full of vigor, is at the same time partly dead: one half of the divided trunk holds skyward a sapless claw, a branch without leaf or bark, baked by the sun and scoured by the wind to a silver finish, where magpies and ravens like to roost when I am not too close.

I've had this tree under surveillance ever since my arrival at Arches, hoping to learn something from it, to discover the significance in its form, to make a connection through its life with whatever falls beyond. Have failed. The essence of the juniper continues to elude me unless, as I presently suspect, its surface is also the essence.

Two living things on the same earth, respiring in a common medium, we contact one another but without direct communication. Intuition, sympathy, empathy, all fail to guide me into the heart of this being—if it has a heart.

At times I am exasperated by the juniper's static pose; something in its stylized gesture of appeal, that dead claw against the sky, suggests catalepsy. Perhaps the tree is mad. The dull, painful creaking of the branches in the wind indicates, however, an internal effort at liberation.

The wind flows around us from the yellow haze in the east, a morning wind, a solar wind. We're in for a storm today, dust and sand and filthy air.

Without flowers as yet but bright and fresh, with leaves of a startling, living green in contrast to the usual desert olive drab, is a shrub known as singleleaf ash, one of the few true deciduous plants in the pinyon-juniper community. Most desert plants have only rudimentary leaves, or no leaves at all, the better to conserve moisture, and the singleleaf ash seems out of place here, anomalous, foredoomed to wither and die. (*Fraxinus anomala* is the botanical name.) But touch the leaves of this plant and you find them dry as paper, leathery in texture and therefore desert-resistant. The singleleaf ash in my garden stands alone along the path, a dwarf tree only three feet high but tough and enduring, clenched to the stone.

Sand sage or old man sage, a lustrous windblown blend of silver and blue and aquamarine, gleams in the distance, the feathery stems flowing like hair. Purple flowers no bigger than your fingernail are half-revealed, half-concealed by the shining leaves. *Purple* sage: crush the leaves between thumb and finger and you release that characteristic odor, pungent and bittersweet, which *means* canyon country, high lonesome mesaland, the winds that blow from far away.

Also worthy of praise is the local pinyon pine, growing hereabouts at isolated points, for its edible nuts that appear in good years, for its ragged raunchy piney good looks, for the superior qualities of its wood as fuel—burns clean and slow, little soot, little ash, and smells almost as good as juniper. Unfortunately, most of the pinyon pines in the area are dead or dying, victims of another kind of pine—the porcupine. This situation came about through the conscientious efforts of a federal agency known formerly as the Wildlife Service, which keeps its people busy in trapping, shooting and poisoning wildlife, particularly coyotes and mountain lions. Having nearly exterminated their natural enemies, the wildlife experts made it possible for the porcupines to multiply so fast and so far that they—the porcupines—have taken to gnawing the bark from pinyon pines in order to survive.

What else? Still within sight of the housetrailer, I can see the princess plume with its tall golden racemes; the green ephedra or Mormon tea, from which Indians and pioneers extracted a medicinal drink (contains ephedrine), the obnoxious Russian thistle, better known as tumbleweed, an exotic; pepperweed, bladderweed, snakeweed, matchweed, skeleton weed—the last-named so delicately formed as to be almost invisible; the scrubby little wavy-leaf oak, stabilizer of sand dunes; the Apache plume, poor cousin of the cliffrose; gray blackbrush, most ubiquitous and humble of desert plants, which will grow where all else has given up; more annuals—primrose, sour-dock, yellow and purple beeplant, rockcress, wild buckwheat, grama grass, and five miles north across the floor of Salt Valley, acres and acres of the coral-colored globemallow.

Not quite within eyeshot but close by, in a shady damp-ish secret place, the sacred datura—moonflower, moon-lily, thornapple—blooms in the night, soft white trumpet-shaped flowers that open only in darkness and close with the coming of the heat. The datura is sacred (to certain cultists) because of its content of atropine, a powerful narcotic of the alkaloid group capable of inducing visionary hallucinations, as the Indians discovered long before the psychedelic craze began. How they could have made such a discovery without poisoning themselves to death nobody knows; but then nobody knows how so-called primitive man made his many other discoveries. We must concede that science is nothing new, that research, empirical logic, the courage to experiment are as old as humanity.

Most of the plants I have named so far belong to what ecologists call the pinyon pine-juniper community, typical of the high, dry, sandy soils of the tablelands. Descend to the alkali flats of Salt Valley and you find an entirely different grouping: shadscale, fourwinged saltbush, greasewood, spiny horsebrush, asters, milk vetch, budsage, galletagrass. Along the washes and the rare perennial streams you'll find a third community: the Fremont poplar or cottonwood tree, willow, tamarisk, rabbitbrush or *chamisa*, and a variety of sedges, tules, rushes, reeds, cattails. The fourth plant community, in the Arches area, is found by the springs and around the seeps on the canyon walls— the hanging gardens of fern, monkey-flower, death camas, columbine, helleborine orchid, bracken, panicgrass, bluestem, poison ivy, squawbush, and the endemic primrose *Primula specuiola*, found nowhere but in the canyonlands.

So much for the inventory. After such a lengthy listing of plant life the reader may now be visualizing Arches National Monument as more a jungle than a desert. Be reassured, it is not so. I have called it a garden, and it is— a *rock* garden. Despite the great variety of living things to be found here, most of the surface of the land, at least three-quarters of it, is sand or sandstone, naked, monolithic, austere and unadorned as the sculpture of the moon. It is undoubtedly a desert place, clean, pure, totally useless, quite unprofitable.

The sun is rising through a yellow, howling wind. Time for breakfast. Inside the trailer now, broiling bacon and frying eggs with good appetite, I hear the sand patter like rain against the metal walls and brush across the windowpanes. A fine silt accumulates beneath the door and on the window ledge. The trailer shakes in a sudden gust. All one to me—sandstorm or sunshine I am content, so long as I have something to eat, good health, the earth to take my stand on, and light behind the eyes to see by.

At eight o'clock I put on badge and ranger hat and go to work, checking in at headquarters by radio and taking my post at the entrance station to greet and orient whatever tourists may appear. None show. After an hour of waiting I climb in the government pickup and begin a patrol of the park, taking lunch and coffee with me. So far as I know there's no one camping in the park at this time, but it won't hurt to make sure.

The wind is coming from the north, much colder than before—we may have sleet or rain or snow or possibly all three before nightfall. Bad weather means that the park entrance road will be impassable; it is part of my job to inform campers and visitors of this danger so that they will have a chance to get out before it's too late.

Taking the Windows road first, I drive beneath the overhanging Balanced Rock, 3500 tons of seamless Entrada sandstone perched on a ridiculous, inadequate pedestal of the Carmel formation, soft and rotten stone eaten away by the wind, deformed by the weight above. One of these days that rock is going to fall—in ten, fifty, or five hundred years. I drive past more free-standing pinnacles, around the edge of outthrust ledges, in and out of the ravines that corrade the rolling terrain—wind-deposited, cross-bedded sand dunes laid down eons ago in the Mesozoic era and since compressed and pertrified by overlaying sediments. Everywhere the cliffrose is blooming, the yellow flowers shivering in the wind.

The heart-shaped prints of deer are plain in the dust of the road and I wonder where the deer are now and how they're doing and if they've got enough to eat. Like the porcupine the deer too become victims of human meddling with the natural scheme of things—not enough coyotes around and the mountain lions close to extinction, the deer have multiplied like rabbits and are eating themselves out of house and home, which means that many each year are condemned to a slow death by starvation. The deerslayers come by the thousands every autumn out of Salt Lake and California to harvest, as they like to say, the surplus deer. But they are not adequate for the task.

The road ends at the Double Arch campground. No one here. I check the garbage can for trapped chipmunks, pick up a few bottlecaps, and inspect the "sanitary facilities," where all appears to be in good order: roll of paper, can of lime, black widow spiders dangling in their usual strategic corners. On the inside of the door someone has written a cautionary note:

> Attention: Watch out for rattlesnakes, coral snakes, whip snakes, vinegaroons, centipedes, millipedes, ticks, mites, black widows, cone-nosed kissing bugs, solpugids, tarantulas, horned toads, Gila monsters, red ants, fire ants, Jerusalem crickets, chinch bugs and Giant Hairy Desert Scorpions before being seated.

I walk out the foot trail to Double Arch and the Windows. The wind moans a dreary tune under the overhanging coves, among the holes in the rock, and through the dead pinyon pines. The sky is obscure and yellow but the air in this relatively sheltered place among the rocks is still clear. A few birds dart about: black-throated sparrows, the cliff swallows, squawking magpies in their handsome academic dress of black and white. In the dust and on the sand dunes I can read the passage of other creatures, from the big track of a buck to the tiny prints of birds, mice, lizards, and insects. Hopefully I look for sign of bobcat or coyote but find none.

We need more predators. The sheepmen complain, it is true, that the coyotes eat some of their lambs. This is true but do they eat enough? I mean, enough lambs to keep the coyotes sleek, healthy and well fed. That is my concern. As for the sacrifice of an occasional lamb, that seems to me a small price to pay for the support of the coyote population. The lambs, accustomed by tradition to their role, do not complain; and the sheepmen, who run their hooved locusts on the public lands and are heavily subsidized, most of them as hog-rich as they are pigheaded, can easily afford these trifling losses.

We need more coyotes, more mountain lions, more wolves and foxes and wildcats, more owls, hawks and eagles. The livestock interests and their hired mercenaries from the Department of the Interior have pursued all of these animals with unremitting ferocity and astonishing cruelty for nearly a century, utilizing in this campaign of extermination everything from the gun and trap to the airplane and the most ingenious devices of chemical and biological warfare. Not content with shooting coyotes from airplanes and hunting lions with dogs, these bounty hunters, self-styled sportsmen, and government agents like to plant poisoned meat all over the landscape, distribute tons of poisoned tallow balls by air, and hide baited cyanide guns in the ground and brush—a threat to humans as well as animals. Still not satisfied, they have developed and begun to use a biochemical compound which makes sterile any animal foolish enough to take the bait.

Absorbed in these thoughts, wind in my eyes, I round a corner of the cliff and there's a doe and her fawn not ten yards away, browsing on the cliffrose. Eating flowers. While she could not have heard or scented me, the doe sees me almost at once. But since I stopped abruptly and froze, she isn't sure that I am dangerous. Puzzled and suspicious, she and the fawn at her side, madonna and child, stare at me for several long seconds. I breathe out, making the slightest of movements, and the doe springs up and away as if bounced from a trampoline, followed by the fawn. Their sharp hooves clatter on the rock.

"Come back here!" I shout. "I want to talk to you."

But they're not talking and in another moment have vanished into the wind. I could follow if I wanted to, track them down across the dunes and through the open parks of juniper and cliffrose. But why should I disturb them further? Even if I found them and somehow succeeded in demonstrating my friendship and good will, why should I lead them to believe that anything manlike can be trusted? That is no office for a friend.

I come to the North Window, a great opening fifty feet high in a wall of rock, through which I see the

clouded sky and the hazy mountains and feel the funneled
rush of the wind. I climb up to it, walk through—like an
ant crawling through the eyesocket of a skull—and down
the other side a half-mile to a little spring at the head of
a seldom-visited canyon. I am out of the wind for a
change, can light up my pipe and look around without
getting dust in my eyes; I can hear myself think.

Here I find the track of a coyote superimposed on the
path of many deer. So there is at least one remaining
in the area, perhaps the same coyote I heard two weeks
ago wailing at the evening moon. His trail comes down
off the sandstone from the west, passes over the sand
under a juniper and up to the seep of dark green water
in its circle of reeds. Under the juniper he has left two
gray-green droppings knitted together with rabbit hair.
With fingertip I write my own signature in the sand to
let him know, to tip him off; I take a drink of water and
leave.

Down below is Salt Creek Canyon, corraded through
an anticline to the bed of the Colorado. If I were lucky I
might find the trail of bighorn sheep, rumored still to
lurk in these rimrock hideaways. In all these years of
prowling on foot through the canyons and desert mountains of the Southwest I have yet to see, free and alive
in the wild, either a lion or a bighorn. In part I can blame
only my ignorance and incompetence, for I know they
are out there, somewhere; I have seen their scat and their
tracks.

As I am returning to the campground and the truck I
see a young cottontail jump from the brush, scamper
across the trail and freeze under a second bush. The rabbit huddles there, panting, ears back, one bright eye on
me.

I am taken by the notion to experiment—on the rabbit.
Suppose, I say to myself, you were out here hungry, starving, no weapon but your bare hands. What would you
do? What *could* you do?

There are a few stones scattered along the trail. I pick
up one that fits well in the hand, that seems to have the

optimum feel and heft. I stare at the cottontail hunched
in his illusory shelter under the bush. Blackbrush, I observe, the common variety, sprinkled with tightly rolled
little green buds, ready to burst into bloom on short notice. Should I give the rabbit a sporting chance, that is,
jump it again, try to hit it on the run? Or brain the little
bastard where he is?

Notice the terminology. A sportsman is one who gives
his quarry a chance to escape with its life. This is known
as fair play, or sportsmanship. Animals have no sense
of sportsmanship. Some, like the mountain lion, are vicious—if attacked they defend themselves. Others, like the
rabbit, run away, which is cowardly.

Well, I'm a scientist not a sportsman and we've got an
important experiment under way here, for which the rabbit has been volunteered. I rear back and throw the stone
with all I've got straight at his furry head.

To my amazement the stone flies true (as if guided by
a Higher Power) and knocks the cottontail head over
tincups, clear out from under the budding blackbush. He
crumples, there's the usual gushing of blood, etc., a brief
spasm, and then no more. The wicked rabbit is dead.

For a moment I am shocked by my deed; I stare at
the quiet rabbit, his glazed eyes, his blood drying in the
dust. Something vital is lacking. But shock is succeeded
by a mild elation. Leaving my victim to the vultures and
maggots, who will appreciate him more than I could—
the flesh is probably infected with tularemia—I continue my
walk with a new, augmented cheerfulness which is hard
to understand but unmistakable. What the rabbit has lost
in energy and spirit seems added, by processes too subtle
to fathom, to my own soul. I try but cannot feel any
sense of guilt. I examine my soul: white as snow. Check
my hands: not a trace of blood. No longer do I feel so
isolated from the sparse and furtive life around me, a
stranger from another world. I have entered into this one.
We are kindred all of us, killer and victim, predator and
prey, me and the sly coyote, the soaring buzzard, the
elegant gopher snake, the trembling cottontail, the foul

worms that feed on our entrails, all of them, all of us. Long live diversity, long live the earth!

Rejoicing in my innocence and power I stride down the trail beneath the elephantine forms of melting sandstone, past the stark shadows of Double Arch. The experiment was a complete success; it will never be necessary to perform it again.

Back in the warm pickup I enjoy a well-earned sandwich and drink my coffee before driving on another six miles, through clouds of wind-driven dust and sand, to the old Turnbow Cabin and the beginning of the trail to Delicate Arch.

Once there was a man named Turnbow who lived in the grimy wastelands of an eastern city which we will not mention here—the name, though familiar to all the world, is not important. This Turnbow had consumption. His doctors gave him six months. Mr. Turnbow in his despair fled to the arid wilds, to this very spot, built the cabin, lived on and on for many years and died, many years ago.

The cabin stands on the banks of the unpotable waters of Salt Creek, a shallow stream on a bed of quicksand. Drinking water is available half a mile upstream at a tributary spring. Turnbow Cabin itself is a well-preserved ruin (nothing decays around here) made of juniper, pinyon and cottonwood logs, no two alike in shape or size. The crudity of the construction followed from the scarcity of wood, not lack of skill. The cracks between the unhewn logs were chinked with adobe; a few fragments still remain. The walls have a morbid greenish hue that matches the coloration of the nearby hills; this is dust from the Morrison formation, a loose friable shale containing copper oxides, agate, chert, and traces of vanadium and uranium. There is a doorway but no door, a single window and no glass. The floor consists of warped, odd-size planks. In one corner is a manger for horses, an addition made long after the death of Mr. Turnbow. Cobwebs complete with black widow spiders adorn the darker corners under the ceiling. In the center of the room is a massive post of juniper shoring up the ancient, sagging roof, which is a thatchwork affair of poles, mud and rock, very leaky. As shelter, the cabin cannot be recommended, except for its shade on a hot day.

Back of the cabin are the lonesome Morrison hills, utterly lifeless piles of clay and shale and broken rock, a dismal scene. In front are the walls of Dry Mesa and Salt Creek Canyon. It is a hot, sunken, desolate place, closed in and still, lacking even a view. As Genghis Khan said of India, "The water is bad and the heat makes men sick." A haunted place, in my opinion, haunted by the ghost of the lonely man who died here. Except for myself no one lives within thirty miles of Turnbow Cabin.

With relief I turn my back on this melancholy ruin and take the golden trail up the long ledge of Navajo sandstone which leads to Delicate Arch. I cross the swinging footbridge over Salt Creek, pestered on the way by a couple of yellow cowflies (cattlemen call them deerflies). The cowfly, or deerfly if you prefer, loves blood. Human blood especially. Persistent as a mosquito, it will keep attacking until either it samples your blood or you succeed in killing it, or both. The most artful among them like to land in your hair and attach themselves to the scalp, where they will not be noticed until too late. But they are home-loving insects; once over the bridge and away from the slimy little creek you leave them behind.

Many have made the climb to Delicate Arch, so many that the erosion of human feet is visible on the soft sandstone, a dim meandering path leading upward for a mile and a half into a queer region of knobs, domes, turrets and coves, all sculptured from a single solid mass of rock. What do the pilgrims see? The trail climbs and winds past isolate pinyons and solitary junipers to a vale of stone where nothing has happened for a thousand years, to judge from the quietude of the place, the sense of *waiting* that seems to hover in the air. From this vale you climb a second ledge blasted across the face of a cliff, round a corner at the end of the trail and Delicate Arch stands before you, a fragile ring of stone on the far side of a natural amphitheater, set on its edge at the brink of a five hundred foot drop-off. Looking through the ring you see the rim of Dry Mesa and far beyond that the peaks of the La Sal Mountains.

There are several ways of looking at Delicate Arch. Depending on your preconceptions you may see the eroded remnant of a sandstone fin, a giant engagement ring cemented in rock, a bow-legged pair of petrified cowboy chaps, a triumphal arch for a procession of angels, an illogical geologic freak, a happening—a something that happened and will never happen quite that way again, a frame more significant than its picture, a simple monolith eaten away by weather and time and soon to disintegrate into a chaos of falling rock (not surprisingly there have been some, even in the Park Service, who advocate spraying Delicate Arch with a fixative of some sort—Elmer's Glue perhaps or Lady Clairol Spray-Net). There are the inevitable pious Midwesterners who climb a mile and a half under the desert sun to view Delicate Arch and find only God ("Goldangit Katherine where's my light meter, this glare is turrible"), and the equally inevitable students of geology who look at the arch and see only Lyell and the uniformity of nature. You may therefore find proof for or against His existence. Suit yourself. You may see a symbol, a sign, a fact, a thing without meaning or a meaning which includes all things.

Much the same could be said of the tamarisk down in the canyon, of the blue-black raven croaking on the cliff, of your own body. The beauty of Delicate Arch explains nothing, for each thing in its way, when true to its own character, is equally beautiful. (There is no beauty in nature, said Baudelaire. A place to throw empty beer cans on Sunday, said Mencken.) If Delicate Arch has any significance it lies, I will venture, in the power of the odd and unexpected to startle the senses and surprise the mind out of their ruts of habit, to compel us into a reawakened awareness of the wonderful—that which is full of wonder.

A weird, lovely, fantastic object out of nature like Delicate Arch has the curious ability to remind us—like rock and sunlight and wind and wilderness—that *out there* is a different world, older and greater and deeper by far than ours, a world which surrounds and sustains the little world of men as sea and sky surround and sustain a ship. The shock of the real. For a little while we are again able to see, as the child sees, a world of marvels. For a few moments we discover that nothing can be taken for granted, for if this ring of stone is marvelous then all which shaped it is marvelous, and our journey here on earth, able to see and touch and hear in the midst of tangible and mysterious things-in-themselves, is the most strange and daring of all adventures.

After Delicate Arch the others are anticlimactic but I go on to inspect them, as I'm paid to do. From Turnbow Cabin I drive northwesterly on a twisting road above Salt Valley past a labyrinth of fins and pinnacles toward the Devil's Garden. On the way I pass Skyline Arch, a big hole in the wall where something took place a few years ago which seems to bear out the hypotheses of geology: one November night in 1940 when no one was around to watch, a big chunk of rock fell out of this arch, enlarging the opening by half again its former size. The photographs, "Before & After," prove it. The event had doubtless been in preparation for hundreds maybe thousands of years—snow falling, melting, trickling into minute fissures, dissolving the cements which knit sandstone particles together, freezing and expanding, wedging apart the tiny cracks, undermining the base—but the cumulative result was a matter, probably, of only a few noisy and dusty minutes in which the mighty slabs cracked and grumbled, shook loose, dropped and slid and smashed upon the older slabs below, shattering the peace of ages. But none were there to see and hear except the local lizards, mice and ground squirrels, and perhaps a pair of outraged, astonished ravens.

I reach the end of the road and walk the deserted trail to Landscape Arch and Double-O Arch, picking up a few candy wrappers left from the weekend, straightening a trail sign which somebody had tried to remove, noting another girdled and bleeding pinyon pine, obliterating from a sandstone wall the pathetic scratchings of some imbeciles who had attempted to write their names across the face of the Mesozoic. (Where are you now, J. Soderlund? Alva T. Sarvis? John De Puy? Wilton Hoy? Malcolm Brown?)

The wind blows, unrelenting, and flights of little gray birds whirl up and away like handfuls of confetti tossed in the air. The temperature is still falling, presaging snow. I am glad to return, several hours later, to the shelter and warmth of the housetrailer. I have not seen a soul anywhere in Arches National Monument today.

In the evening the wind stops. A low gray ceiling of clouds hangs over the desert from horizon to horizon, silent and still. One small opening remains in the west. The sun peers through as it goes down. For a few minutes the voodoo monuments burn with a golden light, then fade to rose and blue and violet as the sun winks out and drops. My private juniper stands alone, one dead claw reaching at the sky. The blossoms on the cliffrose are folding up, the scarlet penstemon and the bayonets of the yucca turn dull and vague in the twilight.

Something strange in the air. I go to the weather station and check the instruments—nothing much, actually, but a rain gauge, an anemometer or wind gauge, and a set of thermometers which record the lows and highs for the day. The little cups on the wind gauge are barely turning, but this breath of air, such as it is, comes from the southwest. The temperature is fifty-five or so, after a low this morning of thirty-eight. It is not going to snow after all. Balanced on a point of equilibrium, hesitating, the world of the high desert turns toward summer.

POLEMIC:
INDUSTRIAL TOURISM
AND THE NATIONAL PARKS

I LIKE my job. The pay is generous; I might even say munificent: $1.95 per hour, earned or not, backed solidly by the world's most powerful Air Force, biggest national debt, and grossest national product. The fringe benefits are priceless: clean air to breathe (after the spring sandstorms); stillness, solitude and space; an unobstructed view every day and every night of sun, sky, stars, clouds, mountains, moon, cliffrock and canyons; a sense of time enough to let thought and feeling range from here to the end of the world and back; the discovery of something intimate—though impossible to name—in the remote.

The work is simple and requires almost no mental effort, a good thing in more ways than one. What little thinking I do is my own and I do it on government time. Insofar as I follow a schedule it goes about like this:

For me the work week begins on Thursday, which I usually spend in patrolling the roads and walking out the trails. On Friday I inspect the campgrounds, haul firewood, and distribute the toilet paper. Saturday and Sunday are my busy days as I deal with the influx of weekend visitors and campers, answering questions, pulling cars out of the sand, lowering children down off the rocks, tracking lost grandfathers and investigating picnics. My Saturday night campfire talks are brief and to the point. "Everything all right?" I say, badge and all, ambling up to what looks like a cheerful group. "Fine," they'll say; "how about a drink?" "Why not?" I say.

By Sunday evening most everyone has gone home and the heavy duty is over. Thank God it's Monday, I say to myself the next morning. Mondays are very nice. I empty the garbage cans, read the discarded newspapers, sweep out the outhouses and disengage the Kleenex from the clutches of cliffrose and cactus. In the afternoon I watch the clouds drift past the bald peak of Mount Tukuhnikivats. (*Someone* has to do it.)

Tuesday and Wednesday I rest. Those are my days off and I usually set aside Wednesday evening for a trip to Moab, replenishing my supplies and establishing a little human contact more vital than that possible with the tourists I meet on the job. After a week in the desert, Moab (pop. 5500, during the great uranium boom), seems like a dazzling metropolis, a throbbing dynamo of commerce and pleasure. I walk the single main street as dazed by the noise and neon as a country boy on his first visit to Times Square. (Wow, I'm thinking, this is great.)

After a visit to Miller's Supermarket, where I stock up on pinto beans and other necessities, I am free to visit the beer joints. All of them are busy, crowded with prospectors, miners, geologists, cowboys, truckdrivers and sheepherders, and the talk is loud, vigorous, blue with blasphemy. Although differences of opinion have been known to occur, open violence is rare, for these men treat one another with courtesy and respect. The general atmosphere is free and friendly, quite unlike the sad, sour gloom of most bars I have known, where nervous men in tight collars brood over their drinks between out-of-tune TV screens and a remorseless clock. Why the difference?

I have considered the question and come up with the following solution:

1. These prospectors, miners, etc. have most of them been physically active all day out-of-doors at a mile or more above sea level; they are comfortably tired and relaxed.

2. Most of them have been working alone; the presence of a jostling crowd is therefore not a familiar irritation to be borne with resignation but rather an unaccustomed pleasure to be enjoyed.

3. Most of them are making good wages and/or doing work they like to do; they are, you might say, happy. (The boom will not last, of course, but this is forgotten. And the ethical and political implications of uranium exploitation are simply unknown in these parts.)

4. The nature of their work requires a combination of skills and knowledge, good health and self-reliance, which tends to inspire self-confidence; they need not doubt their manhood. (Again, everything is subject to change.)

5. Finally, Moab is a Mormon town with funny ways. Hard booze is not sold across the bar except in the semi-private "clubs." Nor even standard beer. These hard-drinking fellows whom I wish to praise are trying to get drunk on three-point-two! They rise somewhat heavily from their chairs and barstools and tramp, with frequency and a squelchy, sodden noise, toward the pissoirs at the back of the room, more waterlogged than intoxicated.

In the end the beer halls of Moab, like all others, become to me depressing places. After a few games of rotation pool with my friend Viviano Jacquez, a reformed sheepherder turned dude wrangler (a dubious reform), I am glad to leave the last of those smoky dens around midnight and to climb into my pickup and take the long drive north and east back to the silent rock, the un-

bounded space and the sweet clean air of my outpost in
the Arches.

Yes, it's a good job. On the rare occasions when I peer
into the future for more than a few days I can foresee
myself returning here for season after season, year after
year, indefinitely. And why not? What better sinecure
could a man with small needs, infinite desires, and
philosophic pretensions ask for? The better part of each
year in the wilderness and the winters in some comple-
mentary, equally agreeable environment—Hoboken perhaps, or Tiajuana, Nogales, Juarez . . . one of the border
towns. Maybe Tonopah, a good tough Nevada mining
town with legal prostitution, or possibly Oakland or even
New Orleans—some place grimy, cheap (since I'd be living on unemployment insurance), decayed, hopelessly
corrupt. I idle away hours dreaming of the wonderful
winter to come, of the chocolate-colored mistress I'll have
to rub my back, the journal spread open between two tall
candles in massive silver candlesticks, the scrambled eggs
with green chile, the crock of homebrew fermenting
quietly in the corner, etc., the nights of desperate laughter
with brave young comrades, burning billboards, and de-
facing public institutions. . . . Romantic dreams, romantic
dreams.

For there is a cloud on my horizon. A small dark cloud
no bigger than my hand. Its name is Progress.

The ease and relative freedom of this lovely job at
Arches follow from the comparative absence of the motorized tourists, who stay away by the millions. And they
stay away because of the unpaved entrance road, the un-
flushable toilets in the campgrounds, and the fact that
most of them have never even heard of Arches National
Monument. (Could there be a more genuine testimonial
to its beauty and integrity?) All this must change.

I'd been warned. On the very first day Merle and Floyd
had mentioned something about developments, improve-
ments, a sinister Master Plan. Thinking that *they* were
the dreamers, I paid little heed and had soon forgotten
the whole ridiculous business. But only a few days ago

something happened which shook me out of my pleasant apathy.

I was sitting out back on my 33,000-acre terrace, shoeless and shirtless, scratching my toes in the sand and sipping on a tall iced drink, watching the flow of evening over the desert. Prime time: the sun very low in the west, the birds coming back to life, the shadows rolling for miles over rock and sand to the very base of the brilliant mountains. I had a small fire going near the table—not for heat or light but for the fragrance of the juniper and the ritual appeal of the clear flames. For symbolic reasons. For ceremony. When I heard a faint sound over my shoulder I looked and saw a file of deer watching from fifty yards away, three does and a velvet-horned buck, all dark against the sundown sky. They began to move. I whistled and they stopped again, staring at me. "Come on over," I said, "have a drink." They declined, moving off with casual, unhurried grace, quiet as phantoms, and disappeared beyond the rise. Smiling, thoroughly at peace, I turned back to my drink, the little fire, the subtle transformations of the immense landscape before me. On the program: rise of the full moon.

It was then I heard the discordant note, the snarling whine of a jeep in low range and four-wheel-drive, coming from an unexpected direction, from the vicinity of the old foot and horse trail that leads from Balanced Rock down toward Courthouse Wash and on to park headquarters near Moab. The jeep came in sight from beyond some bluffs, turned onto the dirt road, and came up the hill toward the entrance station. Now operating a motor vehicle of any kind on the trails of a national park is strictly forbidden, a nasty bureaucratic regulation which I heartily support. My bosom swelled with the righteous indignation of a cop: by God, I thought, I'm going to write these sons of bitches a ticket. I put down the drink and strode to the housetrailer to get my badge.

Long before I could find the shirt with the badge on it, however, or the ticket book, or my shoes or my park ranger hat, the jeep turned in at my driveway and came right

up to the door of the trailer. It was a gray jeep with a
U.S. Government decal on the side—Bureau of Public
Roads—and covered with dust. Two empty water bags
flapped at the bumper. Inside were three sunburned men
in twill britches and engineering boots, and a pile of
equipment: transit case, tripod, survey rod, bundles of
wooden stakes. (*Oh no!*) The men got out, dripping with
dust, and the driver grinned at me, pointing to his parched
open mouth and making horrible gasping noises deep in
his throat.

"Okay," I said, "come on in."

It was even hotter inside the trailer than outside but I
opened the refrigerator and left it open and took out a
pitcher filled with ice cubes and water. As they passed
the pitcher back and forth I got the full and terrible
story, confirming the worst of my fears. They were a
survey crew, laying out a new road into the Arches.

And when would the road be built? Nobody knew for
sure; perhaps in a couple of years, depending on when
the Park Service would be able to get the money. The
new road—to be paved, of course—would cost somewhere
between half a million and one million dollars, depending
on the bids, or more than fifty thousand dollars per linear
mile. At least enough to pay the salaries of ten park rangers for ten years. Too much money, I suggested—they'll
never go for it back in Washington.

The three men thought that was pretty funny. Don't
worry, they said, this road will be built. I'm worried, I
said. Look, the party chief explained, you *need* this road.
He was a pleasant-mannered, soft-spoken civil engineer
with an unquestioning dedication to his work. A very
dangerous man. Who *needs* it? I said; we get very few
tourists in this park. That's why you need it, the engineer
explained patiently; look, he said, when this road is built
you'll get ten, twenty, thirty times as many tourists in
here as you get now. His men nodded in solemn agreement, and he stared at me intently, waiting to see what
possible answer I could have to that.

"Have some more water," I said. I had an answer all

right but I was saving it for later. I knew that I was deal-
ing with a madman.

As I type these words, several years after the little epi-
sode of the gray jeep and the thirsty engineers, all that
was foretold has come to pass. Arches National Monument has been developed. The Master Plan has been ful-
filled. Where once a few adventurous people came on
weekends to camp for a night or two and enjoy a taste
of the primitive and remote, you will now find serpentine
streams of baroque automobiles pouring in and out, all
through the spring and summer, in numbers that would
have seemed fantastic when I worked there: from 3,000
to 30,000 to 300,000 per year, the "visitation," as they
call it, mounts ever upward. The little campgrounds
where I used to putter around reading three-day-old newspapers full of lies and watermelon seeds have now been
consolidated into one master campground that looks, during the busy season, like a suburban village: elaborate
housetrailers of quilted aluminum crowd upon gigantic
camper-trucks of Fiberglas and molded plastic; through
their windows you will see the blue glow of television
and hear the studio laughter of Los Angeles; knobby-
kneed oldsters in plaid Bermudas buzz up and down the
quaintly curving asphalt road on motorbikes; quarrels
break out between campsite neighbors while others gather
around their burning charcoal briquettes (ground camp-
fires no longer permitted—not enough wood) to compare
electric toothbrushes. The Comfort Stations are there,
too, all lit up with electricity, fully equipped inside, though
the generator breaks down now and then and the lights
go out, or the sewage backs up in the plumbing system
(drain fields were laid out in sand over a solid bed of
sandstone), and the water supply sometimes fails, since
the 3000-foot well can only produce about 5gpm—not always enough to meet the demand. Down at the beginning
of the new road, at park headquarters, is the new entrance
station and visitor center, where admission fees are collected and where the rangers are going quietly nuts an-

swering the same three basic questions five hundred times
a day: (1) Where's the john? (2) How long's it take to
see this place? (3) Where's the Coke machine?

Progress has come at last to the Arches, after a million
years of neglect. Industrial Tourism has arrived.

What happened to Arches Natural Money-mint is, of
course, an old story in the Park Service. All the famous
national parks have the same problems on a far grander
scale as everyone knows, and many other problems as yet
unknown to a little subordinate unit of the system in a
backward part of southeastern Utah And the same kind
of development that has so transformed Arches is under
way, planned or completed in many more national parks
and national monuments. I will mention only a few example with which I am personally familiar:

The newly established Canyonlands National Park.
Most of the major points of interest in this park are presently accessible, over passable dirt roads, by car—Grandview Point. Upheaval Dome part of the White Rim,
Cave Spring Squaw Spring campground and Elephant
Hill The more difficult places such as Angel Arch or
Druid Arch can be reached by jeep, on horseback or in a
one- or two-day hike. Nevertheless the Park Service had
drawn up the usual Master Plan calling for modern paved
highways to most of the places named and some not
named.

Grand Canyon National Park. Most of the south rim
of this park is now closely followed by a conventional high-
speed highway and interrupted at numerous places by
large asphalt parking lots. It is no longer easy, on the
South Rim, to get away from the roar of motor traffic,
except by descending into the canyon.

Navajo National Monument. A small, fragile, hidden
place containing two of the most beautiful cliff dwellings
in the Southwest—Keet Seel and Betatakin. This park
will be difficult to protect under heavy visitation, and for
years it was understood that it would be preserved in a
primitive way so as to screen out those tourists unwilling

to drive their cars over some twenty miles of dirt road. No longer so: the road has been paved, the campground enlarged and "modernized," and the old magic destroyed.

Natural Bridges National Monument. Another small gem in the park system, a group of three adjacent natural bridges tucked away in the canyon country of southern Utah. Formerly you could drive your car (over dirt roads, of course) to within sight of and easy walking distance— a hundred yards?—of the most spectacular of the three bridges. From there it was only a few hours walking time to the other two. All three could easily be seen in a single day. But this was not good enough for the developers. They have now constructed a paved road into the heart of the area, between the two biggest bridges.

Zion National Park. The northwestern part of this park, known as the Kolob area, has until recently been saved as almost virgin wilderness. But a broad highway, with banked curves, deep cuts and heavy fills, that will invade this splendid region, is already under construction.

Capitol Reef National Monument. Grand and colorful scenery in a rugged land—south-central Utah. The most beautiful portion of that park was the canyon of the Fremont River, a great place for hiking, camping, exploring. And what did the authorities do? They built a state highway through it.

Lee's Ferry. Until a few years ago a simple, quiet, primitive place on the shores of the Colorado, Lee's Ferry has now fallen under the protection of the Park Service. And who can protect it against the Park Service? Powerlines now bisect the scene; a 100-foot pink water tower looms against the red cliffs; tract-style houses are built to house the "protectors"; natural campsites along the river are closed off while all campers are now herded into an artificial steel-and-asphalt "campground" in the hottest, windiest spot in the area; historic buildings are razed by bulldozers to save the expense of maintaining them while at the same time hundreds of thousands of dollars are spent on an unneeded paved entrance road. And the administrators complain of vandalism.

I could easily cite ten more examples of unnecessary or destructive development for every one I've named so far. What has happened in these particular areas, which I chance to know a little and love too much, has happened, is happening, or will soon happen to the majority of our national parks and national forests, despite the illusory protection of the Wilderness Preservation Act, unless a great many citizens rear up on their hind legs and make vigorous political gestures demanding implementation of the Act.

There may be some among the readers of this book, like the earnest engineer, who believe without question that any and all forms of construction and development are intrinsic goods, in the national parks as well as anywhere else, who virtually identify quantity with quality and therefore assume that the greater the quantity of traffic, the higher the value received. There are some who frankly and boldly advocate the eradication of the last remnants of wilderness and the complete subjugation of nature to the requirements of—not man—but industry. This is a courageous view, admirable in its simplicity and power, and with the weight of all modern history behind it. It is also quite insane. I cannot attempt to deal with it here.

There will be other readers, I hope, who share my basic assumption that wilderness is a necessary part of civilization and that it is the primary responsibility of the national park system to preserve intact and undiminished what little still remains.

Most readers, while generally sympathetic to this latter point of view, will feel, as do the administrators of the National Park Service, that although wilderness is a fine thing, certain compromises and adjustments are necessary in order to meet the ever-expanding demand for outdoor recreation. It is precisely this question which I would like to examine now.

The Park Service, established by Congress in 1916, was

directed not only to administer the parks but also to "provide for the enjoyment of same in such manner and by such means as will leave them unimpaired for the enjoyment of future generations." This appropriately ambiguous language, employed long before the onslaught of the automobile, has been understood in various and often opposing ways ever since. The Park Service, like any other big organization, includes factions and factions. The Developers, the dominant faction, place their emphasis on the words "*provide for the enjoyment.*" The Preservers, a minority but also strong, emphasize the words "*leave them unimpaired.*" It is apparent, then, that we cannot decide the question of development versus preservation by a simple referral to holy writ or an attempt to guess the intention of the founding fathers; we must make up our own minds and decide for ourselves what the national parks should be and what purpose they should serve.

The first issue that appears when we get into this matter, the most important issue and perhaps the only issue, is the one called *accessibility.* The Developers insist that the parks must be made fully accessible not only to people but also to their machines, that is, to automobiles, motorboats, etc. The Preservers argue, in principle at least, that wilderness and motors are incompatible and that the former can best be experienced, understood, and enjoyed when the machines are left behind where they belong—on the superhighways and in the parking lots, on the reservoirs and in the marinas.

What does accessibility mean? Is there any spot on earth that men have not proved accessible by the simplest means—feet and legs and heart? Even Mt. McKinley, even Everest, have been surmounted by men on foot. (Some of them, incidentally, rank amateurs, to the horror and indignation of the professional mountaineers.) The interior of the Grand Canyon, a fiercely hot and hostile abyss, is visited each summer by thousands and thousands of tourists of the most banal and unadventurous type, many of them on foot—self-propelled, so to speak—and the others on the backs of mules. Thousands climb each summer to the summit of Mt. Whitney, highest point in the forty-eight United States, while multitudes of others wander on foot or on horseback through the ranges of the Sierras, the Rockies, the Big Smokies, the Cascades and the mountains of New England. Still more hundreds and thousands float or paddle each year down the currents of the Salmon, the Snake, the Allagash, the Yampa, the Green, the Rio Grande, the Ozark, the St. Croix and those portions of the Colorado which have not yet been destroyed by the dam builders. And most significant, these hordes of nonmotorized tourists, hungry for a taste of the difficult, the original, the real, do not consist solely of people young and athletic but also of old folks, fat folks, pale-faced office clerks who don't know a rucksack from a haversack, and even children. The one thing they all have in common is the refusal to live always like sardines in a can—they are determined to get outside of their motorcars for at least a few weeks each year.

This being the case, why is the Park Service generally so anxious to accommodate that other crowd, the indolent millions born on wheels and suckled on gasoline, who expect and demand paved highways to lead them in comfort, ease and safety into every nook and corner of the national parks? For the answer to that we must consider the character of what I call Industrial Tourism and the quality of the mechanized tourists—the Wheelchair Explorers—who are at once the consumers, the raw material and the victims of Industrial Tourism.

Industrial Tourism is a big business. It means money. It includes the motel and restaurant owners, the gasoline retailers, the oil corporations, the road-building contractors, the heavy equipment manufacturers, the state and federal engineering agencies and the sovereign, all-powerful automotive industry. These various interests are well organized, command more wealth than most modern nations, and are represented in Congress with a strength far greater than is justified in any constitutional or democratic sense. (Modern politics is expensive—power follows money.) Through Congress the tourism industry can bring enormous pressure to bear upon such a slender reed in the executive branch as the poor old Park Service, a pressure which is also exerted on every other possible level—local, state, regional—and through advertising and the well-established habits of a wasteful nation.

When a new national park, national monument, national seashore, or whatever it may be called is set up, the various forces of Industrial Tourism, on all levels, immediately expect action—meaning specifically a road-building program. Where trails or primitive dirt roads already exist the Industry expects—it hardly needs to ask—that these be developed into modern paved highways. On the local level, for example, the first thing that the superintendent of a new park can anticipate being asked, when he attends his first meeting of the area's Chamber of Commerce, is not "Will roads be built?" but rather "When does construction begin?" and "Why the delay?"

(The Natural Money-Mint. With supersensitive antennae these operatives from the C. of C. look into red canyons and see only green, stand among flowers snorting out the smell of money, and hear, while thunderstorms rumble over mountains, the fall of a dollar bill on motel carpeting.)

Accustomed to this sort of relentless pressure since its founding, it is little wonder that the Park Service, through a process of natural selection, has tended to evolve a type of administration which, far from resisting such pressure, has usually been more than willing to accommodate it, even to encourage it. Not from any peculiar moral weakness but simply because such well-adapted administrators are themselves believers in a policy of economic development. "Resource management" is the current term. Old foot trails may be neglected, back-country ranger stations left unmanned, and interpretive and protective services inadequately staffed, but the administrators know from long experience that millions for asphalt can always be found; Congress is always willing to appropriate money for more and bigger paved roads, anywhere—particularly if they form loops. Loop drives are extremely popular with the petroleum industry—they bring the motorist right back to the same gas station from which he started.

Great though it is, however, the power of the tourist business would not in itself be sufficient to shape Park Service policy. To all accusations of excessive development the administrators can reply, as they will if pressed hard enough, that they are giving the public what it wants, that their primary duty is to serve the public not preserve the wilds. "Parks are for people" is the public-relations slogan, which decoded means that the parks are for people-in-automobiles. Behind the slogan is the assumption that the majority of Americans, exactly like the managers of the tourist industry, expect and demand to see their national parks from the comfort, security, and convenience of their automobiles.

Is this assumption correct? Perhaps. Does that justify the continued and increasing erosion of the parks? It does not. Which brings me to the final aspect of the problem of Industrial Tourism: the Industrial Tourists themselves.

They work hard, these people. They roll up incredible mileages on their odometers, rack up state after state in two-week transcontinental motor marathons, knock off one national park after another, take millions of square yards of photographs, and endure patiently the most prolonged discomforts: the tedious traffic jams, the awful food of park cafeterias and roadside eateries, the nocturnal search for a place to sleep or camp, the dreary routine of One-Stop Service, the endless lines of creeping traffic, the smell of exhaust fumes, the ever-proliferating Rules & Regulations, the fees and the bills and the service charges, the boiling radiator and the flat tire and the vapor lock, the surly retorts of room clerks and traffic cops, the incessant jostling of the anxious crowds, the irritation and restlessness of their children, the worry of their wives, and the long drive home at night in a stream of racing cars against the lights of another stream racing in the opposite direction, passing now and then the obscure tangle, the shattered glass, the patrolman's lurid blinker light, of one more wreck.

Hard work. And risky. Too much for some, who have given up the struggle on the highways in exchange for an entirely different kind of vacation—out in the open, on their own feet, following the quiet trail through forest and mountains, bedding down at evening under the stars, when and where they feel like it, at a time when the Industrial Tourists are still hunting for a place to park their automobiles.

Industrial Tourism is a threat to the national parks. But the chief victims of the system are the motorized tourists. They are being robbed and robbing themselves. So long as they are unwilling to crawl out of their cars they will not discover the treasures of the national parks and will never escape the stress and turmoil of the urban-suburban complexes which they had hoped, presumably, to leave behind for a while.

How to pry the tourists out of their automobiles, out of their back-breaking upholstered mechanized wheelchairs and onto their feet, onto the strange warmth and solidity of Mother Earth again? This is the problem which the Park Service should confront directly, not evasively, and which it cannot resolve by simply submitting and conforming to the automobile habit. The automobile, which began as a transportation convenience, has become a bloody tyrant (50,000 lives a year), and it is the responsibility of the Park Service, as well as that of everyone else concerned with preserving both wilderness and civilization, to begin a campaign of resistance. The automotive combine has almost succeeded in strangling our cities; we need not let it also destroy our national parks.

It will be objected that a constantly increasing population makes resistance and conservation a hopeless battle. This is true. Unless a way is found to stabilize the nation's population, the parks cannot be saved. Or anything else worth a damn. Wilderness preservation, like a hundred other good causes, will be forgotten under the overwhelming pressure of a struggle for mere survival and sanity in a completely urbanized, completely industrialized, ever more crowded environment. For my own part I would rather take my chances in a thermonuclear war than live in such a world.

Assuming, however, that population growth will be halted at a tolerable level before catastrophe does it for us, it remains permissible to talk about such things as the national parks. Having indulged myself in a number of harsh judgments upon the Park Service, the tourist industry, and the motoring public, I now feel entitled to make some constructive, practical, sensible proposals for the salvation of both parks and people.

(1) No more cars in national parks. Let the people walk. Or ride horses, bicycles, mules, wild pigs—anything—but keep the automobiles and the motorcycles and all their motorized relatives out. We have agreed not to drive our automobiles into cathedrals, concert halls, art museums, legislative assemblies, private bedrooms and the other sanctums of our culture; we should treat our national parks with the same deference, for they, too, are holy places. An increasingly pagan and hedonistic people (thank God!), we are learning finally that the forests and mountains and desert canyons are holier than our churches. Therefore let us behave accordingly.

Consider a concrete example and what could be done with it: Yosemite Valley in Yosemite National Park. At present a dusty milling confusion of motor vehicles and ponderous camping machinery, it could be returned to relative beauty and order by the simple expedient of requiring all visitors, at the park entrance, to lock up their automobiles and continue their tour on the seats of good workable bicycles supplied free of charge by the United States Government.

Let our people travel light and free on their bicycles—nothing on the back but a shirt, nothing tied to the bike but a slicker, in case of rain. Their bedrolls, their backpacks, their tents, their food and cooking kits will be trucked in for them, free of charge, to the campground of their choice in the Valley, by the Park Service. (Why not? The roads will still be there.) Once in the Valley they will find the concessioners waiting, ready to supply whatever needs might have been overlooked, or to furnish rooms and meals for those who don't want to camp out.

The same thing could be done at Grand Canyon or at Yellowstone or at any of our other shrines to the out-of-doors. There is no compelling reason, for example, why tourists need to drive their automobiles to the very brink of the Grand Canyon's south rim. They could *walk* that last mile. Better yet, the Park Service should build an enormous parking lot about ten miles south of Grand Canyon Village and another east of Desert View. At those points, as at Yosemite, our people could emerge from their steaming shells of steel and glass and climb upon horses or bicycles for the final leg of the journey. On the rim, as at present, the hotels and restaurants will remain to serve the physical needs of the park visitors. Trips along the rim would also be made on foot, on horseback, or—utilizing the paved road which already exists—on bicycles. For those willing to go all the way from one parking lot to the other, a distance of some sixty or seventy miles, we might provide bus service back to their cars, a service which would at the same time effect a convenient exchange of bicycles and/or horses between the two terminals.

What about children? What about the aged and infirm? Frankly, we need waste little sympathy on these two pressure groups. Children too small to ride bicycles and too heavy to be borne on their parents' backs need only wait a few years—if they are not run over by automobiles they will grow into a lifetime of joyous adventure, if we save the parks and *leave them unimpaired for the enjoyment of future generations*. The aged merit even less sympathy: after all they had the opportunity to see the country when it was still relatively unspoiled. However, we'll stretch a point for those too old or too sickly to mount a bicycle and let them ride the shuttle buses.

I can foresee complaints. The motorized tourists, reluctant to give up the old ways, will complain that they can't see enough without their automobiles to bear them swiftly (traffic permitting) through the parks. But this is nonsense. A man on foot, on horseback or on a bicycle will see more, feel more, enjoy more in one mile than the motorized tourists can in a hundred miles. Better to idle through one park in two weeks than try to race through a dozen in the same amount of time. Those who are familiar with both modes of travel know from experience that this is true; the rest have only to make the experiment to discover the same truth for themselves.

They will complain of physical hardship, these sons of the pioneers. Not for long; once they rediscover the pleasures of actually operating their own limbs and senses in a varied, spontaneous, voluntary style, they will complain instead of crawling back into a car; they may even object to returning to desk and office and that dry-wall box on Mossy Brook Circle. The fires of revolt may be kindled —which means hope for us all.

(2) No more new roads in national parks. After banning private automobiles the second step should be easy. Where paved roads are already in existence they will be reserved for the bicycles and essential in-park services, such as shuttle buses, the trucking of camping gear and concessioners' supplies. Where dirt roads already exist they too will be reserved for nonmotorized traffic. Plans for new roads can be discarded and in their place a program of trail-building begun, badly needed in some of the parks and in many of the national monuments. In mountainous areas it may be desirable to build emergency shelters along the trails and bike roads; in desert regions a water supply might have to be provided at certain points —wells drilled and handpumps installed if feasible.

Once people are liberated from the confines of automobiles there will be a greatly increased interest in hiking, exploring, and back-country packtrips. Fortunately the parks, by the mere elimination of motor traffic, will come to seem far bigger than they are now—there will be more room for more persons, an astonishing expansion of space. This follows from the interesting fact that a motorized vehicle, when not at rest, requires a volume of space far out of proportion to its size. To illustrate: imagine a lake approximately ten miles long and on the average one mile wide. A single motorboat could easily circumnavigate the lake in an hour; ten motorboats would begin to crowd it; twenty or thirty, all in operation, would dominate the lake to the exclusion of any other form of activity; and fifty would create the hazards, confusion, and turmoil that makes pleasure impossible. Suppose we banned motorboats and allowed only canoes and rowboats; we would see at once that the lake seemed ten or perhaps a hundred times bigger. The same thing holds true, to an even greater degree, for the automobile. Distance and space are functions of speed and time. Without expending a single dollar from the United States Treasury we could, if we wanted to, multiply the area of our national parks tenfold or a hundredfold—simply by banning the private automobile. The next generation, all 250 million of them, would be grateful to us.

(3) Put the park rangers to work. Lazy scheming loafers, they've wasted too many years selling tickets at toll booths and sitting behind desks filling out charts and tables in the vain effort to appease the mania for statistics which torments the Washington office. Put them to work. They're supposed to be rangers—make the bums range; kick them out of those overheated airconditioned offices, yank them out of those overstuffed patrol cars, and drive them out on the trails where they should be, leading the dudes over hill and dale, safely into and back out of the wilderness. It won't hurt them to work off a little office fat; it'll do them good, help take their minds off each other's wives, and give them a chance to get out of reach of the boss—a blessing for all concerned.

They will be needed on the trail. Once we outlaw the motors and stop the road-building and force the multitudes back on their feet, the people will need leaders. A venturesome minority will always be eager to set off on their own, and no obstacles should be placed in their path; let them take risks, for Godsake, let them get lost, sunburnt, stranded, drowned, eaten by bears, buried alive under avalanches—that is the right and privilege of any

free American. But the rest, the majority, most of them
new to the out-of-doors, will need and welcome assistance,
instruction and guidance. Many will not know how to
saddle a horse, read a topographical map, follow a trail
over slickrock, memorize landmarks, build a fire in rain,
treat snakebite, rappel down a cliff, glissade down a glacier,
read a compass, find water under sand, load a burro, splint
a broken bone, bury a body, patch a rubber boat, portage
a waterfall, survive a blizzard, avoid lightning, cook a
porcupine, comfort a girl during a thunderstorm, predict
the weather, dodge falling rock, climb out of a box canyon, or pour piss out of a boot. Park rangers know these
things, or should know them, or used to know them and
can relearn; they will be needed. In addition to this sort
of practical guide service the ranger will also be a bit of a
naturalist, able to edify the party in his charge with the
natural and human history of the area, in detail and in
broad outline.

Critics of my program will argue that it is too late for
such a radical reformation of a people's approach to the
out-of-doors, that the pattern is too deeply set, and that
the majority of Americans would not be willing to emerge
from the familiar luxury of their automobiles, even
briefly, to try the little-known and problematic advantages
of the bicycle, the saddle horse, and the footpath. This
might be so; but how can we be sure unless we dare the
experiment? I, for one, suspect that millions of our citizens, especially the young, are yearning for adventure, difficulty, challenge—they will respond with enthusiasm.
What we must do, prodding the Park Service into the
forefront of the demonstration, is provide these young
people with the opportunity, the assistance, and the
necessary encouragement.

How could this most easily be done? By following the
steps I have proposed, plus reducing the expenses of wilderness recreation to the minimal level. Guide service by
rangers should, of course, be free to the public. Money
saved by *not* constructing more paved highways into the
parks should be sufficient to finance the cost of bicycles
and horses for the entire park system. Elimination of auto-

mobile traffic would allow the Park Service to save more millions now spent on road maintenance, police work and paper work. Whatever the cost, however financed, the benefits for park visitors in health and happiness—virtues unknown to the statisticians—would be immeasurable.

Excluding the automobile from the heart of the great cities has been seriously advocated by thoughtful observers of our urban problems. It seems to me an equally proper solution to the problems besetting our national parks. Of course it would be a serious blow to Industrial Tourism and would be bitterly resisted by those who profit from that industry. Exclusion of automobiles would also require a revolution in the thinking of Park Service officialdom and in the assumptions of most American tourists. But such a revolution, like it or not, is precisely what is needed. The only foreseeable alternative, given the current trend of things, is the gradual destruction of our national park system.

Let us therefore steal a slogan from the Development Fever Faction in the Park Service. The parks, they say, are for people. Very well. At the main entrance to each national park and national monument we shall erect a billboard one hundred feet high, two hundred feet wide, gorgeously filigreed in brilliant neon and outlined with blinker lights, exploding stars, flashing prayer wheels and great Byzantine phallic symbols that gush like geysers every thirty seconds. (You chould set your watch by them). Behind the fireworks will loom the figure of Smokey the Bear, taller than a pine tree, with eyes in his head that swivel back and forth, watching You, and ears that actually twitch. Push a button and Smokey will recite, for the benefit of children and government officials who might otherwise have trouble with some of the big words, in a voice ursine, loud and clear, the message spelled out on the face of the billboard. To wit:

HOWDY FOLKS. WELCOME. THIS IS YOUR NATIONAL PARK, ESTABLISHED FOR THE PLEASURE OF YOU AND ALL PEO-PLE EVERYWHERE. PARK YOUR CAR, JEEP, TRUCK, TANK, MOTORBIKE, SNOWMOBILE, MOTORBOAT, JETBOAT, AIR-

BOAT, SUBMARINE, AIRPLANE, JETPLANE, HELICOPTER, HOVERCRAFT, WINGED MOTORCYCLE, ROCKETSHIP, OR ANY OTHER CONCEIVABLE TYPE OF MOTORIZED VEHICLE IN THE WORLD'S BIGGEST PARKINGLOT BEHIND THE COMFORT STATION IMMEDIATELY TO YOUR REAR. GET OUT OF YOUR MOTORIZED VEHICLE, GET ON YOUR HORSE, MULE, BICYCLE OR FEET, AND COME ON IN.
ENJOY YOURSELVES. THIS HERE PARK IS FOR people.

The survey chief and his two assistants did not stay very long. Letting them go in peace, without debate, I fixed myself another drink, returned to the table in the backyard and sat down to await the rising of the moon.

My thoughts were on the road and the crowds that would pour upon it as inevitably as water under pressure follows every channel which is opened to it. Man is a gregarious creature, we are told, a social being. Does that mean he is also a herd animal? I don't believe it, despite the character of modern life. The herd is for ungulates, not for men and women and their children. Are men no better than sheep or cattle, that they must live always in view of one another in order to feel a sense of safety? I can't believe it.

We are preoccupied with time. If we could learn to love space as deeply as we are now obsessed with time, we might discover a new meaning in the phrase to live like men.

At what distance should good neighbors build their houses? Let it be determined by the community's mode of travel: if by foot, four miles; if by horseback, eight miles; if by motorcar, twenty-four miles; if by airplane, ninety-six miles.

Recall the Proverb: "Set not thy foot too often in thy neighbor's house, lest he grow weary of thee and hate thee."

The sun went down and the light mellowed over the sand and distance and hoodoo rocks "pinnacled dim in the intense inane." A few stars appeared, scattered liberally through space. The solitary owl called.

Finally the moon came up, a golden globe behind the rocky fretwork of the horizon, a full and delicate moon that floated lightly as a leaf upon the dark slow current of the night. A face that watched me from the other side.

The air grew cool. I put on boots and shirt, stuffed some cheese and raisins in my pocket, and went for a walk. The moon was high enough to cast a good light when I reached the place where the gray jeep had first come into view. I could see the tracks of its wheels quite plainly in the sand and the route was well marked, not only by the tracks but by the survey stakes planted in the ground at regular fifty-foot intervals and by streamers of plastic ribbon tied to the brush and trees.

Teamwork, that's what made America what it is today. Teamwork and initiative. The survey crew had done their job; I would do mine. For about five miles I followed the course of their survey back toward headquarters, and as I went I pulled up each little wooden stake and threw it away, and cut all the bright ribbons from the bushes and hid them under a rock. A futile effort, in the long run, but it made me feel good. Then I went home to the trailer, taking a shortcut over the bluffs.

ROCKS

THE VERY names are lovely—chalcedony, carnelian, jasper, chrysoprase and agate. Onyx and sardonyx. Crypto-crystalline quartz. Quartzite. Flint, chert and sard. Chrysoberyl, spodumene, garnet, zircon and malachite. Obsidian, turquoise, calcite, feldspar, hornblende pyrope, tourmaline, porphyry, arkose, rutile. The rare metals—lithium, cobalt, berylium, mercury, arsenic, molybdenum, titanium and barium. And the basic rocks—basalt, granite, gneiss, limestone, sandstone, marble, slate, gabbro, shale.

Most of them can be found in this area. If you look hard enough and long enough. By this area I mean southeastern Utah: the canyonlands; Abbey's country.

The various forms of chalcedony for example, are strewn liberally over the dismal clay hills along Salt Creek. Here you will find tiny crystals of garnet embedded in a matrix of mica schist—almandite or "common garnet."

Fragments of quartzite are everywhere, some containing pure quartz crystals. You might find a geode: a lump of sandstone the size and shape of an ostrich egg, or sometimes much larger; slice it through with a diamond wheel and you may find inside a glittering treasure trove of crystals. A treasure not in money but in beauty. (Although I have been told by some rockhounds that they can make a better living peddling gemstones and curious rocks than they could mining gold.) In the washes are flintshards, edges scalloped with marks of secondary chipping—manmade. For the Indians were here too. Centuries ago. Trace the drainages upstream and look in shady alcoves under the canyon walls; there in the sand and dust, among the packrat storehouses and the litter of other animals you will find the mother lode, the place where the naked, indolent savages lounged about making jokes, pictures, and conchoidal fractures in flint. Flakes, scales, splinters of failed and incompleted points scatter the ground; if you are extremely lucky you may discover a complete and intact arrowhead. Possibly a spearhead. Some of them in translucent obsidian—volcanic glass, "Apache tears."

Lying within the bounds of a national monument, these rocks and artifacts are protected by law. That is, you are welcome to look, to pick up and examine but not to remove. And justly so. For without such protection the area would soon be picked clean by souvenir hunters, acquisitive rockhounds and the commercial merchandisers of stones. For my own part I seldom take rocks home, no matter where I might find them; in my opinion they are best enjoyed *in situ*, where God Himself, so to speak, and the leisurely economy of Nature have seen fit to deposit them.

Petrified wood is also common in the canyon country. Not so much in the vast formations of sandstone which bulk largest in the landscape but at odd, irregular places where clays, shales and mudstones appear. Among the liver-colored hills along the Paria; under the Orange Cliffs west of the standing rocks; in the exquisitely carved façades that line the Fremont River; and in general in any sort of "badlands" or painted-desert terrain. Nothing so extensive or spectacular as the deposits in Petrified Forest National Park, to be sure, but interesting and beautiful just the same. The gradual cell-by-cell replacement or infiltration of buried logs by hot, silica-bearing waters in a process so exact that the original cellular structure of the wood is preserved in all its detail forms this desert jewelry —agatized rainbows in rock. Coming unexpectedly upon such a trove a man is sometimes overcome by greed; by the mad desire to possess it all, to load his pockets, his knapsack, his truck with these hard lustrous treasures and somehow transport them all from the wilderness to the shop, garage and backyard. An understandable mania; packrats, hoarding string, tinfoil, old shoes and plastic spoons, suffer from the same instinct. So that over the surface of the earth a general redistribution of all that is loose, not nailed or bolted down, takes place, hastening the processes of geology, and continents sag at the edges. Silly perhaps but not in the long run harmful; nothing is really lost except that epiphenomenon known as human delight. This too will be replaced.

Up north in the Roan Cliffs are seams of low-grade coal; and throughout an area larger than many states where Utah, Colorado and Wyoming meet lies an immense reserve of shale oil—riches for somebody. But these are not strictly speaking rock forms. There are traces of gold in the Colorado River and the sunken ruins of gigantic dredges; a few lead, zinc and silver mines scattered about; but the only rock which has so far proved to be of commercial value in the canyon country is that called carnotite. Carnotite, a greenish-yellow ore, is a complex mineral containing radon gas, vanadium and—uranium.

Here was a treasure. Spurred by the exciting demands of the Cold War the Atomic Energy Commission, soon after our technicians had shown what they could do (Hiroshima, Nagasaki), began to promote an intensive search for uranium. With known deposits in the Southwest, the search was concentrated here, attracting fortune-hunters from everywhere. Some struck it rich; the professional geologist Charles Steen after years of patient development and hard-luck frustrations suddenly patented a mine he called (with revealing pathos) *Mi Vida*— My Life. Aided by a discovery bonus from the A.E.C., financed by the bankers of Denver and Salt Lake City, he bought heavy mining equipment and a fleet of ore trucks, hired miners and truckers, built an ore-reduction mill on the banks of the Colorado, and became after years of effort a happy if beleaguered millionaire. He constructed a modest mansion on a rocky waterless ledge overlooking Moab; invited relatives, friends and neighbors in for one great barbecue after another; endured threats of blackmail and kidnaping (he had children) from mysterious strangers; built a garrison-type steel fence topped with barbed wire around his entire property and employed guards and a gatekeeper; planted trees along the fence to soften the warlike aspect; ran for public office and was elected; tried to legalize hard liquor and was defeated; sold his mill to the Vanadium Corporation of America; moved elsewhere; came back; moved again.

Another prospector, an amateur but equally fortunate, was Vernon Pick. Drifting in from somewhere out of the Midwest, he lost himself for weeks at a time among the haunted monoliths and goblin gulches above the Dirty Devil River; poisoned himself drinking its foul waters but survived to locate deep in that intricate voodooland a smoldering radioactive hoard which he named, poetically, The Hidden Splendor.

Some of the native Utahns also made money, particularly the ones shrewd enough the moment the boom took off to hustle out into the boondocks and stake claims on everything in sight. A few of these claims were developed and some yielded a profitable tonnage of uranium ore; but most of the wealth was acquired not in mining but in the trading and selling of claims and shares in mining companies which never got beyond the paperwork. Speculation was the big thing; and the money poured in from all over the United States from those persons, always numerous in our society, eager to profit from the labor of others, anxious to harvest what they had not sown. But here was planting, of a sort—the variety known in the industry as "salting"—and many investors, betrayed by their greed, were taken for a jolly ride.

The serious prospecting was carried out by the technicians of the Atomic Energy Commission. Equipped with powerful scintillometers, they cruised in airplanes back and forth above the Colorado Plateau, mapping the hot spots. The information thus obtained was made available to the public but usually too late. The small-time prospector, grinding in by jeep, would arrive in time to see the helicopters of some big mining company rising skyward and the land neatly staked out in acres and acres of identical claims.

Despite such unfair competition the more persevering among the amateur prospectors, climbing over the landscape with their cheap little Geiger counters in hand, sometimes succeeded in finding a source of radiation all their own. The next step was to stake a claim and have it filed with the county recorder. But now their problems were only beginning. Before they could raise the money to finance a mining operation it was necessary to have core samples taken in order to assay the quality and the extent of the uranium deposit. This meant first of all bulldozing a road into the claim; then if they had any money left or could borrow more they had to hire or lease a drilling rig. All very expensive procedures. If the drilling proved out they might be ready to go into business. Or might not, depending upon still other factors, such as the expense of trucking the ore from mine to mill.

The A.E.C. provided a guaranteed market at a guaranteed price for a period of ten years beginning in 1949 for all of the uranium ore—at or above a specified grade—which the miners could produce. Plus a discovery bonus of ten thousand dollars. But even so it became apparent after a time that only large-scale operations—in this as in most other businesses—would make a profit. Also the many small ore pockets scattered about the canyon country were soon made insignificant by the location of vast contiguous bodies of uranium in the Ambrosia Lake district of New Mexico and in Ontario. The small independent miners in Utah, forced to transport their ore long distances over the tire-busting, axle-breaking, clutch-burning terrain of the canyonlands (where roads run every way but straight), found themselves up against the overwhelming competition of such giants as the Anaconda Corporation, with generals and admirals on its governing board and senators on the invisible payroll. When the A.E.C.'s ten-year guarantee ran out most of the independents went out with it—out of business.

There must have been many who were glad to quit. For in addition to the unnumbered exasperations and frustrations which plague the small businessman, and the customary hazards of work in a mine, suggestions of another danger—nuclear radiation—could not be entirely ignored. The uranium miner down deep in his burrow was not only inhaling rock dust every minute and working daily with dynamite, his body was absorbing far more than the usual dosage of alpha, beta and gamma rays. The miner would disregard this danger, so vague, theoretical and intangible (to him), but for the rest of his life whenever he became sick or his health seemed to be ebbing he might remember and wonder about the rumors he had heard years before in the bars and machine shops of Moab, Monticello, Mexican Hat, Green River. Those hot, dusty, strange and isolated little towns set so far apart from one another, so far from anywhere, in the middle of silence and emptiness and burning rock.

Whatever the cost, there was for all who took part the zest of gambling and the exhilaration of adventure into unknown or little known territory. For a few an adventure which became a nightmare:

Two men, for example, greenhorn treasure-seekers, went down the Colorado in a small motorboat overloaded with canned goods, ore samples, hammers, Geiger counters. Whey they reached the junction with the Green River something went wrong; the motor failed and they drifted helplessly into the forty-mile millrace of Cataract Canyon, a place where they had not planned to go. Nearly a century before Major Powell, the first man to go through and write about it, described a portion of Cataract Canyon as follows:

> July 24, 1869.—We examine the rapids below. Large rocks have fallen from the walls—great, angular blocks which have rolled down the talus and are strewn along the channel. We are compelled to make three portages in succession, the distance being less than three fourths of a mile, with a fall of 75 feet. Among these rocks, in chutes, whirlpools and great waves, with rushing breakers and foam, the water finds its way, still tumbling down. We stop for the night only three fourths of a mile below the last camp. . . . Darkness is coming on; but the waves are rolling with crests of foam so white they almost give a light of their own. Near by, a chute of water strikes the foot of a great block of limestone 50 feet high, and the waters pile up against it and roll back. Where there are sunken rocks the water heaps up in mounds or even in cones. At a point where rocks come very near the surface, the water forms a chute above, strikes, and is shot up 10 or 15 feet, and piles back in gentle curves, as in a fountain; and on the river tumbles and roars.

The two prospectors never got through at all. Near the very beginning their boat overturned, cast them out, and went down the river on its own. The men managed to get ashore still alive. But they could not agree on the best way back to human settlement. One hiked up a side canyon and struck off west across-country toward the hamlet of Hanksville, some forty miles away by airline. The second man, thinking it was wiser to stay close to water, trudged northeast along the Colorado back toward Moab, their starting point. He had twice as far to go, taking into account the meanders of the river, but was in no danger of dying from thirst. Neither had any food.

But the first man had all the luck. Soon after the organized search began he was spotted from the air and promptly rescued. While his former comrade struggled on mile after mile and day after day through the willow thickets and over the talus debris on the river's shore. Search parties in powerboats cruised down the river and back again but incredibly failed to see him. He saw them but was too exhausted to shout, lacked matches to start a fire, and apparently was too frightened or too delirious to stay at one spot and construct some kind of distress signal. "They never looked in the right direction," he would later explain, bitterly. And therefore crawled on over the rocks under the desert sun. Now and then catching a lizard which he ate raw and whole. "Tasted like tuna," he reported. Finally he was discovered ten days after the search began near an abandoned miner's shack below Dead Horse Point. They found him sitting on the ground hammering feebly at an ancient can of beans, trying to open the can with a stone. Hospitalized for exposure, shock and malnutrition, he urged that the entrance to Cataract Canyon be somehow chained off, closed forever to human exploration.

(Some present-day Moabites have suggested that the Federal Government take atomic bombs and blast a straight deep channel through Cataract Canyon so that they—the Moabites—can pilot their new cabin cruisers without hazard all the way down to the new Glen Canyon reservoir.)

In all those years of feverish struggle, buying and selling, cheating and swindling, isolation, loneliness, hardship, danger, sudden fortune and sudden disaster, there is one question about this search for the radiant treasure—the hidden splendor—which nobody ever asked. It is necessary, therefore, to relate one more story concerning the uranium strike, a story based on events which may or may not have actually happened but which all who tell it will swear is true:

Among the thousands drawn to the canyon country by the publicity of the boom was one Albert T. Husk of Star Route 2, Box 17, Flat Rock, Texas. He brought with him his young and pleasant-looking (if somewhat thin and anxious) second wife, his eleven-year-old son Billy-Joe, and two little girls younger than the boy. He had left behind a seventy-acre farm in the East Texas pinelands, a Fordson tractor and lesser implements, two purebred Blue Tick coondogs and his father, A. T. Husk Senior, to look after things. All except the old man had been mortgaged to finance the hunt for new wealth and a new life. For Albert Husk was a man of vision.

The Husk family rattled into Moab one blazing hot day in June riding in a jeep pickup which looked as if it had been rolled down a mountainside and towing without safety chain an antique housetrailer of the type which only sheepherders live in these days: plywood and tar-paper, a thin coat of aluminum paint, tires worn down to the threads (purchased from and guaranteed by a dealer in Lubbock named Sharpe). Husk found a vacant spot in the mouth of Courthouse Wash where, under a splendid cottonwood tree, he set up his base camp. There was a spring nearby, with a pool below it large as a bathtub where his new wife could bathe and wash her flaxen hair. With two charges of blasting powder (one of which failed to go off) Husk excavated a pit toilet in the alluvium (he was in a hurry) and slung a tent over it. The Baptist Church was only five miles away in the heart of downtown Moab behind T. C. Tracey's gas station but once his family had been established in their new home Husk—a somewhat indifferent Christian—went straight to the Club 66, where the smoke-dense air crackled with radioactivity and the smell of honest miners' sweat. Here he met his benefactor, a man known as Charles "Chuck" Graham. Or Ingraham—the name has been obscured by the many variants of the narrative.

Mr. Graham like Husk was also a newcomer to the Moab area, though not so new as the latter. In fact he was already pretty well dug in. He owned a flying service —light planes and helicopters for hire or charter—carried a pilot's license, and operated as well the only car- and truck-rental agency in town. An affable and helpful man, he quickly engaged Husk in a friendly conversation at the bar. From the bar they moved to a table in the corner where Mr. Graham produced a large tectonic map and explained to Husk as well as he could (for Husk had only the dimmest notions of geology) what the prospects were for making fresh uranium discoveries in the Colorado Plateau.

It was soon made apparent to Husk that the better possibilities were already firmly tied up in claims and developments. Mr. Graham advised Husk that it might be wiser in the long run to return to Flat Rock and redeem his farm rather than risk his (no doubt limited) assets in what would probably be a fruitless search for a fool's treasure.

Husk allowed that the odds were against him but declared fervently, over the second pitcher of beer, that he wasn't about to go all the way back to East Texas without even giving his luck a try. Mr. Graham then suggested to Husk that better than rambling off half-cocked into the outback he should buy into a partnership with somebody who already controlled a likely group of claims.

Husk requesting further information, Mr. Graham reluctantly conceded that he himself had a few such properties, including a very promising group of uranium claims along the San Rafael River. Mr. Graham explained that he planned to develop the claims himself sooner or later but that the press of his other business had so far made it impossible; he would therefore be willing to take in a partner if the partner commenced the necessary location work.

Husk was willing, even eager, and inquired as to the terms. Mr. Graham however insisted that Husk think it over and have a look at the claims before they discussed pecuniary details; he wanted Husk to be quite certain beforehand that he was getting his money's worth. He did not, he explained, wish to see any friend of his get into something over his head.

Husk smiled and showed Mr. Graham the corner of a cashier's check from a bank in Flat Rock. He wasn't rich, he said, but he could take care of himself. Mr. Graham frowned and cautioned Husk against displaying his funds too openly in a place like the Club 66. Mormons, he implied, have few compunctions about separating a Gentile from his money. Husk said that Mr. Graham was a genuine Christian gentleman if he ever seen one and invited him home to meet the wife and kids. Mr. Graham accepted. Husk reeled out of the bar into the blinding sunlight, Mr. Graham following, and after some confusion led the way to the camp in Courthouse Wash.

Mrs. Husk was pleased to make his acquaintance and the children also took to Mr. Graham at once except for Billy-Joe who was a very shy boy. Mr. Graham showed him his pilot's license and that helped a little. Certainly Mrs. Husk was impressed. She invited Mr. Graham to stay for supper and he did. He particularly enjoyed the mucilaginous green pods of the okra which Mrs. Husk had prepared, remarking that he'd been practically raised on that vegetable back in Oklahoma during his boyhood. He offered Mrs. Husk a cigarette and lit it for her with his slim butane lighter. Later the children showed him the pool up in the canyon below the spring. An owl hooted softly; and little hog-nosed bats zig-zagged through the twilight.

Before leaving for the night Mr. Graham and Husk agreed to meet the next morning for an inspection trip by air to the claims on the San Rafael. When he was gone the Husk family discussed their new friend and all agreed that he seemed like a very fine person, again except for the boy who thought he "smiled too much."

The flight over the canyons next day was a success, though Husk who'd never been up in an airplane before got slightly airsick on the return. In order to land, Mr. Graham had to make three passes over the unpaved airstrip before some browsing cattle would get out of the runway. But during the flight over the canyons he had shown Husk not only his own properties but also several small uranium mines in the vicinity actually in operation: yes, Husk could see for himself the test holes, the adits and tailings, the winding jeep roads along the verge

of dizzy ledges. And as they flew over the claims Mr.
Graham switched on the scintillometer wired to a case of
storage batteries which he carried in the plane and
pointed out to Husk the pointer readings on the dials,
indicative he explained of radioactive minerals somewhere in the mesa below. It would be his partner's job,
on the ground, to locate those deposits precisely.

Husk nodded eagerly and stared so hard his eyes wa-
tered, trying to see through the lifeless rock the buried
slowly disintegrating hoard. Then Mr. Graham pulled up
sharply to clear a bulging escarpment. Husk felt his
stomach sink into his bowels. He saw the horizon rise in
a queer way far up on his right and to the left where the
earth had been a moment before was only blue sky, empty
space, a bottomless gulf.

That evening they made the deal. For a consideration
of $2250 (half the amount of the cashier's check) Husk
gained a forty per cent interest in Hotrock Mountain
Mineral Development Company, as they decided to call
their joint enterprise. An agreement four pages long was
drawn up by Mr. Graham's secretary, signed by both
parties, notarized by the secretary and witnessed formally
by the grimy hand of a man in oily green coveralls who
crawled out from beneath Mr. Graham's aircraft when
needed. With his carbon copy of the contract in hand
Husk went home to give the good news to his wife.

Early the next day Husk went to work. Mr. Graham provided him with a Geiger counter and probe, a geologist's
hammer, standard uranium ore samples, a canvas ore sack,
and extra cans for water and gasoline.

At first Husk had wanted to take his wife and kids
along to the San Rafael but Mr. Graham talked him out
of it, pointing out that the family would be much more
comfortable in its present camp near the amenities and
conveniences of Moab. He said that he would look after
them in Husk's absence and furnish them transportation
into town when needed. (The claims lay far away beyond
the rivers, more than a hundred miles by road, including
some fifty miles of jeep trail and the last ten miles where

there was no road or trail at all.) So Husk loaded his pickup with tools, bedrolls and enough food for two weeks, said goodby to his wife and little girls and drove off, taking only the boy along.

Late that afternoon during the hottest part of the day Mr. Graham left his office and strolled down the street to the Club 66. After a couple of beers he got in his car and went for a drive. Five miles north of town he stopped his car under the shade of the big cottonwood at the outlet of Courthouse Wash. The sheepherder's trailer stood with its screen door sagging open. Flies drifted in and out and a white butterfly with wilted wings rested on the dust of the doorstep. There seemed to be nobody home. Mr. Graham knocked on the trailer wall. Nobody answered but he thought he heard the sound of laughing children in the distance. He walked slowly up the canyon through the stifling heat, keeping to the shady side. At the first turn he halted. Through a screen of willows he looked at the two little girls splashing in the water, and at Mrs. Husk, half undressed, sitting at the edge of the pool. Her long straight yellow hair, wet now, hung before her eyes; indolently, with languid grace, she was combing it. Mr. Graham watched for a few moments then backed off quietly, returned to the trailer and waited there.

All summer long Husk and his son toiled over the rocks above the trickling stream of the San Rafael. They struggled up the debris of talus slopes, clambered along ledges, pulled themselves up the boulder-choked defiles of side canyons. At every gray outcrop of Morrison and Shinarump, the uranium-bearing formations, they probed with the counter foot by foot, now and then getting a static of excitement from the instrument, and they hammered and picked at the rock and loaded their sack with specimens. During the middle of the day they rested in whatever shade they could find—under an overhang or juniper, sometimes under the truck itself—and in the evenings went painfully down to the stream to wash up a little and lug cans of water back up the trail. Much of the time they spent making a road for the truck, hacking through juniper stands, filling in washouts or blasting a hole down through rimrock in order to reach a slope. At night they camped wherever they happened to be, cooking their supper over an open fire and sleeping in the bed of the truck for fear of scorpions and rattlesnakes. And rose before dawn to resume the hunt, covering as much ground as they could before the glare and withering heat of midday.

About every two weeks Husk and Billy-Joe returned to Moab for fresh supplies and for repairs, parts and sometimes new tires for the truck. Each time Husk showed Mr. Graham the samples he had collected. All of them proved to contain a little uranium or thorium but none, according to the report of Mr. Graham's assayist, were rich enough to be of commercial value. Mr. Graham did his best to encourage Husk, bought him drinks at the Club 66 and staked him to new batteries for the Geiger counter. Husk said that what he really needed was a new truck. Mr. Graham laughed, patted him on the back, and reminded him that he'd soon be riding around in Cadillacs.

Preoccupied—almost obsessed—with his work, Husk was only dimly aware of the change in his wife's response to him. With each visit to the home camp she seemed a little more irritable, more disinclined to intimacy, somehow more distant. She submitted to his love-making with indifference, sometimes with reluctance. Husk was faintly troubled; but grateful on the other hand that she seemed so unconcerned by the rapid reduction of their savings and the so-far worthless results of his prospecting. Therefore he did not attempt to question her but returned to his search with anxious eagerness despite the heaviness in his heart.

One afternoon during the last week in August Mr. Graham sat in his office checking the action of the small pistol which he kept in his desk. He was alone. He loaded a clip and slipped it into the pistol, drew the slide back and pushed it forward, placing a round in the firing chamber. Carefully he let the hammer down and put the pistol into the pocket of a light jacket which he sometimes wore. Taking the jacket he went to his helicopter, filled the fuel tanks, climbed into the pilot's seat in the center of the cockpit and started the engine.

Husk and Billy-Joe were cooking their supper over a fire of juniper sticks when they heard the thrashing racket of noise come over the edge of the mesa. The sun was down, the new half-moon hung nearly overhead. In the blend of sunset and twilight they saw the flickering lights before they saw the machine itself coming like a bright metallic dragonfly out of the east and circling once, twice above them before landing. The gusts of wind blew sand and twigs into their fire, into the open pan of corned beef and beans. Billy-Joe's new straw cowboy hat took off from his head, whirled toward the brink of the mesa and sailed off into space. In silence they watched the tall figure of Mr. Graham emerge from the helicopter's plastic bubble, stoop under the slow-turning blades of the prop and walk toward them.

Billy-Joe did not clearly understand everything that followed during the hour or more of conversation around the campfire. He knew that his father was unhappy, even angry, with Mr. Graham and the tone of the argument did not soften when Mr. Graham unzipped the left-hand pocket of his jacket and produced a half-pint of whiskey which he passed to Billy-Joe's father. Husk accepted the bottle and drank but soon afterwards was saying things which made Mr. Graham sit very still, very quiet, with a look on his face which frightened the boy. And after a pause Billy-Joe heard Mr. Graham say a thing about his new mother—his father's new wife—that was strange and ugly.

His father stood up suddenly and roared. He stepped straight through the flames of the fire toward Mr. Graham. And Mr. Graham already standing, backing away, pulled the dark gleaming thing from his other jacket pocket, cocked it, thrust it forward. There was a flash of light and a small explosion. Billy-Joe saw his father stop, grab at his stomach, and lunge again at Mr.

Graham. Who fired again. His father doubled forward, head close to his knees, and sank to the ground. Mr. Graham shot him a third time, in the back. His father, gasping and clutching at his belly, rolled slowly over onto one side.

Billy-Joe stood up wanting to speak. Mr. Graham shielded his eyes from the glow of the campfire and looked for him with the gun. Where are you, Billy? he said.

The boy could not say a word. But his body, his legs, reacted for him. He stumbled backward, turned, ran. Ran madly into the gloom. He heard the gun go off but felt nothing. He kept running and heard the heavy feet of Mr. Graham coming after him. He plunged through brush, through a tree's branches and over the edge of a ravine. He felt himself falling, falling, then a stunning blow as he crashed into sand and went sliding and tumbling all the way down to the bottom of a great dune, all the way to the ravine floor. He tried to move and a sickening jet of pain coursed through his shoulder. He lay still on his back in the shadows, looking up at the scarp over which he had fallen. There was Mr. Graham silhouetted against the sky, walking back and forth, hunting for a way down. A few pale stars shone through the moonlight. The boy and the desert and the night waited in perfect silence for whatever might happen next.

Breathing hard, for he was really somewhat out of shape, Mr. Graham went back to Husk's camp to get a flashlight. There he discovered that his partner was still alive, crawling inch by inch away from the now fading campfire toward the jeep truck. Mr. Graham paused, stepped carefully around Husk and went to the truck, which was parked with chocked wheels on a slope above the rim of the mesa. Beyond the rim the world dropped away at an angle of ninety degrees, down sheer for eight hundred feet or more to a talus of broken slabs in the bottom of a side canyon of the San Rafael canyon. Mr. Graham found a flashlight in the truck, also Husk's rifle. He sat down on the runningboard to rest, to regain his wind, and watched Husk crawling slowly toward him.

When Husk was nearly close enough to reach the toes of his boots Mr. Graham shot him again, this time in the head and with the rifle. He dragged the body into the cab of the truck and slammed shut the doors. He thought for a while, then opened a five-gallon jerry can and poured gasoline over Husk's body and all over the interior of the cab. He found a second gasoline can, unscrewed the lid and set it in the right-hand corner of the cab, on the floor. Mr. Graham was sweating badly, his hands shaking, his chest painfully constricted. He was about to light a cigarette but thought better of it. He sat down near the truck to rest for a while.

Thinking carefully, Mr. Graham decided to ease the truck down close to the edge of the mesa, stop it there and toss a match in on his partner before pushing the whole works over. The truck was parked parallel to the rim, not facing it, so Mr. Graham after removing the rocks from in front of the wheels climbed into the driver's seat, pushing Husk's legs out of the way, and automatically, out of habit, turned on the switch. He had almost stepped on the starter before he realized the danger. Without starting the motor he disengaged the clutch, took the truck out of gear and turned the wheels downhill. There was an awful lot of loose play in the steering. As the truck began to roll Mr. Graham's right foot groped for the brake pedal, found it and pushed it down to the floorboard without meeting the slightest hint of resistance. In sudden alarm he grabbed for the parking brake and found the handle missing. There was nothing there. All at once Mr. Graham knew that more than anything else in the world he wanted to get out of that truck.

As the end of everything swept toward him he struggled with the battered door, got it open and tried to roll out. But as he tumbled from the fast-moving truck the inside door handle projecting foward, slipped into the open pocket of his jacket. Mr. Graham's feet touched solid ground only briefly before he was jerked like a hooked fish over the verge of the abyss. Lightly attached to one another, weightless and free, the truck with its open door and Mr. Graham went off all together into space. He saw the horizon swing in a queer way far up on his right, and to the left, where the earth had been a moment before, was only the sky, a few stars, the tranquil moon floating far below.

The rising sun discovered the boy still alive, stirring feebly in the sand. After some time, moaning softly, he got up on his knees. One eye was swollen shut. His left arm hung limply from a dislocated shoulder. When he tried to lift the arm a wave of pain surged through his body. Nausea rose from his bowels. He waited and when the pain and sickness subsided he hugged the injured limb to his chest with his good arm and got slowly to his feet.

The pain came again, ebbed and returned. His shirt hung in tatters from his shoulder. With a shred of it he made several turns around his left forearm and slung it from his neck. Slowly, tentatively, he started down the bed of the ravine, downhill. Going through a willow thicket the rags of his shirt caught on the branches. He freed himself by stripping off what was left of the shirt. And trudged on.

Not once did he look back or upward.

At noon he found water. Beneath the shade of boulders jammed in the middle of the streambed lay a basin of quicksand with a pool at its center. The heart-shaped prints of deer led in and out. Billy-Joe waded through the mud, went down on his belly, cleared the slime from the surface of the water and drank. Through most of the afternoon he lay there. When the sun had moved beyond the canyon wall he crawled out of the sucking sand and went on.

Now he was hungry. He found a bush with red berries like currants and ate them. In a dank and shady place he found a cluster of plants with large white trumpetlike flowers the color of moonlight. The flowers were fragrant, tender, inviting; he ate them. He walked on, following the downward course of the dry streambed. When he began to feel a little dizzy he sat down again to rest.

Although it was still day the new moon could be seen in the slot between the canyon walls, drifting among clouds. Staring at the moon the boy saw it surrounded with hazy rings, rust-colored. The dark vibrations in the sky hurt his eyes. He looked down at the sand between his legs.

The dry sand, scattered with pebbles, seemed alive. The surface of the ground was palpitating softly, steadily, as if breathing. And each pebble, formerly so dull and sun-bleached, now shone like a jewel. He had never seen anything before so beautiful. He passed his free hand before his eyes and saw the bones glowing through his translucent flesh. He stared and stared and then something off in the corner of his field of vision caught his attention.

There was a bush. A bush growing out of the hard sun-baked mud. And the bush was alive, each of its many branches writhing in a sort of dance and all clothed in a luminous aura of smoky green, fiery blue, flame-like yellow. As he watched the bush became larger, more active, brighter and brighter. Suddenly it exploded into fire.

Whimpering, Billy-Joe pressed his hands to his eyes and felt the joints of his bones grate together like glass. He held himself rigid against the convulsions that swelled with a droning murmur through his body. They grew more powerful, overwhelmed him, possessed him. Yielding, the agony passed out of him and beyond and all became quiet again, marvelously still.

He lowered his hand, opened his eyes. The bush was in place as before, writhing and glowing but not in fire. The walls of the canyon towered over him, leaning in toward him then moving back, in and then back, but without sound. They were radiant, like heated iron. The moon had passed out of sight. He saw the stars caught in a dense sky like moths in a cobweb, alive, quivering, struggling to escape. He understood their fear, their desperation, and wept in sympathy with their helplessness.

He watched and a meteor passed beneath the web, gliding more slowly than a ship across what seemed an infinite sea of vibrant, curling waves. In the wake of the meteor streamers of flame expanded with languorous, unhurried

ease, fading out as they grew larger but leaving the sky
in some way transmuted, stained by their burning passage.

The boy looked down at the bush, at the pebbles on
the sand, at his hand. When he looked up again the
meteor had crossed about two-thirds of the interval between canyon walls and was still advancing. Before it
passed over the farther wall he fell asleep. And when he
awoke late the next morning he remembered all that he
had seen but no longer as anything strange. For everything
appeared to him as equally strange.

The still-smoking wreckage of a truck which he passed
in the middle of the day, with ravens picking at fragments of burnt meat crammed inside the crumpled black-
ened steel—this did not seem to Billy-Joe in any way ex-
traordinary. Farther down the canyon he stepped over
parts of a human body—an arm encased in the sleeve of
a jacket, the shoulder gnawed down to the bone—and a
head, the head of a man, separated from its trunk by a
blow of some incredible violence. He looked at these
things and he saw them but did not pause. He shuffled
past them without glancing back, neither slowing nor
increasing his pace.

The ravens watched him go, croaking with satisfaction,
and swept down again upon the remnants. They approached their meat in a stylized, formal fashion with
little dancing steps and covered it under widespread,
glossy, blue-black wings.

In the afternoon he came into a larger canyon, through
which flowed a small stream. The place should have been
familiar to the boy—the warm, unpleasant-smelling water, the mudbanks encrusted with alkali white as salt, the
tamarisk and pickleweed—but he did not recognize it. He
drank the water and bathed his eye. The swelling was
beginning to go down and he could open the lids enough
to see through. He followed the water.

All through the day clouds gathered in the sky, wind
whistled above the walls, and by evening he could hear
from far away the mutter of thunder. At night whenever
he awoke for a few moments he saw flashes of lightning

reflected in the sky. But no rain fell where he was. His hunger made him sick with misery, worse than the pain of his arm and shoulder to which he was now accustomed, or the fiery discomfort of his sunburned back.

When morning came he got up and tried to go on but could not walk very far. He crawled into the shade of a giant cottonwood tree, long dead, that lay across the streambed with its roots exposed and its bare limbs pointing up the canyon. The cool damp sand felt good to the boy, with the water trickling over his feet and ankles. He was not going to walk any more. He would wait now for whatever had to happen. He was tired. And everything was strange.

He might not even have heard the coming of the flash flood. It began as a dim toneless resonance in the distance, like the sound made by a train entering the far end of a very long tunnel. Gradually the vibrations grew in volume until the canyon filled with a dull and heavy roar. But the flood itself did not yet appear. Half-conscious, Billy-Joe dreamed of home.

One two three four small gray birds fluttered out of the willows beside the stream and flew in circles to a perch high on the canyon wall.

Now.

Around the bend up-canyon poured a red snout of liquid mud, which seemed to mumble to itself as it advanced. Sliding greasily forward the snout of mud dashed against the undercut wall on the outside of the bend, wallowed over ledges and swung back to the main channel in the center of the canyon floor. The clear perennial stream which flowed there was suddenly buried, extinguished. Swaying from side to side in the rhythm of its pendulous momentum, like a locomotive on uneven rails, the flood rumbled down upon the boy and the dead tree and everything else in its path. Dust sailed into the air as it crashed into mudbanks; cracks rippled like lightning over the surface of the alluvium, yawning wide apart as chunks and blocks and sections of dried-out earth slid or toppled into the torrent. On the crest of the flood as it

came, above the churning debris of bushes, vines, weeds
and logs, floated a delicate and rosy vapor, a fine pink
mist suffused with the glow of sunlight.

Billy-Joe watched the flood surge toward him, saw the
light shine on the roiling tomato-red waters. Instinctively
he crawled deeper in among the roots of the tree and
clung there with his good arm and both legs as the deluge
smashed over him.

The big cottonwood shuddered under the impact,
stirred, swung loose and rose, becoming buoyant. As the
flood widened and deepened, filling the canyon floor from
wall to wall, the tree began to float with it, slowly at first
and then faster and faster as it was caught in the central
current. The limbs spreading out on either side, like out-
riggers, kept the tree from rolling as it sailed toward its
destiny.

Gasping for air Billy-Joe crawled onto the trunk and
rode it all the way through the canyon, all the way while
boulders clashed in the foam beneath him and slabs of
sandstone shook free of their ancient fastenings, spalled
from the cliffs and crashed with a sound like thunder into
the heave and roar of the flood. He was still leeched to
the tree, part drowned but alive, when it caromed off a
jutting outcrop at the canyon's mouth and glided majesti-
cally out onto the flow of a wide and gleaming, deep and
golden river.

Now began for the boy what was for him an unrec-
koned, uncountable series of days and nights. His life became dreamlike. The nightmare with its unacceptable dis-
asters was left behind, submerged in chaos. He lived now
a dream. A golden dream which grew day by day more
golden, more dreamlike, on the golden water under the
inescapable eye of the golden desert sun. He clung to the
tree as if it were the only thing he knew; he had neither
the thought nor the power to leave it. And as the tree
drifted southward and west through the labyrinthine canyons of the river, through the immense silence, the light
came down on his naked body from above, from the
burnished walls on either side, from the dazzling play and
sparkle of the water itself.

At first during the early days he may have made feeble efforts to cool his body by slipping off the trunk of the tree and floating with it, one arm bent over a limb. But as his strength diminished he would have found it always more difficult to pull himself out of the water and back onto the trunk. Finally he must have given up those efforts and remained entirely on the tree, making no move whatever as the rays of the sun, direct and reflected, seared his flesh, baked his brain within its skull, poisoned the marrow of his bones. Each night brought relief, enough to stir his drugged consciousness and arouse his agony. Each day brought the golden sun, more than enough to burn him deeper into the dream. At last he surrendered and passed through his pain into a deeper state of bliss.

Sixteen days after Mr. Graham's last flight Billy-Joe was discovered by the ferryman at Hite's Crossing. He saw the tree lodged against his landing dock and what resembled a shriveled human figure attached to the trunk of it. He called for help. Carefully they removed the body which was covered with a mass of second and third degree burns. The boy certainly appeared to be quite dead. But then they detected a trace of life. Or thought they did. Someone radioed for an airplane, the boy was flown to a hospital in Flagstaff. The doctors there believed that Billy-Joe was still alive. They put him into an oxygen tent and pumped quarts of glucose into his veins. Mrs. Husk was contacted and came down to see him. But he never saw her. He never came back, never opened his eyes, never spoke. He could not live anymore and after three days even the strongest of the doctors let him go. Then he died.

Mrs. Husk survived, even after the remains of her husband and her lover were found, and with her two little daughters went back home to Texas. (But not to the farm—that was gone. Along with Grandpaw.) About a year after the incident in Utah she was approached cautiously by a lawyer, an affable young fellow from Austin. After the usual sociable preliminaries the attorney said that he understood that Mrs. Husk, as inheritor of the estate of her late husband, held a 40 per cent interest in a group of uranium claims known as the Hotrock Mountain Mineral Development Company. Mrs. Husk said that this was true. The lawyer said that he had been authorized by an interested party to negotiate with Mrs. Husk the purchase of her share in these properties. Mrs. Husk said how much? The lawyer said that he had been authorized to offer Mrs. Husk $4500—twice what her late husband had paid for them. Mrs. Husk said that she would settle for $150,000. The lawyer smiled and said that he was quite serious. Mrs. Husk said that she was serious too and that on second thought perhaps $237,000 would be a more reasonable figure. The lawyer smiled again and revealed confidentially that he had been authorized to offer, *if absolutely necessary*, as much as $15,000. Mrs. Husk said that $192,761 seemed to her a fair price. The lawyer offered her a cigarette. She took it. He lit it for her with a trim-shaped lighter bearing on its fuselage the emblem of the USAF. They agreed shortly thereafter on the sum of one hundred thousand ($100,000) dollars.

COWBOYS AND INDIANS

JUNE IN the desert. The sun roars down from its track in space with a savage and holy light, a fantastic music in the mind. Up in the mountains the snow has receded to timberline—Old Tukuhnikivats and the other peaks take on a soft spring green along their flanks; the aspen is leafing out. The roads up into the meadows and forests are open again and all the Moab cattlemen who hold grazing permits up there (and some who don't) are moving their stock out of the desert and into the national forest, where the animals will stay until September and the return of the snow.

Springtime on the mountains. Summer down here.

Yesterday I helped Roy Scobie clear his cows out of Courthouse Wash, which runs mostly to the west of the park but through the south end of it. We started early, about six, after a hot breakfast in the morning twilight.

Three of us—Roy, his Basque hired man Viviano Jacquez, myself.

Roy is a leather-hided, long-connected, sober-sided old man with gray hair, red nose and yellow teeth; he is kind, gentle, well-meaning, but worries too much, takes things too seriously. For instance, he's afraid of having a heart attack, falling off the horse, dying there on the sand, under the sun, among the flies and weeds and indifferent cattle. I'm not inferring this—he told me so.

What could I say? I was still young myself, or thought I was, enjoying good health, not yet quite to the beginning of the middle of the journey. I listened gravely as he spoke of death, nodding in an agreement I did not feel. His long yellow fingers, holding a cigarette, trembled.

Roy's no Mormon and not much of a Christian, and does not honestly believe in an afterlife. Yet the manner of death he fears does not sound bad to me; to me it seems like a decent, clean way of taking off, surely better than the slow rot in a hospital oxygen tent with rubber tubes stuck up your nose, prick, asshole, with blood transfusions and intravenous feeding, bedsores and bedpans and bad-tempered nurses' aides—the whole nasty routine to which most dying men, in our time, are condemned.

But how could I tell him so? What did I know of it? To me death was little more than a fascinating abstraction, the conclusion to a syllogism or the denouement of a stage drama. What do old men who don't believe in Heaven think about? I used to wonder. Now we know: they think about their blood pressure, their bladders, their aortas, their lower intestines, ice on the doorstep, too much sun at noon.

I met Roy and Viviano at a place called Willow Seep near the upper end of Courthouse Wash and there we began the drive. We were only about ten miles from the stockpens near Moab, but would have to check out all the side canyons along the way.

We unloaded the horses from Roy's truck, gave them each a little grain, saddled up, and moved out with the old man in the middle. A fine morning—a sweet cool

stark sunlit silent desert morning—before the heat moved
in and the deerflies, the sweat, the dust and the thirst
came down on us.

Not far down the canyon we found the first small bunch
of cows and calves. They saw us coming and trotted off
in various directions through the brush, making things
more difficult than was really necessary. In the cool of the
morning they were feeling lively; also, not having seen a
man or a horse all winter, they were half-wild. The little
calves had never seen *anything* like us and were, under-
standably, terrified.

We collected them all after a time and got them moving together down the wash, pushing them steadily but
not fast. Only half the cows wore Roy's brand and ear-
marks but in accordance with custom we herded everything we found toward Moab; the other ranchers would
do the same and in the stockpens each man would sort
out his own property from the rest. Any cow without a
brand—"slick"—belonged to the finder. (Many a famous
cattle outfit had been started with no more than a rope
and a good horse.) Cooperation is necessary because in
this part of Utah there are not many fences. The cattle
wander far over the open range, driven by hunger and
thirst, and forget who they belong to. Why no fences?
Because in much of the canyon country there is no ground
to dig postholes in—nothing but solid rock.

Old Roy had something on his mind. When the sun
burst out above the canyon rim, flaring like a white scream,
and its hot breath burned my neck, I knew what he was
thinking about.

The cattle plodded before us, slowing down as the heat
rose, reluctant to keep moving. When they stopped we
yelled and whistled at them, beat their gaunt hipbones
with our bridle reins, kicked them in the ribs. They jogged
ahead, half-trotting, and the green dung streamed down
their legs. Ugly brutes, bound for a summer in the high
meadows and then the slaughter house—too bloody good
for them, I was thinking.

Side canyons appeared. Viviano took one, I took the

other, while Roy stayed with the bunch we already had. The canyon I faced was choked with brush, impossible to ride through; the prickly pear grew knee-high in great clumps hairy with spines, scrub oak obstructed the path, the branches of juniper and pinyon pine struck at my face, knocked my hat off. I had to tie the horse and go in on foot. The heavy air was swarming with flies and the numerous trails in the thickets were well beaten and dusty, strewn with cow droppings. Real cattle country all right. I picked up a club, went on, stooping under the tangle. The canyon was short and boxed in and at the head was a cow and her calf; I drove them out and back to the main canyon. I was glad to get on my horse and rejoin Viviano and Roy.

Viviano was happy that morning. He sang and whistled continually, winked and grinned when he caught my eye and charged after straying cattle like a maniac, spurring his thin-skinned palomino through the brush, up over rocks, down mudbanks and between trees with what looked to me like complete indifference to life and limb, the vulnerability of the flesh. Not showing off, for I'd seen his exhibitions of recklessness at other times, but simply out of high spirits, for the fun and the hell of it.

Viviano Jacquez, born in the Pyrenees somewhere (he never cared to tell me more), had been imported with his parents into Utah to herd sheep for some congressman's favorite constituent, then drifted from job to job until he came to Roy Scobie's combination dude and cattle ranch. He's a good cowboy, I suppose; at least he knows the basic skills of the trade: can shoe a horse, rope and brand and castrate a calf, fix a flat tire, stretch barbed wire, dynamite a beaver dam or lay out an irrigation ditch. His English is about fifty per cent profanity, rough but intelligible, and he can sing, play the guitar, and read your fortune in the cards, the rewards of what I would call his liberal education. He is short, dark and savage, like most good Basques, with large brown glamorous eyes which seem to appeal to the ladies; from fourteen to forty-five he pursues them all, and if I can believe his lies, makes out with every one.

What else about him? This: he does not understand American clock time and has no sense of responsibility; he is completely and dependably totally unreliable. But, in his favor, he is inexpensive; he is economical; he works full-time seven days a week for room and board and a hundred dollars a month. Employers like that; but it would be false to say that Viviano is exploited. How can you exploit a man who enjoys his work? He'll work for nothing, almost, if necessary, requiring only a token wage or salary in recognition of his professional status.

Not that he never bitches and grumbles. When he isn't singing or whistling or telling lies in some woman's ear he complains loud and bitterly about his pay, the long hours, the lousy food, the skunks under the bunkhouse, the treacherous and conniving women, the stupid dudes. He threatens to quit, gets drunk and disappears for a couple of days. But always comes back. Or has so far.

Poor Viviano with so much to his credit has one problem which he'll never be able to outlive. Two or three beers and he reveals it to me. He has been infected by the poison of prejudice. Infected and victimized. With his dark skin and Spanish accent he is often taken for a Mexican, which he resents, because he despises Mexicans. He also despises Indians. Even his own heritage: "dumb Basko" he once called himself. Inadvertently when drunk he exposes the wistful desire to somehow disappear and merge into the pale-faced millions who own and operate America.

Useless to try and reassure him that he has more to lose than gain by such assimilation; somewhere, in a way we all know, his pride was damaged and his confidence shaken. In our occasional rambles through the beer halls of Moab I have not seen him rebuffed in any way; but he may be alert to signals of rejection too subtle for me. In any case, at one time or another, perhaps unknown even to Viviano himself, the damage was done. And his reaction is the typical one; he responds to prejudice by cultivating a prejudice of his own against those whom he feels are even lower in the American hierarchy than he is: against the Indians, the Mexicans, the Negroes. He knows where the bottom is.

Too late to make a liberal out of Viviano Jacquez.

The sun climbed noon-high, the heat grew thick and heavy on our brains, the dust clouded our eyes and mixed with our sweat—Viviano's white teeth gleam through a kind of pancake makeup of sweat and dirt when he laughs at me or at the hardmouth beast I'm riding. The cows groan against the forced migration as if they know where it will eventually bring them. I think of the second movement from Beethoven's Eroica. *Marcia funebre*. My canteen is nearly empty and I'm afraid to drink what little water is left—there may never be any more. I'd like to cave in for a while, crawl under yonder cottonwood and die peacefully in the shade, drinking dust. . . . I look aside covertly under my hat brim at old man Scobie who thinks he is going to have a heart attack and fall off his horse: he rides steadily forward, eyes sad and thoughtful, watching the green rumps of his cattle, cigarette hanging from his lower lip, flicking the reins casually back and forth across the mane of his equally thoughtful, abstracted horse. Lunchtime maybe? I think, glancing at the sun. But nobody says anything about lunch. Maybe they aren't even planning to stop for lunch? Maybe they aren't human?

Some of the cows bunched up in the shade under an overhang in the canyon wall. They refused to move. Their calves stumbled close to them, bawling piteously. The drive was starting to drag. Have mercy on us all, I thought. But Viviano like a sun-crazed madman rode savagely into the cattle, screaming and whistling, lashing at the cows with a length of rope. "Crazy son of my bitches," he was screaming, "let's pick up the feet!"

Roy raised a hand. "That's all right, Viviano," he said, "we'll take a break now. Don't want to run them little beeves right into the ground."

Good man, I thought, heading at once for the nearest
shade, where I tied my horse to a log, unsaddled, and
dropped. I was too hot and tired at first even to care about
food or water. Viviano and Roy joined me, unhurried,
lay down in the shade nearby and lit up cigarettes. Above
us was the green canopy of the cottonwood tree filtering
the light to a tolerable dimness. A few red ants crawled
over my belly; I didn't care. *Tengo sed,* I said to myself.
I finished my water. But appeasing thirst brought back
hunger. Who brought the lunch? I began to worry, realiz-
ing for the first time that no one had said a word about it
yet. I didn't say anything either. But I was worried.

"I'm worried," old Roy said.

Tengo mucho hambre, hombre—I'm worried too. How
did it go in that other language? *Faim? J'ai faim? Je suis
famine?* I looked toward Viviano. He was already asleep,
the fancy twenty dollar Stetson over his eyes, a pair of flies
circling above his open mouth. For a hatband he wore a
sterling silver chain—in the mouth a golden tooth. The
goddamned lady killer.

"You know what happened to Ernie Faye?" Roy said,
evidently addressing me though he was staring up at the
leaves.

"No," I said; "what happened to him?"

"You wouldn't know him; this happened three years
ago." Roy paused. "He was picking peaches one day in
his own backyard, taking it easy, and he had a stroke.
When his wife went out to look for him he was on the
ground on top of a bushel basket and he was dead. A
big strong man, too. Sixty-six years old. That's for a
fact."

"It happens. Did you bring any lunch, Roy?"

"Lunch?" He continued to stare at nothing. Thinking.
Worrying. "Sixty-six years old," he said.

"It happens. But only once."

"Once is enough."

"Did you bring any lunch?"

"Lunch?" At last he turned his head to look at me.
"Well no, I didn't. You hungry?"

"A little bit, now that you mention it."

"Sorry we didn't bring anything. We'll eat good when we get back."

"That's all right," I said. "I'll survive, maybe."

But Roy had lost interest in the subject. He wasn't listening to me. The vacant look was in his eyes as he resumed the study of his problem. After a while he let his head drop back against his saddle and closed his eyes. The red nose, the gray hair, the yellow teeth and fingers, a white stubble of whiskers on his bony jaw, his leathery flat cheeks—he looked like an old horse all right but still tough and viable. He was only about seventy years old.

Old Roy is a good man in most ways, but he has his troubles. I'd been spending some of my days off at his ranch, doing a little work around the place in return for room and board. (There's a girl there, one of the paying guests.) I was sharing a bunkhouse room with Viviano one night when I heard the shuffling of feet, the sound of a mumbling voice. It was very late; Viviano was sound asleep. I got up and stepped outside and saw Roy walking by in his long underwear and boots, a revolver in his hand, talking to himself. What's up? I asked him. Insomnia, he said. Try getting a little sleep. I tried, he said, and I can't. What's the gun for? Skunks, he said—they been at the chickens again. We'll they're no chickens here, I said. No but there's skunks, and they're living right under that room where you're sleeping. And he walked away, unhappy and preoccupied.

He has troubles, God knows. He fights with his wife—third or fourth wife—and has difficulties with the bank, with his horses, with his hired help, with the ranch machinery. Mortgaged over his head, he tries to economize by getting by with old trucks and a second-hand tractor, and by hiring cheap and irresponsible help like me and Viviano. He thinks he is saving money by always paying Viviano one month late. Worst of all he skimps on food.

His pack trips are notorious for their frugality. He does the cooking, of course, so that someone else is morally obliged to wash the dishes, and so that he can control the consumption of supplies. "One egg or two?" he'll ask at breakfast time, when you are hungry enough to eat the skin off a bear. Slowly, his old yellow hands shaking, he shovels two little Grade C eggs onto your plate. Then he says. "You want any bacon with that?"

He tries to justify his miserliness with food by pretending that he is observing some time-honored Western tradition. "It's a fact," he will claim, "them old timers never ate much when they was out working on the range. A man rides better on a hard stomach. It's a fact. But we'll eat good when we get back."

The lying old bastard. He hopes that by starving his employees they won't live long enough to collect their wages. The paying guests don't fare much better and as a result seldom come back for a second season at Roy Scobie's Redrock Ranch. It's a beautiful ranch and his pack trips take them into an unknown world—but they don't often return. As a small businessman Roy is getting smaller every season. Bankruptcy and heart attacks loom ahead.

I've endeavored to warn him. He is interested in my opinion and listens at first with some care. Then his attention wanders. The habits of a lifetime are impossible to break. When we bed down at night, out in the open, he always looks for a slab of sandstone to spread his bedroll on. "Rock is softer than sand," he explains. "That's a fact." His words trail off into the vague mumble, "Slept on rock all my life, goddamnit. . . ." The empty stare follows: a foolish thrift is driving him to ruin and all he cares about is his heart; he is thinking about falling off his horse again like Ernie Faye fell off the ladder picking peaches. Dead on the rock.

I can help him with that question, too, I sometimes think; I have a supply of classic philosophical lore ready to offer at the slightest provocation. Our life on earth is but the shadow of a higher life, I could tell him. Or, Life is but a dream. Or, Who wants to live forever? Vanity, vanity. Recall Sophocles, Roy: Lucky are those who die in infancy but best of all is never to have been born. You know.

All kinds of ideas spring to mind, but an instinctive

prudence makes me hold my tongue. What right have I to interfere with an old man's antideath wish? He knows what he's doing; let him savor it to the full. He'll never have another chance as good as this. Each man in his humor. Every cobbler gets clobbered at last, etc. Let him shamble through the dark at night in his underwear, looking for the black skunk with the white stripe down its back, the ultimate enemy.

The weird silence woke me up. I looked around. Everything seemed to be withering in the heat, blasted and shrunken under the furnace of the sun. I dreamed of water and wondered if it would be worth the effort to dig a hole through the ceramic mud of the canyon floor. While I debated the matter in my head, Roy opened his eyes, staggered up, glanced blearily at me to see that I was awake, nudged Viviano in the ribs with the toe of his boot. "Let's get on, boys," he said.

We saddled our horses and got on. On with the death march, *marcia funebre*, the stations of the cross, *el jornado del muerto*. The cows faced us stubbornly, their red eyes full of hatred. The poor little white-faced calves trembled on their shaky legs, hides coated with dust, hind-ends crusted with sunbaked excrement. *Miserere*.

Roy moved his horse stolidly against them, implacable. Viviano, undaunted by the heat and still showing off, sprang on his horse—yes, literally vaulted into the saddle —and rode yelling and flailing and whistling into the herd. (One leap and he was in the saddle; five beers and he was on the floor.) I climbed onto my horse like a man dragging himself through a bad dream, got both feet in the stirrups and rode after the others. After a few minutes of milling struggle the weary beasts gave up and headed down the canyon, moving in the right direction toward their fate.

Not that their fate was so terrible: a summer in the high mountain meadows eating flowers, far above the heat and hay fever of the desert; I envied them. The cows would live to breed again, those that didn't eat too much larkspur; the new crop of calves had a life expectancy of at least one full year; only the yearling steers would be shipped off in the fall to meet the hook and the hammer. I nursed my sympathies, saving them chiefly for myself, who could better appreciate them and deserved them more —hungry, tired, dirty and thirsty as I was.

More side canyons came into view—Two-Mile, Sleepy Hollow, and others without names—and we had to separate, explore each one in search of the outlaws and the fugitives, drive them out of the thickets where they were shaded up and add them to the herd.

There is water in Sleepy Hollow, a big pool under a seep in the canyon wall, fenced off from the cows. We paused for a few minutes to drink and refill canteens, then moved on. No time for a swim today. The drive continued.

As the herd became bigger the dust and the heat got worse. The cattle complained but we were merciless. One old cow, followed by her calf, slipped aside into the tamarisk and lay down. Since she was on my flank of the drive I had to get her out. Again I had to dismount and go in on foot, fighting my way through the brush and clouds of gnats and the vicious yellow-backed flies. The cow didn't want to get up; she preferred the shade. I beat her with the club, kicked her in the ribs, yanked at her tail. At last, groaning and farting with exaggerated self-pity, she hoisted her rear end, then her front end, and plodded off to rejoin the gang. When I got back to my horse I was too tired to climb immediately into the saddle; it seemed easier for a while to walk and lead the horse.

Second movement, seventh symphony, Beethoven again —the slow, ponderous dirge. Had the sun moved at all? Not that I could tell. But as I came up with the others, Viviano, grinning through his dusty face, yelled at me:

"Around the bend, only nine son of bitch more, we get the Jesus Christ out of here."

"Good," I said but something in my face must have given me away; Viviano laughed, spurred his horse and dashed off singing.

I parked my beast for a minute close to a mudbank and hauled myself onto the saddle the easy way. But dropped the reins and nearly fell off retrieving them. Recovered. Both feet in stirrups, I took a few gulps of water and proceeded.

Puddles of quicksand lay ahead of us. We drove the herd around to the side but one cow, stubborn and stupid, managed to get into the stuff. Deliberately, I was sure. The sand quivered like jelly beneath the cow's hooves, broke open, sucked at the plunging feet. Panicked, the cow struggled through, splashing mud and sand. Safe. As we went on I looked back and saw the holes the cow had made fill up and brim over with water, like suppurating sores.

More quicksand. This time we weren't so lucky. The pool extended clear across the canyon floor from one sheer wall to the other. We rushed the herd through but one cow, the same one as before, got herself bogged down. Really trapped this time. Bellydeep in the soup, willing to give up, she neither struggled nor bellowed. This cow didn't want to fight anything anymore.

The sun beat down on our backs and the sweat trickled into our eyes. Roy and Viviano discussed the situation briefly; we went to work. Keeping their mounts clear of the quicksand, they each tossed a loop over the cow's head, drew the knot firm around her neck, taking in the slack, and dallied each rope to the horns of their respective saddles. As the ropes tautened and the horses prepared to pull, I slogged into the mud and tugged at the cow's tail to give her hindquarters whatever life I could.

We were ready. Roy and Viviano urged their horses forward; the horses squatted, braced, heaved; the ropes squeaked under the strain. For a moment nothing seemed to be happening. Then something was happening. Like a cork from a bottle the cow was being drawn from the suction of the quicksand. She struggled feebly, the horses swung ahead, the mud made a violent raw gasping noise, exploded, and out she came.

Roy and Viviano stopped and gave me some slack; I

removed the ropes from the cow's neck as she stood trembling on firm ground. Her eyeballs protruded like a pair of onion bulbs; the tongue, purple in hue and coated with scum, hung loosely from the side of her mouth like a rag of spoiled meat. It was the longest tongue I had ever seen outside of a butcher's shop.

"Seventy dollars worth of cow," Roy explained, coiling his rope. "A fact. Couldn't hardly afford to leave it there."

The cow had still not moved. Viviano rode up and lashed it across the rump. "Heeyah!" he shouted, "lez go man, Jesus Christ!" The cow stumbled toward the herd, Viviano pressing it hard. "Heeyah! goddamn!" Whacking it across the rear with his heavy, wet rope. "Goddamn son of bitch cow!"

The herd began to move, the choking dust filled the air. I climbed on my horse, loading the poor brute down not only with my own weight but with two bootfuls of mud and water.

An hour later we descended the jump-off, a stairway of stone ledges in the canyon floor where trickles of water oozed down over mats of algae, through slick sculptured grooves and into the sandy basins below. The cattle clattered and skidded on the bare rock; sparks flew from the iron-shod hooves of the horses. Lagging behind, I stopped to admire a tiny spring bubbling out of the sand above the ledges, well off to one side of the trail. The water was so clear, so perfectly transparent, that only the dance of grains of sand in the bottom of the spring, where the flow came up through a fissure in the rock, revealed that it was under pressure and in motion. I took a quick drink—cool and sweet—and rode on through the blessed shade of the canyon walls; the sun had finally dropped below the rim. Life began to seem plausible again after an afternoon of doubt.

We went on for another mile and emerged abruptly and to me unexpectedly into full day again, the glare of the sun and the scalding heat. We were in the mouth of the canyon. Ahead lay the highway, the Colorado River, the outskirts of Moab. We pushed the cattle on over the bridge, across the cement and asphalt, and into the big corrals in the fields beyond. We unsaddled the horses and brushed them as best we could with handfuls of juniper twigs and turned them loose in the pasture. Free at last, frolicking like colts, they galloped after one another in circles, lay down and rolled in the dust, got up and galloped some more. I knew how they felt.

Roy's station wagon was parked near the stockpens. We adjourned the field for a pitcher of beer in Moab. It was, of course, only the usual Mormon 3.2—for which may God forgive them—but never had beer tasted better, or been drunk by more deserving men. Old Roy treated us each to a bag of peanuts and talked a little about tomorrow's work: trucking the cattle up to his allotment on the southern slope of Tukuhnikivats. A tedious job in which I would not participate—back to the Arches for me, I reminded him. Roy's expression saddened; he would have to hire someone to take my place for the day, someone who would probably expect to be paid in United States hard dollars. He looked away and into the emptiness, thinking again; the smoke from his forgotten cigarette rose slowly into the haze beneath the ceiling.

Stop that, I wanted to tell him. *Stop that thinking.* I wanted to put my arm around his old shoulders and stroke his thin gray hair and tell him the truth about everything, the entire wild beautiful utterly useless truth. But I didn't.

Viviano ordered a second pitcher of beer, got up suddenly from his chair, tripped over my outstretched legs and fell flat on the floor. He pulled himself slowly to his feet and scowled about through the gloom to see if anyone had noticed; nobody had. Nobody could have cared less. I should have apologized and helped him get up but I didn't. He tramped bitterly, soggily, toward the men's room and disappeared in a dim, rancid, yellowish light. He was a cowboy, *muy macho, mucho hombre*. Very sensitive.

Years later, still wandering in circles, I will come back to the Arches and the canyon country and inquire about my old acquaintances. Where are they? I will ask and the people will say to me:

Viviano Jacquez? You mean that little Mexican that worked for Roy Scobie? Well, who knows? Some say he went to Ouray, Colorado, to work in a silver mine; some say he married Scobie's cook, that white girl from Oklahoma, and they went to California; some say he went back to sheepherding; some say he went to Spain.

And old Roy? You didn't hear? Well he had to sell out a couple years after you left. He went down to Arizona and started an Indian jewelry store near Sedona. He's dead now. He was hanging a picture on the wall of his store and had a heart attack. He was standing on a chair at the time.

COWBOYS AND INDIANS
PART II

THERE ARE lonely hours. How can I deny it? There are times when solitaire becomes solitary, an entirely different game, a prison term, and the inside of the skull as confining and unbearable as the interior of the house-trailer on a hot day.

To escape both, I live more and more in the out-of-doors. First I built the fireplace on a level bench of sandstone about fifty yards to the rear of the trailer. I dragged the wooden picnic table close to the fireplace and this became my office and dining room. Next I built a *ramada* or sunshelter over both. The ramada is a simple affair: four upright posts about ten feet tall tied and braced with crosspoles and supporting a thatched roof of juniper branches, which keeps out the sunlight but lets smoke and heat filter up through. There are of course no walls to this structure. The floor is sandstone, swept clean by the winds, with a couple of wild shrubs—cliffrose and blackbush—growing in one corner. The windbells and the red bandana, my private flag, hang from the projecting end of one of the crosspoles. Finally I set up a cot near the ramada—not under it—and my home without walls was complete. I can sleep at night with nothing but space between me and the stars, comforted in the knowledge that I am not likely to miss anything important up there.

The housetrailer serves now chiefly as storage place and kitchen. Although I sometimes cook at the fireplace outside, it is certainly easier to use the gas stove in the trailer, despite the heat. When the meal is ready I carry it out to the picnic table under the ramada and eat it there. The refrigerator, too, is a useful machine. Not indispensable but useful. It is in fact one of the few positive contributions of scientific technology to civilization and I am grateful for it. Raised in the backwoods of the Allegheny Mountains, I remember clearly how we used to chop blocks of ice out of Crooked Creek, haul them with team and wagon about a mile up the hill to the farmhouse and store them away in sawdust for use in the summer. Every time I drop a couple of ice cubes into a glass I think with favor of all the iron and coal miners, bargemen, railroaders, steelworkers, technicians, designers, factory assemblers, wholesalers, truckdrivers and retailers who have combined their labors (often quite taxing) to provide me with this simple but pleasant convenience, without which the highball or the *Cuba libre* would be poor things indeed.

Once the drink is mixed, however, I always go *outside*, out in the light and the air and the space and the breeze, to enjoy it. Making the best of both worlds, that's the thing.

But how, you might ask, does living outdoors on the terrace enable me to escape that other form of isolation, the solitary confinement of the mind? For there are the bad moments, or were, especially at the beginning of my life here, when I would sit down at the table for supper inside the housetrailer and discover with a sudden shock that I was alone. There was nobody, nobody at all, on the other side of the table. Alone-ness became loneliness and the sensation was strong enough to remind me (how could I have forgotten?) that the one thing better than solitude, the only thing better than solitude, is society.

By society I do not mean the roar of city streets or the cultured and cultural talk of the schoolmen (reach for your revolver!) or human life in general. I mean the society of a friend or friends or a good, friendly woman.

Strange as it might seem, I found that eating my supper out back made a difference. Inside the trailer, surrounded by the artifacture of America, I was reminded insistently of all that I had, for a season, left behind; the plywood walls and the dusty venetian blinds and the light bulbs and the smell of butane made me think of Albuquerque. But taking my meal outside by the burning juniper in the fireplace with more desert and mountains than I could explore in a lifetime open to view, I was invited to contemplate a far larger world, one which extends into a past and into a future without any limits known to the human kind. By taking off my shoes and digging my toes in the sand I made contact with that larger world—an exhilarating feeling which leads to equanimity. Certainly I was still by myself, so to speak—there were no other people around and there still are none—but in the midst of such a grand tableau it was impossible to give full and serious consideration to Albuquerque. All that is human melted with the sky and faded out beyond the mountains and I felt, as I feel—is it a paradox? —that a man can never find or need better companionship than that of himself.

As for the "solitary confinement of the mind," my theory is that solipsism, like other absurdities of the professional philosopher, is a product of too much time wasted in library stacks between the covers of a book, in smoke-filled coffeehouses (bad for the brains) and conversation-clogged seminars. To refute the solipsist or the metaphysical idealist all that you have to do is take him out and throw a rock at his head: if he ducks he's a liar. His logic may be airtight but his argument, far from revealing the delusions of living experience, only exposes the limitations of logic.

In the evenings after work I sit at the table outside and watch the sky condensing in the form of twilight over the desert. I am alone but loneliness has passed like a shadow, has come and is gone. I hear the mutter of the flames in the fireplace, eating wood. Far away to the south I can see the headlights of a car or truck approaching Moab. It is so far away, that merged point of light, that unless you watch it steadily you will not perceive that it is in motion; relative to the distance the light moves as the stars move or about as fast as the sun fades from the sky or the fire consumes the log.

I am not alone. From the vicinity of Balanced Rock comes the cry of the great horned owl. Suppertime, for the owl. The mice, squirrels, gophers, rabbits know what I mean. What is he up to? Rather than hunt for his supper the owl seems to be calling his supper to come to him. He calls again, always from the same place, not moving, in a voice which seems to come from not one spot alone but—anywhere. A war of nerves.

His nervous, timorous prey, terribly insecure, hear that cry and tremble. Where exactly is the owl? Perhaps the next shrub, the next rock, would offer better concealment than this. They hesitate. The great horned owl cries again and a rabbit breaks, dashes for what might be a better place, revealing his position. Quiet as a moth the owl swoops down.

The horned owl may be the natural enemy of the rabbit but surely the rabbit is the natural friend of the horned owl. The rabbit feels the owl. One can imagine easily the fondness, the sympathy, the genuine affection with which the owl regards the rabbit before rending it into edible portions.

Is the affection reciprocated? In that moment of truce, of utter surrender, when the rabbit still alive offers no resistance but only waits, is it possible that the rabbit also loves the owl? We know that the condemned man, at the end, does not resist but submits passively, almost gratefully, to the instruments of his executioner. We have seen millions march without a whimper of protest into an inferno. Is it love? Or only teamwork again—good sportsmanship?

Fear betrays the rabbit to the great horned owl. Fear does the hard work, making the owl's job easy. After a lifetime of dread it is more than likely that the rabbit yields to the owl during the last moment with a sense of gratitude, as pleased to be eaten—finally!—as the owl is to eat. For the one a consummation, for the other fulfillment. How can we speak of natural enemies in such a well-organized system of operations and procedures? All the time, everywhere, something or someone is dying to please.

The great horned owl calls again, once or twice every few minutes, concerned but not anxious. Supper will come. A few bats flicker through the air near the ramada making tiny clicking noises—sonar. There is no moon tonight. Stars appear one by one, forming incomplete constellations: Scorpio, Cassiopeia, Draco, Sagittarius and the Big Dipper. Like a solitary diamond Venus glows on the soft flare in the west, following the sun.

> Thou fair-haired angel of the evening,
> Now, whilst the sun rests on the mountains, light
> Thy bright torch of love; thy radiant crown
> Put on, and smile upon our evening bed.
> Smile on our loves. . . .

In the mixture of starlight and cloud-reflected sunlight in which the desert world is now illuminated, each single object stands forth in preternatural though transient brilliance, a final assertion of existence before the coming of night: each rock and shrub and tree, each flower, each stem of grass, diverse and separate, vividly isolate, yet joined each to every other in a unity which generously includes me and my solitude as well.

Or so it seems at the moment, as my fire dies to a twist of smoke and a heap of rubies, and for a moment I think I've almost caught a falling star: there is no mystery; there is only paradox, the incontrovertible union of contradictory truths. A falling star which melts into vapor as I grasp it, which flows through my fingers like water, like smoke.

What about the Indians? There are no Indians in the Arches country now; they all left seven hundred years ago and won't be back for a long time. But here as elsewhere in the canyonlands they left a record of their passage. Near springs and under overhanging cliffs, good camping spots, you may find chipping grounds scattered with hundreds of fragments of flint or chert where the Anasazi hunters worked their arrowpoints. You may find shards of pottery. At other places you will see their writing on the canyon walls—the petroglyphs and pictographs.

Petroglyphs are carved in the rock; pictographs are painted on the rock. Whether in one form or the other they consist of representations of birds, snakes, deer and many other animals, of human, semihuman and superhuman figures, and of designs purely abstract or symbolic. In some places you find only petroglyphs, in other places only pictographs, in some places both. The explicitly representational often comes side by side with the highly abstract.

In style the inscriptions and paintings range from the crude and simple to the elegant, sophisticated and subtle. They seem to include the work of different cultures and a great extent of time: on a wall of rock near Turnbow Cabin is pictured a man on horseback, which must have been made after the arrival of the Spanish in North America; on another rock wall a few miles southwest of Moab is the petroglyph of what appears to be a mastodon—a beast supposedly extinct more than twenty thousand years ago.

Whether crude or elegant, representational or abstract, very old or relatively new, all of the work was done in a manner pleasing to contemporary taste, with its vogue for the stylized and primitive. The ancient canyon art of Utah belongs in that same international museum without walls which makes African sculpture, Melanesian masks, and the junkyards of New Jersey equally interesting— those voices of silence which speak to us in the first world language. As for the technical competence of the artists, its measure is apparent in the fact that these pictographs and petroglyphs though exposed to the attack of wind, sand, rain, heat, cold and sunlight for centuries still survive vivid and clear. How much of the painting and sculpture being done in America today will last—in the merely physical sense—for even a half-century?

The pictures (to substitute one term for the petroglyph-pictograph combination) are found on flat surfaces along the canyon walls, often at heights now inaccessible to a man on foot. (Because of erosion.) They usually appear in crowded clusters, with figures of a later date sometimes superimposed on those of an earlier time. There is no indication that the men who carved and painted the figures made any attempt to compose them into coherent murals; the endless variety of style, subject and scale suggests the work of many individuals from different times and places who for one reason or another came by, stopped, camped for days or weeks and left a sign of their passing on the rock.

What particular meaning, if any, have these pictures on the canyon walls? No one has a definite answer to that question but several possible explanations come to mind when you see them, in their strange and isolated settings, for the first time.

They could be the merest doodling—that is an easy first impression. Yet there's quite a difference between scribbling on paper and on sandstone. As anyone knows who has tried to carve his name in rock, the task requires persistence, patience, determination and skill. Imagine the effort required to inscribe, say, the figure of a dancer, with no tool but a flint chisel and in such a way as to make it last five hundred years.

Perhaps these stone walls served as community bulletin boards, a form of historical record-keeping, a "newspaper rock" whereon individuals carved and painted their clan or totemic signatures. Or the frequently repeated figures of deer, beaver, bighorn sheep and other animals might represent the story of successful hunting parties.

While many of the pictures may have had for their makers a religious or ceremonial significance, others look like apparitions out of bad dreams. In this category belong the semihuman and superhuman beings with horned heads, immensely broad shoulders, short limbs and massive bodies that taper down to attenuated legs. Some of them have no legs at all but seem to rise ghostlike out of nothing, floating on air. These are sinister and supernatural figures, gods from the underworld perhaps, who hover in space, or dance, or stand solidly planted on two feet carrying weapons—a club or sword. Most are faceless but some stare back at you with large, hollow, disquieting eyes. Demonic shapes, they might have meant protection and benevolence to their creators and a threat to strangers:

Beware, traveler. You are approaching the land of the horned gods. . . .

Whatever their original intention, the long-dead artists and hunters confront us across the centuries with the poignant sign of their humanity. I was here, says the artist. We were here, say the hunters.

One other thing is certain. The pre-Columbian Indians of the Southwest, whether hunting, making arrowpoints, going on salt-gathering expeditions or otherwise engaged, clearly enjoyed plenty of leisure time. This speaks well of the food-gathering economy and also of its culture, which encouraged the Indians to employ their freedom in the creation and sharing of a durable art. Unburdened by the necessity of devoting most of their lives to the production, distribution, sale and servicing of labor-saving machinery, lacking proper recreational facilities, these primitive savages were free to do that which comes as naturally to men as making love—making graven images.

But now they are gone, some six or seven hundred years later, though not as a race extinguished: their descendants survive in the Hopi, Zuñi and other Pueblo tribes of Arizona and New Mexico. What drove the ancient ones out of the canyonlands? Marauding enemies? Drouth and starvation? Disease? The fear born of nightmares, the nightmares that rise from fear? A combination of these and other causes? The old people have left no record of disaster on the mural walls of the canyons; we can do no more than make educated guesses based on what is known about climatic changes, tribal warfare and Indian village life in the Southwest. Their departure from the high plateau country may have been gradual, an emigration spread out over many years, or it may in some places have been a sudden, panicky flight. In almost all of the cliff dwellings valuable property was abandoned—arrowheads, pottery, seed corn, sandals, turquoise and coral jewelry—which suggests that something happened which impelled the inhabitants to leave in a great hurry. But other explanations are possible. Personal property would have been buried with the dead, to be later dug up by pillagers and animals or exposed by erosion. Or the departing Indians, having no domesticated animals except dogs, may simply have been unable to carry away all of their possessions. Or the abandoned articles may have been under a curse, associated with disease and death.

Today, outside the canyon country and particularly in Arizona and New Mexico, the Indians are making a great numerical comeback, outbreeding the white man by a ratio of three to two. The population of the Navajo tribe, to take the most startling example, has increased from approximately 9500 in 1865 to about 90,000 a century later—a multiplication almost tenfold in only three generations. The increase is the indirect result of the white man's medical science as introduced on the Navajo reservation, which greatly reduced the infant mortality rate and thereby made possible such formidable fecundity. This happened despite the fact that infant mortality rates among the Indians are still much higher than among the American population as a whole. Are the Navajos grateful? They are not. To be poor is bad enough; to be poor and multiplying is worse.

In the case of the Navajo the effects of uncontrolled population growth are vividly apparent. The population, though ten times greater than a century ago, must still exist on a reservation no bigger now than it was then. In a pastoral economy based on sheep, goats and horses the inevitable result, as any child could have foreseen, was severe overgrazing and the transformation of the range— poor enough to start with—from a semiarid grassland to an eroded waste of blowsand and nettles. In other words the land available to the Navajos not only failed to expand in proportion to their growing numbers; it has actually diminished in productive capacity.

In order to survive, more and more of the Navajos, or The People as they used to call themselves, are forced off the reservation and into rural slums along the major highways and into the urban slums of the white man's towns which surround the reservation. Here we find them today doing the best they can as laborers, gas station attendants, motel maids and dependents of the public welfare system. They are the Negroes of the Southwest—red black men. Like their cousins in the big cities they turn for solace, quite naturally, to alcohol and drugs; the peyote cult in particular grows in popularity under the name of The Native American Church.

Unequipped to hold their own in the ferociously competitive world of White America, in which even the language is foreign to them, the Navajos sink ever deeper into the culture of poverty, exhibiting all of the usual and well-known symptoms: squalor, unemployment or irregular and ill-paid employment, broken families, disease, prostitution, crime, alcoholism, lack of education, too many children, apathy and demoralization, and various forms of mental illness, including evangelical Protestantism.

Whether in the *favelas* of Rio de Janeiro, the *barrios* of Caracas, the ghettos of Newark, the mining towns of West Virginia or the tarpaper villages of Gallup, Flagstaff and Shiprock, it's the same the world over—one big wretched family sequestered in sullen desperation, pawed over by social workers, kicked around by the cops and prayed over by the missionaries.

There are interesting differences, of course, both in kind and degree between the plight of the Navajo Indians and that of their brothers-in-poverty around the world. For one thing the Navajos have the B.I.A. looking after them—the Bureau of Indian Affairs. The B.I.A. like everything else is a mixture of good and bad, with policies that change and budgets that fluctuate with every power shift in Washington, but its general aim over the long run has been to change Indians into white men, a process called "assimilation." In pursuit of this end the little Indians are herded into schools on and off the reservation where, under the tutelage of teachers recruited by the B.I.A. from Negro colleges deep in the Bible Belt, the Navajo children learn to speak American with a Southern accent. The B.I.A., together with medical missions set up by various churches, also supplies the Navajos with basic medical services, inadequate by national standards but sufficient nevertheless to encourage the extravagant population growth which is the chief cause, though not the only cause, of the Navajos' troubles.

A second important difference in the situation of the Navajo Indians from that of others sunk in poverty is that the Navajos still have a home of their own—the reservation, collective property of the tribe as a whole. The land is worn out, barren, eroded, hopelessly unsuited to support a heavy human population but even so, however poor in economic terms, it provides the Navajo people with a firm base on earth, the possibility of a better future and for the individual Navajo in exile a place where, when he has to go back there, they have to take him in. Where they would not think of doing otherwise.

Poor as the land is it still attracts the avarice of certain whites in neighboring areas who can see in it the opportunity for profit if only the present occupants are removed. Since the land belongs to the tribe no individual within the tribe is legally empowered to sell any portion of it. Periodic attempts are made, therefore, by false friends of the Navajos, to have the reservation broken up under the guise of granting the Indians "property rights" so that they will be "free" to sell their only tangible possession—the land—to outsiders. So far the tribe has been wise enough to resist this pressure and so long as it continues to do so The People will never be completely separated from their homeland.

Retaining ownership of their land, the Navajos have been able to take maximum advantage through their fairly coherent and democratic tribal organization of the modest mineral resources which have been found within the reservation. The royalties from the sale of oil, uranium, coal and natural gas, while hardly enough to relieve the Indians' general poverty, have enabled them to develop a tribal timber business, to provide a few college scholarships for the brainiest (not necessarily the best) of their young people, to build community centers and finance an annual tribal fair (a source of much enjoyment to The People), and to drill a useful number of water wells for the benefit of the old sheep and goat raising families still hanging on in the backlands.

The money is also used to support the small middle class of officials and functionaries which tribal organization has created, and to pay the costs of a tribal police force complete with uniforms, guns, patrol cars and two-way radios. These unnecessary evils reflect the influence of the Bureau of Indian Affairs and the desire on the part of the more ambitious Navajos to imitate as closely as they can the pattern of the white man's culture which surrounds them, a typical and understandable reaction. Despite such minor failures the Navajos as a tribe have made good use of what little monetary income they have. It is not entirely their fault if the need remains far greater than tribal resources can satisfy.

Meanwhile the tribal population continues to grow in geometric progression: 2... 4 ... 8 ... 16 ... 32 ... 64, etc., onward and upward, as the majority of The People settle more deeply into the second-class way of life, American style, to which they are fairly accustomed, with all of its advantages and disadvantages: the visiting caseworker from the welfare department, the relief check, the derelict automobiles upside down on the front yard, the tarpaper shack next to the hogan and ramada, the repossessed TV set, the confused adolescents, and the wine bottles in the kitchen midden.

Various solutions are proposed: industrialization; tourism; massive federal aid; better education for the Navajo children; relocation; birth control; child subsidies; guaranteed annual income; four-lane highways; moral rearmament. None of these proposals are entirely devoid of merit and at least one of them—birth control—is obviously essential though not in itself sufficient if poverty is to be alleviated among the Navajo Indians. As for the remainder, they are simply the usual banal, unimaginative if well-intentioned proposals made everywhere, over and over again, in reply to the demand for a solution to the national and international miseries of mankind. As such they fail to take into account what is unique and valuable in the Navajo's traditional way of life and ignore altogether the possibility that the Navajo may have as much to teach the white man as the white man has to teach the Navajo.

Industrialization, for example. Even if the reservation could attract and sustain large-scale industry heavy or light, which it cannot, what have the Navajos to gain by becoming factory hands, lab technicians and office clerks? The Navajos are *people*, not *personnel*; nothing in their nature or tradition has prepared them to adapt to the regimentation of application forms and time clock. To force them into the machine would require a Procrustean mutilation of their basic humanity. Consciously or unconsciously the typical Navajo senses this unfortunate truth, resists the compulsory miseducation offered by the Bureau, hangs on to his malnourished horses and cannibalized automobiles, works when he feels like it and quits when he has enough money for a party or the down payment on a new pickup. He fulfills other obligations by getting his wife and kids installed securely on the public welfare rolls. Are we to condemn him for this? Caught in a no-man's-land between two worlds the Navajo takes what advantage he can of the white man's system—the radio, the pickup truck, the welfare—while clinging to the liberty and dignity of his old way of life. Such a man would rather lie drunk in the gutters of Gallup, New Mexico, a disgrace to his tribe and his race, than button on a clean white shirt and spend the best part of his life inside an air-conditioned office building with windows that cannot be opened.

Even if he wanted to join the American middle class (and some Indians do wish to join and have done so) the average Navajo suffers from a handicap more severe than skin color, the language barrier or insufficient education: his acquisitive instinct is poorly developed. He lacks the drive to get ahead of his fellows or to figure out ways and means of profiting from other people's labor. Coming from a tradition which honors sharing and mutual aid above private interest, the Navajo thinks it somehow immoral for one man to prosper while his neighbors go without. If a member of the tribe does break from this pattern, through luck, talent or special training, and finds a niche in the affluent society, he can also expect to find his family and clansmen camping on his patio, hunting in his kitchen, borrowing his car and occupying his bedrooms at any hour of the day or night. Among these people a liberal hospitality is taken for granted and selfishness regarded with horror. Shackled by such primitive attitudes, is it any wonder that the Navajos have not yet been able to get in step with the rest of us?

If industrialism per se seems an unlikely answer to the problems of the Navajo (and most of the other tribes) there still remains industrial tourism to be considered. This looks a little more promising, and with the construction of new highways, motels and gas stations the tribe has taken steps to lure tourists into the reservation and relieve them of their dollars. The chief beneficiaries will be the oil and automotive combines far away, but part of the take will remain on the reservation in the form of wages paid to those who change the sheets, do the laundry, pump the gas, serve the meals, wash the dishes, clean the washrooms and pump out the septic tanks—simple tasks for which the Navajos are available and qualified.

How much the tourist industry can add to the tribal economy, how many Indians it may eventually employ, are questions not answerable at this time. At best it provides only seasonal work and this on a marginal scale—ask any chambermaid. And whether good or bad in strictly pecuniary terms, industrial tourism exacts a spiritual price from those dependent upon it for their livelihood. The natives must learn to accustom themselves to the spectacle of hordes of wealthy, outlandishly dressed strangers invading their land and their homes. They must learn the automatic smile. They must expect to be gaped at and photographed. They must learn to be quaint, picturesque and photogenic. They must learn that courtesy and hospitality are not simply the customs of any decent society but are rather a special kind of commodity which can be peddled for money.

I am not sure that the Navajos can learn these things. For example, the last time I was in Kayenta I witnessed the following incident:

One of the old men, one of the old Longhairs with a Mongolian mustache and tall black hat, is standing in the dust and sunlight in front of the Holiday Inn, talking with two of his wives. A big car rolls up—a Buick Behemoth I believe it was, or it may have been a Cadillac Crocodile, a Dodge Dinosaur or a Mercury Mastodon, I'm not sure which—and this *lady* climbs out of it. She's wearing golden stretch pants, green eyelids' and a hiveshaped head of hair that looks both in color and texture exactly like 25¢ worth of candy cotton. She has a camera in her hands and is aiming it straight at the old Navajo. "Hey!" she says. "Look this way." He looks, sees the woman, spits softly on the ground and turns his back. Naturally offended, the lady departs without buying even a postcard.

But he was an old one. The young are more adaptable and under the pressure to survive may learn to turn tricks for the tourist trade. That, and a few coal mines here and there, and jobs away from the reservation, and more welfare, will enable the Navajos to carry on through the near future. In the long run their economic difficulties can only be solved when and if our society as a whole is willing to make an honest effort to eliminate poverty. By honest effort, as opposed to the current dishonest effort with its emphasis on phoney social services which benefit no one but the professional social workers, I mean a direct confrontation with the two actual basic causes of poverty: (1) too many children and—(here I reveal the secret, the elusive and mysterious key to the whole problem)—(2) too little money. Though simple in formula, the solution will seem drastic and painful in practice. To solve the first part of the problem we may soon have to make birth control compulsory; to solve the second part we will have to borrow from Navajo tradition and begin a more equitable sharing of national income. Politically unpalatable? No doubt. Social justice in this country means social surgery—carving some of the fat off the wide bottom of the American middle class.

Navajo poverty can be cured and in one way or the other—through justice or war—it will be cured. It is doubtful, however, that the Navajo way of life, as distinguished from Navajos, can survive. Outnumbered, surrounded and overwhelmed, the Navajos will probably be forced in self-defense to malform themselves into the shape required by industrial econometrics. Red-skinned black men at present, they must learn to become dark-brown white men with credit cards and crew-cut sensibilities.

It will not be easy. It will not be easy for the Navajos to forget that once upon a time, only a generation ago, they were horsemen, nomads, keepers of flocks, painters in sand, weavers of wool, artists in silver, dancers, singers of the Yei-bei-chei. But they will have to forget or at least learn to be ashamed of these old things and to bring them out only for the amusement of tourists.

A difficult transitional period. Tough on people. For instance, consider an unfortunate accident which took place only a week ago here in the Arches country. Parallel to the highway north of Moab is a railway, a spur line to the potash mines. At one point close to the road this railway cuts through a hill. The cut is about three hundred feet deep, blasted through solid rock with sides that are as perpendicular as the walls of a building. One afternoon two young Indians—Navajos? Apaches? beardless Utes?— in an old perverted Plymouth came hurtling down the highway, veered suddenly to the right, whizzed through a fence and plunged straight down like helldivers into the Big Cut. Investigating the wreckage we found only the broken bodies, the broken bottles, the stain and smell of Tokay, and a couple of cardboard suitcases exploded open and revealing their former owners' wordly goods— dirty socks, some underwear, a copy of *True West* magazine, a comb, three new cowboy shirts from J. C. Penney's, a carton of Marlboro cigarettes. But nowhere did we see any eagle feathers, any conchos of silver, any buffalo robes, any bows, arrows, medicine pouch or drums.

Some Indians.

Well . . . the cowboys have their troubles too. Viviano, old Roy Scobie, they're finished. Cowboyism rides rampant as never before on a field of golden neon dollar signs but job openings for working cowboys are scarce. The cattlegrowing industry like almost everything else has been mechanized and automated. There was a time and not so very long ago when ranching was a way of life, and a good one. Now it is simply a component of the lab to market food-processing apparatus: you take a steer, drop a hormone tablet in his ear and step back quickly.

The steer bloats up suddenly like a poisoned pup and you've got two hundred dollars worth of marbled beef on the hoof, waiting for the meat hook.

Most of the cowboys I know are out of work or about to lose their jobs or doing something else. My friend Ralph Newcomb studies Sri Aurobindo and Bill Eastlake has sunk to writing novels. Others play the electric guitar, drive trucks, or break their bones with an unpleasant crunching sound on the rodeo circuit. Many are committing slow suicide on skid row (like the Indians) or at best (as Viviano used to do) working overtime in hopes of collecting back pay.

While the actual working cowboy disappears, along with the genuine nonworking Indian, the make-believe cowboys flourish and multiply like flies on a pecan pie. Everywhere you see them now, from California to Florida, from Texas to Times Square, crowding the streets in their big white hats, tight pants, flowered shirts, and high-heeled fruity boots. From the rear many of them look like women; many of them *are* women. Especially in the small towns west of the Mississippi, where cowboyism as a cult grows in direct ratio to the disappearance of cattle-herding as an occupation, you will see the latest, the Mr. and Mrs. Cattleman couple in authentic matching Western costume—the husband with sunburnt nose and belly bulging over a steerhorn buckle heavy enough to kill a horse with, and his wife, a tall tough broad in gabardines and boots with a look on her face that would make a Comanche blanch.

But it wasn't always a fake. I think of Viviano, of old Roy, and of another I knew for a while, Leslie McKee, who was both cowboy and cattleman, since he ran a one-man outfit. His career followed an irregular course; every other year the bank took his little ranch away from him and every other year Leslie managed to get it back. Between ranches he worked at whatever he could find. In his youth—long before asphalt—he had driven the first motor stage between Monticello and Moab, a unique bus line which, according to Les, carried three classes of passengers: first class rode, second class walked, third class pushed. He rode as an extra in the movies and got hit in the eye with one of Geronimo's rubber-tipped arrows. One day on Grand Mesa he came on a bear and roped it, planning to lead it home; he changed his mind when the bear took the rope in both paws and walked toward Les and his horse, coiling up the rope as he came. He'd made a little money in the rodeo game and offered me this advice on riding the broomtails:

"Always give a bronc a fair shake. Don't pull its head up and don't grab leather. Better yet don't get on."

Like most other cowboys I have known Leslie was getting on in years. Also, he suffered from sciatica and shingles and like me was allergic to tumbleweed. Leslie too went the way of the others, leaving no sons.

Cowboys and Indians disappear, dying off or transforming themselves by tortuous degrees into something quite different. The originals are nearly gone and will soon be lost forever in the overwhelming crowd. Legendary enemies, their ghosts ride away together—buddies at last—into the mythic sunset of the West.

> Weep, all you little rains,
> wail, winds wail—
> all along, along, along
> the Colorado Trail. . . .

Twilight is over, night is here, the sky is rich with frosty, burning, glittering stars. I become aware that the great horned owl near Balanced Rock has stopped calling; presumably he has found a satisfactory dinner. Bon appetit, mon frère.

My little fire is now completely dead, too cold to rekindle, and I must decide whether to rebuild it or unroll the sleeping bag on the cot and turn in. Not an easy decision. The air is still and cool and I am glad that the heat of the day is finally gone. Tomorrow—or is it the day after?—will be the first of July. I have come to the midpoint of my season in the desert.

WATER

"THIS WOULD be good country," a tourist says to me, "if only you had some water."

He's from Cleveland, Ohio.

"If we had water here," I reply, "this country would not be what it is. It would be like Ohio, wet and humid and hydrological, all covered with cabbage farms and golf courses. Instead of this lovely barren desert we would have only another blooming garden state, like New Jersey. You see what I mean?"

"If you had more water more people could live here."

"Yes sir. And where then would people go when they wanted to see something besides people?"

"I see what you mean. Still, I wouldn't want to live here. So dry and desolate. Nice for pictures but my God I'm glad I don't have to live here."

"I'm glad too, sir. We're in perfect agreement. You

129

wouldn't want to live here, I wouldn't want to live in Cleveland. We're both satisfied with the arrangement as it is. Why change it?"

"Agreed."

We shake hands and the tourist from Ohio goes away pleased, as I am pleased, each of us thinking he has taught the other something new.

The air is so dry here I can hardly shave in the mornings. The water and soap dry on my face as I reach for the razor: aridity. It is the driest season of a dry country. In the afternoons of July and August we may get thundershowers but an hour after the storms pass the surface of the desert is again bone dry.

It seldom rains. The geography books credit this part of Utah with an annual precipitation of five to nine inches but that is merely a statistical average. Low enough, to be sure. And in fact the rainfall and snowfall vary widely from year to year and from place to place even within the Arches region. When a cloud bursts open above the Devil's Garden the sun is blazing down on my ramada. And wherever it rains in this land of unclothed rock the runoff is rapid down cliff and dome through the canyons to the Colorado.

Sometimes it rains and still fails to moisten the desert —the falling water evaporates halfway down between cloud and earth. Then you see curtains of blue rain dangling out of reach in the sky while the living things wither below for want of water. Torture by tantalizing, hope without fulfillment. And the clouds disperse and dissipate into nothingness.

Streambeds are usually dry. The dry wash, dry gulch, *arroyo seco*. Only after a storm do they carry water and then but briefly—a few minutes, a couple of hours. The spring-fed perennial stream is a rarity. In this area we have only two of them, Salt Creek and Onion Creek, the first too salty to drink and the second laced with arsenic and sulfur.

Permanent springs or waterholes are likewise few and far between though not so rare as the streams. They are secret places deep in the canyons, known only to the deer and the coyotes and the dragonflies and a few others. Water rises slowly from these springs and flows in little rills over bare rock, over and under sand, into miniature fens of wire grass, rushes, willow and tamarisk. The water does not flow very far before disappearing into the air and under the ground. The flow may reappear farther down the canyon, surfacing briefly for a second time, a third time, diminishing in force until it vanishes completely and for good.

Another type of spring may be found on canyon walls where water seeps out between horizontal formations through cracks thinner than paper to support small hanging gardens of orchids, monkeyflower, maidenhair fern, and ivy. In most of these places the water is so sparingly measured that it never reaches the canyon floor at all but is taken up entirely by the thirsty plant life and transformed into living tissue.

Long enough in the desert a man like other animals can learn to smell water. Can learn, at least, the smell of things associated with water—the unique and heartening odor of the cottonwood tree, for example, which in the canyonlands is the tree of life. In this wilderness of naked rock burnt to auburn or buff or red by ancient fires there is no vision more pleasing to the eyes and more gratifying to the heart than the translucent acid green (bright gold in autumn) of this venerable tree. It signifies water, and not only water but also shade, in a country where shelter from the sun is sometimes almost as precious as water.

Signifies water, which may or may not be on the surface, visible and available. If you have what is called a survival problem and try to dig for this water during the heat of the day the effort may cost you more in sweat than you will find to drink. A bad deal. Better to wait for nightfall when the cottonwoods and other plants along the streambed will release some of the water which they have absorbed during the day, perhaps enough to allow a potable trickle to rise to the surface of the sand. If the water still does not appear you may then wish to attempt to dig for it. Or you might do better by marching farther up the canyon. Sooner or later you should find a spring or at least a little seep on the canyon wall. On the other hand you could possibly find no water at all, anywhere. The desert is a land of surprises, some of them terrible surprises. Terrible as derived from terror.

When out for a walk carry water; not less than a gallon a day per person.

More surprises. In places you will find clear-flowing streams, such as Salt Creek near Turnbow Cabin, where the water looks beautifully drinkable but tastes like brine.

You might think, beginning to die of thrist, that any water however salty would be better than none at all. Not true. Small doses will not keep you going or alive and a deep drink will force your body to expend water in getting rid of the excess salt. This results in a net loss of bodily moisture and a hastening of the process of dehydration. Dehydration first enervates, then prostrates, then kills.

Nor is blood, your own or a companion's, any adequate substitute for water; blood is too salty. The same is true of urine.

If it's your truck or car which has failed you, you'd be advised to tap the radiator, unless it's full of Prestone. If this resource is not available and water cannot be found in the rocks or under the sand and you find yourself too tired and discouraged to go on, crawl into the shade and wait for help to find you. If no one is looking for you write your will in the sand and let the wind carry your last words and signature east to the borders of Colorado and south to the pillars of Monument Valley—someday, never fear, your bare elegant bones will be discovered and wondered and marveled at.

A great thirst is a great joy when quenched in time. On my first walk down into Havasupai Canyon, which is a branch of the Grand Canyon, never mind exactly where, I took with me only a quart of water, thinking that would be enough for a mere fourteen-mile downhill hike on a warm day in August. At Topocoba on the rim of the canyon the temperature was a tolerable ninety-six degrees but it rose about one degree for each mile on and downward. Like a fool I rationed my water, drank frugally, and could have died of the heatstroke. When late in the afternoon I finally stumbled—sun-dazed, bleareyed, parched as an old bacon rind—upon that blue stream which flows like a miraculous mirage down the floor of the canyon I was too exhausted to pause and drink soberly from the bank. Dreamily, deliriously, I waded into the waist-deep water and fell on my face. Like a sponge I soaked up moisture through every pore, letting the current bear me along beneath a canopy of overhanging willow trees. I had no fear of drowning in the water—I intended to drink it all.

In the Needles country high above the inaccessible Colorado River there is a small spring hidden at the heart of a maze of fearfully arid grabens and crevasses. A very small spring: the water oozes from the grasp of moss to fall one drop at a time, one drop per second, over a lip of stone. One afternoon in June I squatted there for an hour—two hours? three?—filling my canteen. No other water within miles, the local gnat population fought me for every drop. To keep them out of the canteen I had to place a handkerchief over the opening as I filled it. Then they attacked my eyes, drawn irresistibly by the liquid shine of the human eyeball. Embittered little bastards. Never have I tasted better water.

Other springs, more surprises. Northeast of Moab in a region of gargoyles and hobgoblins, a landscape left over from the late Jurassic, is a peculiar little waterhold named Onion Spring. A few wild onions grow in the vicinity but more striking, in season, is the golden princess plume, an indicator of selenium, a mild poison often found in association with uranium, a poison not so mild. Approaching the spring you notice a sulfurous stink in the air though the water itself, neither warm nor cold, looks clear and drinkable.

Unlike most desert waterholes you will find around Onion Spring few traces of animal life. Nobody comes to drink. The reason is the very good one that the water of Onion Spring contains not only sulfur, and perhaps selenium, but also arsenic. When I was there I looked at the water and smelled it and ran my hands through it and after a while, since the sampling of desert water is in my line, I tasted it, carefully, and spat it out. Afterwards I rinsed my mouth with water from my canteen.

This poison spring is quite clear. The water is sterile, lifeless. There are no bugs, which in itself is a warning sign, in case the smell were not sufficient. When in doubt about drinking from an unknown spring look for life. If the water is scummed with algae, crawling with worms, grubs, larvae, spiders and liver flukes, be reassured, drink hearty, you'll get nothing worse than dysentery. But if it appears innocent and pure, beware. Onion Spring wears such a deceitful guise. Out of a tangle of poison-tolerant weeds the water drips into a basin of mud and sand, flows from there over sandstone and carries its potent solutions into the otherwise harmless waters of the creek.

There are a number of springs similar to this one in the American desert. Badwater pool in Death Valley, for example. And a few others in the canyonlands, usually in or below the Moenkopi and Shinarump formations—mudstone and shales. The prospector Vernon Pick found a poison spring at the source of the well-named Dirty Devil River, when he was searching for uranium over in the San Rafael Swell a few years ago. At the time he needed water; he *had* to have water; and in order to get a decent drink he made something like a colander out of his canteen, punching it full of nail holes, filling it with charcoal from his campfire and straining the water through the charcoal. How much this purified the water he had no means of measuring but he drank it anyway and although it made him sick he survived, and is still alive today to tell about it.

There are rumors that when dying of the thirst you can save your soul *and* body by extracting water from the barrel cactus. This is a dubious proposition and I don't know anyone who has made the experiment. It might be possible in the Sonoran desert where the barrel cactus grows tall as a man and fat as a keg of beer. In Utah, however, its nearest relative stands no more than a foot high and bristles with needles curved like fishhooks. To get even close to this devilish vegetable you need leather gloves and a machete. Slice off the top and you find inside not water but only the green pulpy core of the living plant. Carving the core into manageable chunks you might be able to wring a few drops of bitter liquid into your cup. The labor and the exasperation will make you sweat, will cost you dearly.

When you reach this point you are doomed. Far better to have stayed at home with the TV and a case of beer. If the happy thought arrives too late, crawl into the shade and contemplate the lonely sky. See those big black scrawny wings far above, waiting? Comfort yourself with the reflection that within a few hours, if all goes as planned, your human flesh will be working its way through the gizzard of a buzzard, your essence transfigured into the fierce greedy eyes and unimaginable consciousness of a turkey vulture. Whereupon you, too, will soar on motionless wings high over the ruck and rack of human suffering. For most of us a promotion in grade, for some the realization of an ideal.

In July and August on the high desert the thunderstorms come. Mornings begin clear and dazzling bright, the sky as blue as the Virgin's cloak, unflawed by a trace of cloud in all that emptiness bounded on the north by the Book Cliffs, on the east by Grand Mesa and the La Sal Mountains, on the south by the Blue Mountains and on the west by the dragon-tooth reef of the San Rafael. By noon, however, clouds begin to form over the mountains, coming it seems out of nowhere, out of nothing, a special creation.

The clouds multiply and merge, cumuli-nimbi piling up like whipped cream, like mashed potatoes, like sea foam, building upon one another into a second mountain range greater in magnitude than the terrestrial range below.

The massive forms jostle and grate, ions collide, and

the sound of thunder is heard over the sun-drenched land.
More clouds emerge from empty sky, anvil-headed giants
with glints of lightning in their depths. An armada as-
sembles and advances, floating on a plane of air that
makes it appear, from below, as a fleet of ships must look
to the fish in the sea.

At my observation point on a sandstone monolith the
sun is blazing down as intensely as ever, the air crackling
with dry heat. But the storm clouds continue to spread,
gradually taking over more and more of the sky, and as
they approach the battle breaks out.

Lightning streaks like gunfire through the clouds, vol-
leys of thunder shake the air. A smell of ozone. While
the clouds exchange their bolts with one another no rain
falls, but now they begin bombarding the buttes and pinnacles below. Forks of lightning—illuminated nerves—
join heaven and earth.

The wind is rising. For anyone with sense enough to
get out of the rain now is the time to seek shelter. A lash
of lightning flickers over Wilson Mesa, scorching the
brush, splitting a pine tree. Northeast over the Yellowcat
area rain is already sweeping down, falling not vertically
but in a graceful curve, like a beaded curtain drawn lightly
across the desert. Between the rain and the mountains,
among the tumbled masses of vapor, floats a segment of
a rainbow—sunlight divided. But where I stand the storm
is only beginning.

Above me the clouds roll in, unfurling and smoking
billows in malignant violet, dense as wool. Most of the
sky is lidded over but the sun remains clear halfway
down the west, shining in under the storm. Overhead
the clouds thicken, then crack and split with a roar like
that of cannonballs tumbling down a marble staircase;
their bellies open—too late to run now—and the rain
comes down.

Comes down: not softly not gently, with no quality of
mercy but like heavy water in buckets, raindrops like
pellets splattering on the rock, knocking the berries off
the junipers, plastering my shirt to my back, drumming

on my hat like hailstones and running in a waterfall off the brim.

The pinnacles, arches, balanced rocks, fins and elephant-backs of sandstone, glazed with water but still in sunlight, gleam like old gray silver and everything appears transfixed in the strange wild unholy light of the moment. The light that never was.

For five minutes the deluge continues under the barrage of thunder and lightning, then trails off quickly, diminishing to a shower, to a sprinkling, to nothing at all. The clouds move off and rumble for a while in the distance. A fresh golden light breaks through and now in the east, over the turrets and domes, stands the rainbow sign, a double rainbow with one foot in the canyon of the Colorado and the other far north in Salt Wash. Beyond the rainbow and framed within it I can see jags of lightning still playing in the stormy sky over Castle Valley.

The afternoon sun falls lower; above the mountains and the ragged black clouds hangs the new moon, pale fragment of what is to come; in another hour, at sundown, Venus too will be there, planet of love, to glow bright as chromium down on the western sky. The desert storm is over and through the pure sweet pellucid air the cliff swallows and the nighthawks plunge and swerve, making cries of hunger and warning and—who knows?—maybe of exultation.

Stranger than the storms, though not so grand and symphonic, are the flash floods that follow them, bursting with little warning out of the hills and canyons, sometimes an hour or more after the rain has stopped.

I have stood in the middle of a broad sandy wash with not a trickle of moisture to be seen anywhere, sunlight pouring down on me and on the flies and ants and lizards, the sky above perfectly clear, listening to a queer vibration in the air and in the ground under my feet—like a freight train coming down the grade, very fast—and looked up to see a wall of water tumble around a bend and surge toward me.

A wall of water. A poor image. For the flash flood of

the desert poorly resembles water. It looks rather like a loose pudding or a thick dense soup, thick as gravy, dense with mud and sand, lathered with scuds of bloody froth, loaded on its crest with a tangle of weeds and shrubs and small trees ripped from their roots.

Surprised by delight, I stood there in the heat, the bright sun, the quiet afternoon, and watched the monster roll and roar toward me. It advanced in crescent shape with a sort of forelip about a foot high streaming in front, making hissing sucking noises like a giant amoeba, nosing to the right and nosing to the left as if on the spoor of something good to eat. Red as tomato soup or blood it came down on me about as fast as a man could run. I moved aside and watched it go by.

> A flick of lightning to the north
> where dun clouds grumble—
> while here in the middle of the wash
> black beetles tumble
> and horned toads fumble
> over sand as dry as bone
> and hard-baked mud and glaring stone.
>
> Nothing here suggests disaster
> for the ants' shrewd play;
> their busy commerce for tomorrow
> shows no care for today;
> but a mile away
> and rolling closer in a scum of mud
> comes the hissing lapping blind mouth of the flood.
>
> Through the tamarisk whine the flies
> in pure fat units of conceit
> as if the sun and the afternoon
> and blood and the smells and the heat
> and something to eat
> would be available forever, never die
> beyond the fixed imagination of a fly.

The flood comes, crawls thickly by, roaring
with self-applause, a brown
spongy smothering liquid avalanche:
great ant-civilizations drown,
worlds go down,
trees go under, the mud bank breaks
and deep down underneath the bedrock shakes.

A few hours later the bulk of the flood was past and
gone. The flow dwindled to a trickle over bars of quicksand. New swarms of insect life would soon come to recover the provinces of those swept away. Nothing had
changed but the personnel, a normal turnover, and the
contours of the watercourse, that not much.

Now we've mentioned quicksand. What is quicksand
anyway? First of all, quicksand is *not* as many think a
queer kind of sand which has the hideous power to draw
men and animals down and down into a bottomless pit.
There can be no quicksand without water. The scene of
the sand-drowned camel boy in the movie *Lawrence of
Arabia* is pure fakery. The truth about quicksand is that
it is simply a combination of sand and water in which the
upward force of the water is sufficient to neutralize the
frictional strength of the particles of sand. The greater
the force and saturation, the less weight the sand can bear.

Ordinarily it is possible for a man to walk across quicksand, if he keeps moving. But if he stops, funny things
begin to happen. The surface of the quicksand, which
may look as firm as the wet sand on an ocean beach, begins to liquefy beneath his feet. He finds himself sinking
slowly into a jelly-like substance, soft and quivering, which
clasps itself around his ankles with the suction power of
any viscous fluid. Pulling out one foot, the other foot
necessarily goes down deeper, and if a man waits too long,
or cannot reach something solid beyond the quicksand,
he may soon find himself trapped. The depth to which
he finally sinks depends upon the depth and the fluidity of
the quicksand, upon the nature of his efforts to extricate

himself, and upon the ratio of body weight to volume of quicksand. Unless a man is extremely talented, he cannot work himself in more than waist-deep. The quicksand will not *pull* him down. But it will not let him go either. Therefore the conclusion is that while quicksand cannot drown its captive, it could possibly starve him to death. Whatever finally happens, the immediate effects are always interesting.

My friend Newcomb, for instance. He has only one good leg, had an accident with the other, can't hike very well in rough country, tends to lag behind. We were exploring a deep dungeon-like defile off Glen Canyon one time (before the dam). The defile turned and twisted like a snake under overhanging and interlocking walls so high, so close, that for most of the way I could not see the sky. The floor of this cleft was irregular, wet, sandy, in places rather soupy, and I was soon far ahead and out of sight of Newcomb.

Finally I came to a place in the canyon so narrow and dark and wet and ghastly that I had no heart to go farther. Retracing my steps I heard, now and then, a faint and mournful wail, not human, which seemed to come from abysmal depths far back in the bowels of the plateau, from the underworld, from subterranean passageways better left forever unseen and unknown. I hurried on, the cries faded away. I was glad to be getting out of there. Then they came again, louder and as it seemed from all sides, out of the rock itself, surrounding me. A terrifying caterwauling it was, multiplied and amplified by echoes piled on echoes, overlapping and reinforcing one another. I looked back to see what was hunting me but there was only the naked canyon in the dim, bluish light that filtered down from far above. I thought of the Minotaur. Then I thought of Newcomb and began to run.

It wasn't bad. He was in only a little above the knees and sinking very slowly. As soon as he saw me he stopped hollering and relit his pipe. Help, he said, simply and quietly.

What was all the bellowing about? I wanted to know.

I'm sorry, he said, but it's a horrible way to die. Get out of that mud, I said, and let's get out of here. It ain't just mud, he said. I don't care what it is, get out of there; you look like an idiot. I'm sinking, he said.

And he was. The stuff was now halfway up his thighs.

Don't you ever read any books? I said. Don't you have sense enough to know that when you get in quicksand you have to lie down flat? Why? he asked. So you'll live longer, I explained. Face down or face up? he asked next.

That stumped me. I couldn't remember the answer to that one. You wait here, I said, while I go back to Albuquerque and get the book.

He looked down for a moment. Still sinking, he said; please help?

I stepped as close to him as I could without getting bogged down myself but our extended hands did not quite meet. Lean forward, I said. I am, he said. All the way, I said; fall forward.

He did that and then I could reach him. He gripped my wrist and I gripped his and with a slow steady pull I got him out of there. The quicksand gurgled a little and made funny, gasping noises, reluctant to let him go, but when he was free the holes filled up at once, the liquid sand oozing into place, and everything looked as it had before, smooth and sleek and innocent as the surface of a pudding. It was in fact the same pool of quicksand that I had walked over myself only about an hour earlier.

Quicksand is more of a menace to cattle and horses, with their greater weight and smaller feet, than it is to men, and the four-legged beasts generally avoid it when they can. Sometimes, however, they are forced to cross quicksand to reach water, or are driven across, and then the cattleman may have an unpleasant chore on his hands. Motor vehicles, of course, cannot negotiate quicksand; even a four-wheel-drive jeep will bog down as hopelessly as anything else.

Although I hesitate to deprive quicksand of its sinister glamour I must confess that I have not yet heard of a case where a machine, an animal or a man has actually sunk *completely* out of sight in the stuff. But it may have happened; it may be happening to somebody at this very moment. I sometimes regret that I was unable to perform a satisfactory experiment with my friend Newcomb when the chance presented itself; such opportunities come but rarely. But I needed him; he was among other things a good camp cook.

After the storms pass and the flash floods have dumped their loads of silt into the Colorado, leaving the stream-beds as arid as they were before, it is still possible to find rainwater in the desert. All over the slickrock country there are natural cisterns or potholes, tubs, tanks and basins sculptured in the soft sandstone by the erosive force of weathering, wind and sand. Many of them serve as little catchment basins during rain and a few may contain water for days or even weeks after a storm, the length of time depending on the shape and depth of the hole and the consequent rate of evaporation.

Often far from any spring, these temporary pools attract doves, ravens and other birds, and deer and coyotes; you, too, if you know where to look or find one by luck, can slake your thirst and fill your water gourd. Such pools may be found in what seem like the most improbable places: out on the desolate White Rim below Grand-view Point, for example, or on top of the elephant-back dome above the Double Arch. At Toroweap in Grand Canyon I found a deep tank of clear sweet water almost over my head, countersunk in the summit of a sandstone bluff which overhung my campsite by a hundred feet. A week after rain there was still enough water there to fill my needs; hard to reach, it was well worth the effort. The Bedouin know what I mean.

The rain-filled potholes, set in naked rock, are usually devoid of visible plant life but not of animal life. In addition to the inevitable microscopic creatures there may be certain amphibians like the spadefoot toad. This little animal lives through dry spells in a state of estivation under the dried-up sediment in the bottom of a hole.

When the rain comes, if it comes, he emerges from the mud singing madly in his fashion, mates with the handiest female and fills the pool with a swarm of tadpoles, most of them doomed to a most ephemeral existence. But a few survive, mature, become real toads, and when the pool dries up they dig into the sediment as their parents did before, making burrows which they seal with mucus in order to preserve that moisture necessary to life. There they wait, day after day, week after week, in patient spadefoot torpor, perhaps listening—we can imagine—for the sound of raindrops pattering at last on the earthen crust above their heads. If it comes in time the glorious cycle is repeated; if not, this particular colony of *Bufonidae* is reduced eventually to dust, a burden on the wind.

Rain and puddles bring out other amphibia, even in the desert. It's a strange, stirring, but not uncommon thing to come on a pool at night, after an evening of thunder and lightning and a bit of rainfall, and see the frogs clinging to the edge of their impermanent pond, bodies immersed in water but heads out, all croaking away in tricky counterpoint. They are windbags: with each croak the pouch under the frog's chin swells like a bubble, then collapses.

Why do they sing? What do they have to sing about? Somewhat apart from one another, separated by roughly equal distances, facing outward from the water, they clank and croak all through the night with tireless perseverance. To human ears their music has a bleak, dismal, tragic quality, dirgelike rather than jubilant. It may nevertheless be the case that these small beings are singing not only to claim their stake in the pond, not only to attract a mate, but also out of spontaneous love and joy, a contrapuntal choral celebration of the coolness and wetness after weeks of desert fire, for love of their own existence, however brief it may be, and for joy in the common life.

Has joy any survival value in the operations of evolution? I suspect that it does; I suspect that the morose and fearful are doomed to quick extinction. Where there is no joy there can be no courage; and without courage all other virtues are useless. Therefore the frogs, the toads, keep on singing even though we know, if they don't, that the sound of their uproar must surely be luring all the snakes and ringtail cats and kit foxes and coyotes and great horned owls toward the scene of their happiness.

What then? A few of the little amphibians will continue their metamorphosis by way of the nerves and tissues of one of the higher animals, in which process the joy of one becomes the contentment of the second. Nothing is lost, except an individual consciousness here and there, a trivial perhaps even illusory phenomenon. The rest survive, mate, multiply, burrow, estivate, dream, and rise again. The rains will come, the potholes shall be filled. Again. And again. And again.

More secure are those who live in and around the desert's few perennial waterholes, those magical hidden springs that are scattered so austerely through the barren vastness of the canyon country. Of these only a rare few are too hot or too briny or too poisonous to support life— the great majority of them swarm with living things. Here you will see the rushes and willows and cottonwoods, and four-winged dragonflies in green, blue, scarlet and gold, and schools of minnows in the water, moving from sunlight to shadow and back again. At night the mammals come—deer, bobcat, cougar, coyote, fox, jackrabbit, bighorn sheep, wild horse and feral burro—each in his turn and in unvarying order under the declaration of a truce. They come to drink, not to kill or be killed.

Finally, in this discussion of water in the desert, I should make note of a distinctive human contribution, one which has become a part of the Southwestern landscape no less typical than the giant cactus, the juniper growing out of solid rock or the red walls of a Navajo canyon. I refer to the tiny oasis formed by the drilled well, its windmill and storage tank. The windmill with its skeleton tower and creaking vanes is an object of beauty as significant in its way as the cottonwood tree, and the open tank at its foot, big enough to swim in, is a thing of joy to man and beast, no less worthy of praise than the desert spring.

Water, water, water. . . . There is no shortage of water

in the desert but exactly the right amount, a perfect ratio of water to rock, of water to sand, insuring that wide, free, open, generous spacing among plants and animals, homes and towns and cities, which makes the arid West so different from any other part of the nation. There is no lack of water here, unless you try to establish a city where no city should be.

The Developers, of course—the politicians, businessmen, bankers, administrators, engineers—they see it somewhat otherwise and complain most bitterly and interminably of a desperate water shortage, especially in the Southwest. They propose schemes of inspiring proportions for diverting water by the damful from the Columbia River, or even from the Yukon River, and channeling it overland down into Utah, Colorado, Arizona and New Mexico.

What for? "In anticipation of future needs, in order to provide for the continued industrial and population growth of the Southwest." And in such an answer we see that it's only the old numbers game again, the monomania of small and very simple minds in the grip of an obsession. They cannot see that growth for the sake of growth is a cancerous madness, that Phoenix and Albuquerque will not be better cities to live in when their populations are doubled again and again. They would never understand that an economic system which can only expand or expire must be false to all that is human.

So much by way of futile digression: the pattern is fixed and protest alone will not halt the iron glacier moving upon us.

No matter, it's of slight importance. Time and the winds will sooner or later bury the Seven Cities of Cibola, Phoenix, Tucson, Albuquerque, all of them, under dunes of glowing sand, over which blue-eyed Navajo bedouin will herd their sheep and horses, following the river in winter, the mountains in summer, and sometimes striking off across the desert toward the red canyons of Utah where great waterfalls plunge over silt-filled, ancient, mysterious dams.

Only the boldest among them, seeking visions, will

camp for long in the strange country of the standing rock, far out where the spadefoot toads bellow madly in the moonlight on the edge of doomed rainpools, where the arsenic-selenium spring waits for the thirst-crazed wanderer, where the thunderstorms blast the pinnacles and cliffs, where the rust-brown floods roll down the barren washes, and where the community of the quiet deer walk at evening up glens of sandstone through tamarisk and sage toward the hidden springs of sweet, cool, still, clear, unfailing water.

THE HEAT OF NOON:
ROCK AND TREE
AND CLOUD

At lunchtime I leave my post at the entrance station, hurrying from its shade through the blaze to the housetrailer, where I take a pitcher from the refrigerator and still in a hurry gulp down about a pint of fruit juice without stopping for breath. There are times in this hot and arid place when my thirst becomes so intense I cannot seem to drink any liquid fast enough to quench it.

July. Though all the windows are wide open and the blinds rattle in a breeze the heat is terrific. The inside of the trailer is like the inside of a kiln, a fierce dry heat that warps the loose linoleum on the floor, turns an exposed slice of bread into something like toast within half an hour, makes my papers crackle like parchment.

I take off my shirt and hang it over a chair; the sweat-soaked armpits will dry within five minutes, leaving a rime of salt along the seams. Hastily I assemble a couple of sandwiches: lettuce, leftover bacon from breakfast, sliced ham, peanut butter, salami, longhorn cheese, cashews, raisins, horseradish, anything else that will fit comfortably between two slices of bread—and take the dewy-cold pitcher of juice and hasten outside and through the storm of sunlight over the baking sandstone of the 33,000-acre terrace to the shade and relative coolness of the ramada.

The thermometer nailed to a post reads 110° F., but in the shade, with a breeze and almost no humidity, such a temperature is comfortable, even pleasant. I sit down at the table, pull off my boots and socks, dig my toes into the gritty, cleansing sand. Fear no more the heat of the sun. This is comfort. More, this is bliss, pure smug animal satisfaction. I relax beneath the sheltering canopy of juniper boughs and gaze out squinting and blinking at a pink world being sunburned to death.

Yes, July. The mountains are almost bare of snow except for patches within the couloirs on the northern slopes. Consoling nevertheless, those shrunken snowfields, despite the fact that they're twenty miles away by line of sight and six to seven thousand feet higher than where I sit. They comfort me with the promise that if the heat down here becomes less endurable I can escape for at least two days each week to the refuge of the mountains—those islands in the sky surrounded by a sea of desert. The knowledge that refuge is available, when and if needed, makes the silent inferno of the desert more easily bearable. Mountains complement desert as desert complements city, as wilderness complements and completes civilization.

A man could be a lover and defender of the wilderness without ever in his lifetime leaving the boundaries of asphalt, powerlines, and right-angled surfaces. We need wilderness whether or not we ever set foot in it. We need a refuge even though we may never need to go there. I may never in my life get to Alaska, for example, but I am grateful that it's there. We need the possibility of escape as surely as we need hope; without it the life of the cities would drive all men into crime or drugs or psychoanalysis.

A familiar and plaintive admonition; I would like to introduce here an entirely new argument in what has now become a stylized debate: the wilderness should be preserved for political reasons. We may need it someday not only as a refuge from excessive industrialism but also as a refuge from authoritarian government, from political oppression. Grand Canyon, Big Bend, Yellowstone and the High Sierras may be required to function as bases for guerrilla warfare against tyranny. What reason have we Americans to think that our own society will necessarily escape the world-wide drift toward the totalitarian organization of men and institutions?

This may seem, at the moment, like a fantastic thesis. Yet history demonstrates that personal liberty is a rare and precious thing, that all societies tend toward the absolute until attack from without or collapse from within breaks up the social machine and makes freedom and innovation again possible. Technology adds a new dimension to the process by providing modern despots with instruments far more efficient than any available to their classical counterparts. Surely it is no accident that the most thorough of tyrannies appeared in Europe's most thoroughly scientific and industrialized nation. If we allow our own country to become as densely populated, overdeveloped and technically unified as modern Germany we may face a similar fate.

The value of wilderness, on the other hand, as a base for resistance to centralized domination is demonstrated by recent history. In Budapest and Santo Domingo, for example, popular revolts were easily and quickly crushed because an urbanized environment gives the advantage to the power with the technological equipment. But in Cuba, Algeria and Vietnam the revolutionaries, operating in mountain, desert and jungle hinterlands with the active or tacit support of a thinly dispersed population, have been able to overcome or at least fight to a draw official establishment forces equipped with all of the terrible weapons of twentieth century militarism. Rural insurrections can then be suppressed only by bombing and burning villages and countryside so thoroughly that the mass of the population is forced to take refuge in the cities, there the people are then policed and if necessary starved into submission. The city, which should be the symbol and center of civilization, can also be made to function as a concentration camp. This is one of the significant discoveries of contemporary political science.

How does this theory apply to the present and future of the famous United States of North America? Suppose we were planning to impose a dictatorial regime upon the American people—the following preparations would be essential:

1. Concentrate the populace in megalopolitan masses so that they can be kept under close surveillance and where, in case of trouble, they can be bombed, burned, gassed or machine-gunned with a minimum of expense and waste.

2. Mechanize agriculture to the highest degree of refinement, thus forcing most of the scattered farm and ranching population into the cities. Such a policy is desirable because farmers, woodsmen, cowboys, Indians, fishermen and other relatively self-sufficient types are difficult to manage unless displaced from their natural environment.

3. Restrict the possession of firearms to the police and the regular military organizations.

4. Encourage or at least fail to discourage population growth. Large masses of people are more easily manipulated and dominated than scattered individuals.

5. Continue military conscription. Nothing excels military training for creating in young men an attitude of prompt, cheerful obedience to officially constituted authority.

6. Divert attention from deep conflicts within the society by engaging in foreign wars; make support of these wars a test of loyalty, thereby exposing and isolating potential opposition to the new order.

7. Overlay the nation with a finely reticulated network of communications, airlines and interstate *autobahns*.

8. *Raze the wilderness*. Dam the rivers, flood the canyons, drain the swamps, log the forests, strip-mine the hills, bulldoze the mountains, irrigate the deserts and improve the national parks into national parking lots.

Idle speculations, feeble and hopeless protest. It was all foreseen nearly half a century ago by the most cold-eyed and clear-eyed of our national poets, on California's shore, at the end of the open road. Shine, perishing republic.

The sun reigns, I am drowned in light. At this hour, sitting alone at the focal point of the universe, surrounded by a thousand square miles of largely uninhabited no-man's-land—or all-men's-land—I cannot seriously be disturbed by any premonitions of danger to my vulnerable wilderness or my all-too-perishable republic. All dangers seem equally remote. In this glare of brilliant emptiness, in this arid intensity of pure heat, in the heart of a weird solitude, great silence and grand desolation, all things recede to distances out of reach, reflecting light but impossible to touch, annihilating all thought and all that men have made to a spasm of whirling dust far out on the golden desert.

The flowers that graced the red dunes in April and May have withered now, all gone to seed except for a few drooping sunflowers. The cliffrose has faded, the yucca stalks have bloomed, blown, died, cracked and dried, the seedpods now only empty husks. Under the daily sweep of the parching May winds almost everything that was green has been burned to soft, sere tones of saffron and auburn. But the summer thunderstorms have not yet begun. When they come, as they soon will, we'll see a resurgence of hairy green across the land—the succulent scratchy allergenic tumbleweed, that exotic import from the Mongolian steppes.

The majority of living things retreat before the stunning glare and heat of midday. A snake or lizard exposed to the noon sun for more than ten minutes would die; having no internal cooling mechanism the reptiles must at all costs avoid extremes of temperature, especially in the desert where the temperature on the surface of the ground is much higher than it is in the air a few feet above. The snakes therefore seek shade, waiting until sundown to come out to hunt for supper. The insect-eating lizards dart from shelter to shelter, never lingering for more than a few moments in the open blaze.

The other creatures do the same. Like myself, they stay in the shade as much as possible. To conserve bodily moisture and energy the rodents remain in their burrows during the day. Scorpions and spiders go underground for the duration. Deer, antelope, bighorn sheep, bobcats, foxes and coyotes all shade up beneath rock ledges, oakbrush, pinyon and juniper trees, till the sun goes down.

Even the red ants keep to the inside of their evil nests at noon, though they will come spilling out eager to fight if riled with a stick—I've tried it, naturally.

Flowers curl up. Leaves fold inward. Everything shrinks, contracts, shrivels; somewhere a desiccated limb on an ancient dying cottonwood tree splits off from the trunk, and the rending fibers make a sound like the shriek of a woman.

The birds are muted, inactive. Now and then I can hear the faraway call of a mourning dove—a call that always sounds far away. A few gray desert sparrows fly from one tree to the next, stop there, do not reappear. The ravens and magpies stay in the shade, the former up on the rimrock, the latter in the trees. The owls, of course, and the nighthawks keep to holes and crevices during the day.

Insect life, sparse to begin with on the open desert, diminishes to near total invisibility and inaudibility during the heat of the day, although at times, during the very hottest and stillest hour, you may hear the eerie ticking noise of a sun-demented cricket or locust, a small sad music that seems to have—like a Bach partita—a touch of something ageless, out of time, eternal in its primeval vibrations.

In this static period even the domestic livestock—horses, sheep, goats, cattle—have sense enough to take it easy, relaxing in the shade. Of all the featherless beasts only man, chained by his self-imposed slavery to the clock, denies the elemental fire and proceeds as best he can about his business, suffering quietly, martyr to his madness. Much to learn.

Among the wild things only the hawks, vultures and eagles seem to remain fully active during the hottest days and hottest hours of the desert. I have seen them circling and soaring far in the sky at high noon, dark wings against the blue, above the heat.

What are they doing up there in the middle of the sky at the apex of the day? I watch them for hour after hour with the naked eye and with binoculars and never see either hawk or eagle stoop and strike at such a time. And no wonder, for there's precious little fresh meat abroad. Nor does the buzzard descend for lunch or make any effort of any kind. The hawks appear most frequently and most briefly, gliding overhead on some invisible stream in the air. The golden eagle does not come into sight often but stays longer than the hawk, floating toward the horizon in overlapping circles until out of sight.

The vulture or buzzard, master of soaring flight, is most common and most often seen. He stays aloft for hours at a time without ever stirring his long black white-trimmed wings, recognizable at a great distance by their dihedral inclination. Never in a hurry to get anywhere or do anything, an indolent and contemplative bird, he hovers on a thermal, rocking slightly, rising slowly, slips off, sails forward and upward without lifting a feather, primaries extended like fingers at his wingtips. He soars around and around in expanding spirals, lingering at a thousand feet above the landscape, bleak eyes missing nothing that moves below. Or maybe—who can be sure?—he is fast alseep up there, dreaming of a previous incarnation when wings were only a dream. Still without a stroke the vulture rises higher, higher, in ever wider circles, until nothing can be seen of this gaunt, arrogant, repellent bird but the coal-dark V-sign of his wings against the blue dome of heaven.

Around noon the heat waves begin flowing upward from the expanses of sand and bare rock. They shimmer like transparent, filmy veils between my sanctuary in the shade and all the sun-dazzled world beyond. Objects and forms viewed through this tremulous flow appear somewhat displaced or distorted, as a stick seems bent when half-immersed in water.

The great Balanced Rock floats a few inches above its pedestal, supported by a layer of superheated air. The buttes, pinnacles and fins in the Windows area bend and undulate beyond the middle ground like a painted backdrop stirred by a draft of air. The peaks of the Sierra La Sal—Mount Nass, Mount Tomaski, Mount Peale, Mount Tukuhnikivats and the others—seem to melt into one another, merging like cloud forms so that the profile of one mountain cannot be distinguished from that of another closer or farther away.

In the foreground the dwarf trees of pinyon pine and juniper waver like algae under water without, however, losing any of their sharpness of detail. There is in fact no illusion of the sort called mirage, only the faint deception of motion where nothing is actually moving but the overheated air. You are not likely to see a genuine mirage on the high desert of canyon and mesa country; for that spectacle we must go west or southwest into the basin-and-range provinces of Arizona, Nevada, Southern California and Sonora. There the dry lake beds between the parallel mountain ranges fill with planes of hot air which reflect sky and mountains in mirror fashion, creating the illusory lakes of blue water, the inverted mountains, the strange vision of men and animals walking through or upon water—Palestinian miracles.

Dehydration: the desert air sucks moisture from every pore. I take a drink from the canvas water-bag dangling near my head, the water cooled by evaporation. Noontime here is like a drug. The light is psychedelic, the dry electric air narcotic. To me the desert is stimulating, exciting, exacting; I feel no temptation to sleep or to relax into occult dreams but rather an opposite effect which sharpens and heightens vision, touch, hearing, taste and smell. Each stone, each plant, each grain of sand exists in and for itself with a clarity that is undimmed by any suggestion of a different realm. *Claritas, integritas, veritas.* Only the sunlight holds things together. Noon is the crucial hour: the desert reveals itself nakedly and cruelly, with no meaning but its own existence.

My lone juniper stands half-alive, half-dead, the silvery wind-rubbed claw of wood projected stiffly at the sun. A single cloud floats in the sky to the northeast, motionless, a magical coalescence of vapor where a few minutes before there was nothing visible but the hot, deep, black-grained blueness of infinity.

Life has come to a standstill, at least for the hour. In this forgotten place the tree and I wait on the shore of time, temporarily free from the force of motion and process and the surge toward—what? Something called the *future?* I am free, I am compelled, to contemplate the world which underlies life, struggle, thought, ideas, the human labyrinth of hope and despair.

Through half-closed eyes, for the light would otherwise be overpowering, I consider the tree, the lonely cloud, the sandstone bedrock of this part of the world and pray —in my fashion—for a vision of truth. I listen for signals from the sun—but that distant music is too high and pure for the human ear. I gaze at the tree and receive no response. I scrape my bare feet against the sand and rock under the table and am comforted by their solidity and resistance. I look at the cloud.

THE MOON-EYED HORSE

WHEN WE reached Salt Creek we stopped to water the horses. I needed a drink myself but the water here would make a man sick. We'd find good water farther up the canyon at Cigarette Spring.

While Mackie indulged himself in a smoke I looked at the scenery, staring out from under the shelter of my hat brim. The glare was hard on the eyes and for relief I looked down, past the mane and ears of my drinking horse, to something near at hand. There was the clear shallow stream, the green wiregrass standing stiff as bristles out of the alkali-encrusted mud, the usual deerflies and gnats swarming above the cattle tracks and dung.

I noticed something I thought a little odd. Cutting directly across the cattle paths were the hoofprints of an unshod horse. They led straight to the water and back again, following a vague little trail that led into the nearest side canyon, winding around blackbrush and cactus, short-cutting the meanders of the wash.

I studied the evidence for a while, trying to figure everything out for myself before mentioning it to Mackie, who knew this country far better than I ever would. He was a local man, a Moabite, temporarily filling in for Viviano Jacquez, who'd had another quarrel with old Roy Scobie and disappeared for a few days.

"There's a horse living up that canyon," I announced; "a wild horse. And a big one—feet like frying pans."

Slowly Mackie turned his head and looked where I pointed. "Wrong again," he said, after a moment's consideration.

"What do you mean, wrong again? If it's not a horse it must be a unicorn. Or a centaur? Look at those tracks—unshod. And from the wear and tear on that trail it's been living out here for a long time. Who runs horses out here?" We were about twenty miles from the nearest ranch.

"Nobody," Mackie agreed.

"You agree it's a horse."

"Of course it's a horse."

"Of course it's a horse. Well thank you very much. And no shoes, living out here in the middle of nothing, it must be a *wild* horse."

"Sorry," Mackie said. "Wrong again."

"Then what the hell is it?"

"Old Moon-Eye is what you might call an independent horse. He don't belong to anybody. But he ain't wild. He's a gelding and he's got Roy Scobie's brand on his hide."

I stared up the side canyon to where the tracks went out of sight around the first bend. "And this Moon-Eye lives up there all by himself?"

"That's right. He's been up in that canyon for ten years."

"Have you seen him?"

"No. Moon-Eye is very shy. But I heard about him."

Our mounts had raised their heads from the water and shifting restlessly under our weight, they seemed anxious to move on. Mackie turned his horse up the main trail along the stream and I followed, thinking.

"I want that horse," I said.

"What for?"

"I don't know."

"You can have him."

We rode steadily up the canyon, now and then splashing through the water, passing under the high red walls, the hanging gardens of poison ivy and panicgrass, the flowing sky. Where the trail widened I jogged my horse beside Mackie's and after a while, with a little prodding, extracted from him the story of the independent horse.

First of all, Moon-Eye had suffered. He had problems. His name derived from an inflamed condition of one of his eyes called moonblindness, which affected him periodically and inflamed his temper. The gelding operation had not improved his disposition. On top of that he'd been dude-spoiled, for old Roy had used him for many years—since he made a poor cow horse—in his string of horses for hire. The horse Moon-Eye seemed safe and well-behaved but his actual feelings were revealed one day on a sight-seeing tour through the Arches when all his angers came to a boil and he bucked off a middle-aged lady from Salt Lake City. Viviano Jacquez, leading the ride, lost his temper and gave the horse a savage beating. Moon-Eye broke away and ran off into the canyons with a good saddle on his back. He didn't come back that night. Didn't come back the next day. Never came back at all. For two weeks Viviano and Roy tracked that horse not because they wanted the horse but because Roy wanted his saddle back. When they found the saddle, caught on the stub of a limb, the cinch straps broken, they gave up the search for the horse. The bridle they never recovered. Later on a few boys from town came out to try to catch the horse and almost got him boxed up in Salt Creek Canyon. But he got away, clattering over the slickrock wall at an angle of 45 degrees, and was seldom seen afterward. After that he stayed out of box canyons and came down to the creek only when he needed a drink. That was the story of Moon-Eye.

We came at noon to the spring, dismounted, unsaddled the horses and let them graze on the tough brown grass near the cottonwoods. We dipped our cupped hands in the water and drank, leaned back against a log in the cool of the shade and ate some lunch. Mackie lit a cigarette. I stared out past the horses at the sweet green of the willows and cottonwoods under the hot red canyon wall. Far above, a strip of blue sky, cloudless. In the silence I heard quite clearly the buzzing of individual flies down by the creek, the shake and whisper of the dry cottonwood leaves, the bright tinkling song of a canyon wren. The horses shuffled slowly through the dead leaves, ripping up the grass with their powerful, hungry jaws—a solid and pleasing sound. The canyon filled with heat and stillness.

"Look, Mackie," I said, "what do you suppose that horse does up in there?"

"What horse?"

"Moon-Eye. You say he's been up that dry canyon by himself for ten years."

"Right."

"What does he *do* up in there?"

"That is a ridiculous question."

"All right it's a ridiculous question. Try and answer it."

"How the hell should I know? Who cares? What difference does it make?"

"Answer the question."

"He eats. He sleeps. He walks down to the creek once a day for a drink. He turns around and walks back. He eats again. He sleeps again."

"The horse is a gregarious beast," I said, "a herd animal, like the cow, like the human. It's not natural for a horse to live alone."

"Moon-Eye is not a natural horse."

"He's supernatural?"

"He's crazy. How should I know? Go ask the horse."

"Okay, I'll do that."

"Only not today," Mackie said. "Let's get on up and out of here."

We'd laid around long enough. Mackie threw away the butt of his cigarette; I tanked up on more water. We mounted again, rode on to the head of the canyon where a forty-foot overhang barred the way, turned and rode back the way we'd come, clearing out the cattle from the brush and tamarisk thickets, driving them before us in a growing herd as we proceeded. By the time we reached the mouth of the canyon we had a troop of twenty head plodding before us through the dust and heat, half of them little white-faced calves who'd never seen a man or a horse before. We drove them into the catchpen and shut them up. Tomorrow the calves would be branded, castrated, ear-marked, dehorned, inoculated against blackleg, and the whole herd trucked to the mountains for the summer. But that would be a job for Mackie and Roy, not for me; for me tomorrow meant a return to sentry duty at the entrance of the Monument, the juniper guard and the cloud-formation survey.

As we loaded the horses into the truck for the return to the ranch I asked Mackie how he liked this kind of work. He looked at me. His shirt and the rag around his neck were dark with sweat, his face coated with dust; there was a stripe of dried blood across his cheek where a willow branch had struck him when he plunged through the brush after some ignorant cow.

"Look at yourself," he said.

I looked; I was in the same condition. "I do this only for fun," I explained. "If I did it for pay I might not like it. Anyway you haven't answered my question. How do *you* like this kind of work?"

"I'd rather be rich."

"What would you do if you were rich?"

He grinned through the dust. "Buy some cows of my own."

I hadn't forgotten the moon-eyed horse. A month later I was back at the spot by Salt Creek where I'd first seen the tracks, this time alone, though again on horseback. We were deep into the desert summer now and the stream had shrunk to a dribble of slimy water oozing along between sunbaked flats of mud.

As before I let my pony drink what he wanted from the

stream while I pondered the view from beneath the meager shelter of my hat. The alkali, white as lime, dazzled the eyes; the wiregrass looked sere and shriveled and even the hosts of flies and gnats had disappeared, hiding from the sun.

There was no sound but the noise of my drinking mount, no sight anywhere of animate life. In the still air the pinkish plumes of the tamarisk, light and delicate as lace, drooped from the tips of their branches without a tremor. Nothing moved, nothing stirred, except the shimmer of heat waves rising before the red canyon walls.

I could hardly have picked a more hostile day for a venture into the canyons. If anyone had asked I'd have said that not even a mad horse would endure a summer in such a place. Yet there were the tracks as before, coming down the pathway out of the side canyon and leading back again. Moon-Eye was still around. Or at any rate his tracks were still here, fresh prints in the dust that looked as if they might have been made only minutes before my arrival.

Out of the heat and stillness came an inaudible whisper, a sort of telepathic intimation that perhaps the horse did not exist at all—only his tracks. You ought to get out of this heat, I told myself, taking a drink from the canteen. My saddle horse raised his dripping muzzle from the water and waited. He turned his head to look at me with one drowsy eye; strings of algae hung from the corner of his mouth.

"No," I said, "we're not going home yet." I prodded the animal with my heels; slowly we moved up into the side canyon following the narrow trail. As we advanced I reviewed my strategy: since Moon-Eye had learned to fear and distrust men on horseback I would approach him on foot; I would carry nothing in my hands but a hackamore and a short lead rope. Better yet, I would hide these inside my shirt and go up to Moon-Eye with empty hands. Others had attempted the violent method of pursuit and capture and had failed. I was going to use nothing but sympathy and understanding, in direct violation of common sense and all precedent, to bring Moon-Eye home again.

I rounded the first bend in the canyon and stopped. Ahead was the typical scene of dry wash, saltbush and prickly pear, talus slopes at the foot of vertical canyon walls. No hint of animal life. Nothing but the silence, the stark suspension of all sound. I rode on. I was sure that Moon-Eye would not go far from water in this weather.

At the next turn in the canyon, a mile farther, I found a pile of fresh droppings on the path. I slid from the saddle and led my pony to the east side of the nearest boulder and tied him. Late in the afternoon he'd get a little shade. It was the best I could do for him; nothing else was available.

I pulled off the saddle and sat down on the ground to open a can of tomatoes. One o'clock by the sun and not a cloud in the sky: hot. I squatted under the belly of the horse and ate my lunch.

When I was finished I got up, reluctantly, stuffed hackamore and rope inside my shirt, hung the canteen over my shoulder and started off. The pony watched me go, head hanging, the familiar look of dull misery in his eyes. I know how you feel, I thought, but by God you're just going to have to stand there and suffer. If I can take it you can. The midday heat figured in my plan: I believed that in such heat the moon-eyed outlaw would be docile as a plow horse, amenable to reason. I thought I could amble close, slip the hackamore over his head and lead him home like a pet dog on a leash.

A mile farther and I had to take refuge beneath a slight overhang in the canyon wall. I took off my hat to let the evaporation of my sweaty brow cool my brains. Tilted the canteen to my mouth. Already I was having visions of iced drinks, waterfalls, shade trees, clear deep emerald pools.

Forward. I shuffled through the sand, over the rocks,

around the prickly pear and the spiny hedgehog cactus. I found a yellowish pebble the size of a crab apple and put it in my mouth. Kept going, pushing through the heat.

If you were really clever, I thought, you'd go back to Moon-Eye's watering place on Salt Creek, wait for him there, catch him by starlight. But you're not clever, you're stupid, I reminded myself: stick to the plan. I stopped to swab the sweat from my face. The silence locked around me again like a sphere of glass. Even the noise I made unscrewing the cap from the canteen seemed harsh and exaggerated, a gross intrusion.

I listened:

Something breathing nearby—I was in the presence of a tree. On the slope above stood a giant old juniper with massive, twisted trunk, its boughs sprinkled with the pale-blue inedible berries. Hanging from one of the limbs was what looked at first glance like a pair of trousers that reached to the ground. Blinking the sweat out of my eyes I looked harder and saw the trousers transform themselves into the legs of a large animal, focused my attention and distinguished through the obscurity of the branches and foliage the outline of a tall horse. A very tall horse.

Gently I lowered my canteen to the ground.

I touched the rope and hackamore bunched up inside my shirt. Still there. I took the pebble from my mouth, held it in my palm, and slowly and carefully and quietly stepped toward the tree. Out of the tree a gleaming eyeball watched me coming.

I said, "That you, Moon-Eye?"

Who else? The eyeball rolled, I saw the flash of white. The eye in the tree.

I stepped closer. "What are you doing out here, you old fool?"

The horse stood not under the tree—the juniper was not big enough for that—but within it, among its branches. There'd be an awful smashing and crashing of dry wood if he tried to drive out of there.

"Eh? What do you think you're up to anyway? Damned old idiot. . . ." I showed him the yellowish stone in my hand, round as a little apple. "Why don't you answer me, Moon-Eye? Forgotten how to talk?"

Moving closer. The horse remained rigid, ears up. I could see both eyes now, the good one and the bad one—moonstruck, like a bloodshot cueball.

"I've come to take you home, old horse. What do you think of that?"

He was a giant about seventeen hands high, with a buckskin hide as faded as an old rug and a big ugly coffin-shaped head.

"You've been out here in the wilderness long enough, old man. It's time to go home."

He looked old, all right, he looked his years. He looked more than old—he looked like a spectre. Apocalyptic, a creature out of a bad dream.

"You hear me, Moon-Eye? I'm coming closer...."

His nineteen ribs jutted out like the rack of a skeleton and his neck, like a camel's, seemed far too gaunt and long to carry that oversize head off the ground.

"You old brute," I murmured, "you hideous old gargoyle. You goddamned nightmare of a horse.... Moon-Eye, look at this. Look at this in my hand, Moon-Eye."

He watched me, watched my eyes. I was within twenty feet of him and except for the eyes he had yet to reveal a twitch of nerve or muscle; he might have been petrified. Mesmerized by sun and loneliness. He hadn't seen a man for—how many years?

"Moon-Eye," I said, approaching slowly, one short step, a pause, another step, "how long since you've stuck that ugly face of yours into a bucket of barley and bran? Remember what alfalfa tastes like, old pardner? How about grass, Moon-Eye? Green sweet fresh succulent grass, Moon-Eye, what do you think of that, eh?"

We were ten feet apart. Only the branches of the juniper tree separated us. Standing there watching the horse I could smell the odor of cedarwood, the fragrance of the tree.

Another step. "Moon-Eye...."

I hesitated; to get any closer I'd have to push through

the branches or stoop underneath them. "Come on, Moon-Eye, I want to take you home. It's time to go home, oldtimer."

We stared at each other, unmoving. If that animal was breathing I couldn't hear it—the silence seemed absolute. Not a fly, not a single fly crawled over his arid skin or whined around his rheumy eyeballs. If it hadn't been for the light of something like consciousness in his good eye I might have imagined I was talking to a scarecrow, a dried stuffed completely mummified horse. He didn't even smell like a horse, didn't seem to have any smell about him at all. Perhaps if I reached out and touched him he would crumble to a cloud of dust, vanish like a shadow.

My head ached from the heat and glare and for a moment I wondered if this horselike shape in front of me was anything more than hallucination.

"Moon-Eye. . . .?" Keep talking.

I couldn't stand there all afternoon. I took another step forward, pressing against a branch. Got to keep talking.

"Moon-Eye. . . ."

He lowered his head a couple of inches, the ears flattened back. Watch out. He was still alive after all. For the first time I felt a little fear. He was a big horse and that moon-glazed eye was not comforting. We watched each other intently through the branches of the tree. If I could only wait, only be patient, I might yet sweet-talk him into surrender. But it was too hot.

"Look here, old horse, have a sniff of this." I offered him the pebble with one hand and with the other unbuttoned a button of my shirt, preparing to ease out the rope when the chance came. "Go on, have a look. . . ."

I was within six feet of the monster.

"Now you just relax, Moon-Eye old boy. I'm coming in where you are now." I started to push through the boughs of the juniper. "Easy boy, easy now. . . ."

He backed violently, jarring the whole tree. Loose twigs and berries rained around us. The good eye glared at me, the bad one shone like a boiled egg—monocular vision.

"Take it easy, old buddy." Speaking softly. I had one

hand on the rope. I stepped forward again, pushing under the branches. Softly—"Easy, easy, don't be scared—"

Moon-Eye tried to back again but his retreat was blocked. Snorting like a truck he came forward, right at me, bursting through the branches. Dry wood snapped and popped, dust filled the air, and as I dove for the ground I had a glimpse of a lunatic horse expanding suddenly, growing bigger than all the world and soaring over me on wings that flapped like a bat's and nearly tore the tree out of the earth.

When I opened my eyes a second later I was still alive and Moon-Eye was down in the wash fifty feet away, motionless as a statute, waiting. He stood with his ragged broomtail and his right angled pelvic bones toward me but had that long neck and coffin head cranked around, watching me with the good eye, waiting to see what I would do next. He didn't intend to exert himself unless he was forced to.

The shade of the tree was pleasant and I made no hurry to get up. I sat against the trunk and checked for broken bones. Everything seemed all right except my hat a few feet away, crushed into the dirt by a mighty hoof. I was thirsty though and looked around for the canteen before remembering where I'd left it; I could see it down in the wash, near the horse.

Moon-Eye didn't move. He stood rigid as stone, conserving every drop of moisture in his body. But he was in the sun now and I was in the shade. Perhaps if I waited long enough he'd be forced to come back to the tree. I made myself comfortable and waited. The silence settled in again.

But that horse wouldn't come, though I waited a full hour by the sun. The horse moved only once in all that time, lowering his head for a sniff at a bush near his foreleg.

The red cliffs rippled behind the veil of heat, radiant as hot iron. Thirst was getting to me. I stirred myself, got up painfully, and stepped out of the wreckage of the juniper. The horse made no move.

"Moon-Eye," I said—he listened carefully—"let's get out

of here. What do you say? Let's go home, you miserable old bucket of guts. Okay?"

I picked up my flattened hat, reformed it, put it on.

"Well, what do you say?"

I started down the slope. He raised his head, twitched one ear, watching me. "Are you crazy, old horse, standing out here in the heat? Don't you have any sense at all?"

I did not approach him directly this time but moved obliquely across the slope, hoping to head him down the canyon toward the creek and the trail to the corral. Moon-Eye saw my purpose and started up the canyon. I hurried; the horse moved faster. I slowed to a walk; he did the same. I stopped and he stopped.

"Moon-Eye, let me tell you something. I can outrun you if I have to. These Utah cowboys would laugh themselves sick if I ever mentioned it out loud but it's a fact and you ought to know it. Over the long haul, say twenty or thirty miles, it's a known fact that a healthy man can outrun a horse."

Moon-Eye listened.

"But my God, in this heat, Moon-Eye, do you think we should? Be sensible. Let's not make fools of ourselves."

He waited. I squatted on my heels and passed my forefinger, like a windshield wiper, across my forehead, brushing off the streams of sweat. My head felt hot, damp, feverish.

"What's the matter with you, Moon-Eye?"

The horse kept his good eye on me.

"Are you crazy, maybe? You don't want to die out here, do you, all alone like a hermit? In this awful place. . . ." He watched me and listened. "The Turkey buzzards will get you, Moon-Eye. They'll smell you dying, they'll come flapping down on you like foul and dirty kites and roost on your neck and drink your eyeballs while you're still alive. Yes, they do that. And just before that good eye is punctured you'll see those black wings shutting off the sky, shutting out the sun, you'll see a crooked yellow beak and a red neck crawling with lice and a pair of insane eyes looking into yours. You won't like that, old horse. ..."

I paused. Moon-Eye was listening, he seemed attentive, but I sensed that he wasn't really much interested in what I was saying. Perhaps it was all an old story to him. Maybe he didn't care.

I continued with the sermon. "And when the buzzards are through with you, Moon-Eye—and you'll be glad when *that's* over—why then a quiet little coyote will come loping down the canyon in the middle of the night under the moon, Moon-Eye, nosing out your soul. He'll come to within fifty yards of you, old comrade, and sit for a few hours, thinking, and then he'll circle around you a few times trying to smell out the hand of man. Pretty soon his belly will get the best of his caution—maybe he hasn't eaten for two weeks and hasn't had a chance at a dead horse for two years—and so he'll come nosing close to you, tongue out and eyes bright with happiness, and all at once when you're hardly expecting it he'll pounce and hook his fangs into your scrawny old haunch and tear off a steak. Are you listening to me, Moon-Eye? And when he's gorged himself sick he'll retire for a few hours of peaceful digestion. In the meantime the ants and beetles and blowflies will go to work, excavating tunnels through your lungs, kidneys, stomach, windpipe, brains and entrails and whatever else the buzzards and the coyote leave."

Moon-Eye watched me as I spoke; I watched him. "And in a couple of weeks you won't even stink anymore and after a couple of months there'll be nothing left but your mangled hide and your separated bones and —get this, Moon-Eye get the picture—way out in eternity somewhere, on the far side of the sun, they'll hang up a brass plaque with the image of your moon-eyed soul stamped on it. That's about all. Years later some tired and dirty cowboy looking for a lost horse, some weary prospector looking for potash or beryllium will stumble up this way and come across your clean white rib cage, your immaculate skull, a few other bones. ..."

I stopped talking. I was tired. Would that sun never go down beyond the canyon wall? Wasn't there a cloud in the whole state of Utah?

The horse stood motionless as a rock. He looked like part of that burnt-out landscape. He looked like the steed of Don Quixote carved out of wood by Giacometti. I could see the blue of the sky between his ribs, through the eyesockets of his skull. Dry, odorless, still and silent, he looked like the idea—without the substance—of a horse.

My brain and eyes ached, my limbs felt hollow, I had to breathe deliberately, making a conscious effort. The thought of the long walk back to my saddle pony, the long ride back to the pickup truck, made my heart sink. I didn't want to move. So I'd wait, too, wait for sundown before starting the march home, the *anabasis* in retreat. I glanced toward the sun. About four o'clock. Another hour before that sun would reach the rim of the canyon. I crawled back to the spotted shade of the juniper and waited.

We waited then, the horse and I, enduring the endless afternoon, the heartbreaking heat, and passed the time as best we could in one-sided conversation. I'd speak a sentence and wait about ten minutes for the next thought and speak again. Moon-Eye watched me all the time and made no move.

At last the sun touched the skyline, merged with it for a moment in a final explosive blaze of light and heat and sank out of sight. The shadow of the canyon wall advanced across the canyon floor, included the horse, touched the rocks and brush on the far side. A wave of cooling relief like a breeze, like an actual movement of air, washed through the canyon. A rock wren sang, a few flies came out of hiding and droned around the juniper tree. I could almost see the leaves of the saltbush and blackbush relax a little, uncurling in the evening air.

I stood up and emerged from the shelter of the broken tree. Old Moon-Eye took a few steps away from me, stopped. Still watching. We faced each other across some fifty feet of sand and rock. No doubt for the last time.

I tried to think of something suitable to say but my mouth was so dry, my tongue so stiff, my lips so dried-out and cracked, I could barely utter a word.

"You damned stupid harrr. . . ." I croaked, and gave it up.

Moon-Eye blinked his good eye once, twitched his hide and kept watching me as all around us, along the wash and on the canyon walls and in the air the desert birds and desert bugs resumed their inexplicable careers. A whiptail lizard scurried past my feet. A primrose opened its petals a few inches above the still-hot sand. Knees shaking, I stepped toward the horse, pulled the ropy hackamore out of my shirt—to Moon-Eye it must have looked as if I were pulling out my intestines—and threw the thing with all the strength I had left straight at him. It slithered over his back like a hairy snake, scaring him into a few quick steps. Again he stopped, the eye on me.

Enough. I turned my back on the horse and went to the canteen, picked it up. The water was almost too hot to drink but I drank it. Drank it all, except a few drops which I poured on my fingers and dabbed on my aching forehead. Refusing to look again at the spectre horse, I slung the canteen over my shoulder and started homeward, trudging over the clashing stones and through the sand down-canyon toward my pony and Salt Creek.

Once, twice, I thought I heard footsteps following me but when I looked back I saw nothing.

DOWN THE RIVER

THE BEAVERS had to go and build another god-damned dam on the Colorado. Not satisfied with the enormous silt trap and evaporation tank called Lake Mead (back of Boulder Dam) they have created another even bigger, even more destructive, in Glen Canyon. This reservoir of stagnant water will not irrigate a single square foot of land or supply water for a single village; its only justification is the generation of cash through electricity for the indirect subsidy of various real estate speculators, cottongrowers and sugarbeet magnates in Arizona, Utah and Colorado; also, of course, to keep the engineers and managers of the Reclamation Bureau off the streets and out of trouble.

The impounded waters form an artificial lake named Powell, supposedly to honor but actually to dishonor the memory, spirit and vision of Major John Wesley Powell, first American to make a systematic exploration of the Colorado River and its environs. Where he and his brave men once lined the rapids and glided through silent canyons two thousand feet deep the motorboats now smoke and whine, scumming the water with cigarette butts, beer cans and oil, dragging the water skiers on their endless rounds, clockwise.

PLAY SAFE, read the official signboards; SKI ONLY IN CLOCKWISE DIRECTION; LET'S ALL HAVE FUN TOGETHER! With regulations enforced by water cops in government uniforms. Sold. Down the river.

Once it was different there. I know, for I was one of the lucky few (there could have been thousands more) who saw Glen Canyon before it was drowned. In fact I saw only a part of it but enough to realize that here was an Eden, a portion of the earth's original paradise. To grasp the nature of the crime that was committed imagine the Taj Mahal or Chartres Cathedral buried in mud until only the spires remain visible. With this difference: those man-made celebrations of human aspiration could conceivably be reconstructed while Glen Canyon was a living thing, irreplaceable, which can never be recovered through any human agency.

(Now, as I write these words, the very same coalition of persons and avarice which destroyed Glen Canyon is preparing a like fate for parts of the Grand Canyon.)

What follows is the record of a last voyage through a place we knew, even then, was doomed.

One day in late June Ralph Newcomb and I arrive on the shore of the Colorado River at a site known variously as Hite, White Canyon or Dandy Crossing, about one hundred and fifty miles upriver from the new dam already under construction. In my pickup truck, badly shaken by a long drive down one of the roughest roads in Utah, we carry camping gear, enough grub for two weeks, and two little rubber boats folded up in suitcase-size cartons.

We spend half a day on the shore, preparing our boats and ourselves for the journey. The river looks terribly immense and powerful, swollen with snow-melt from the western slope of the Rockies and from the Wind River

Range in Wyoming, a veritable Mississippi of a river rolling between redrock walls. Our rubber boats, after we inflate them, seem gaudy, flimsy and much too small. Inevitably we've forgotten a few things, among them life jackets, and I can't help thinking that maybe we should make the trip some other time. One of the things that worries me, besides the missing life jackets and the obvious fragility of our Made-in-Japan vessels, is the fact that Ralph has only one good leg. He can walk but not hike; he can swim but not very far.

However, I keep my cowardly doubts to myself, waiting for Ralph to speak of them first. But he doesn't. Imperturbable as the river itself, tranquil as the sky overhead, he puffs on his corncob pipe, limping back and forth between the truck and the launching point with canned goods and bedrolls.

We divide our supplies, mostly bacon and beans, into equal parts, bind them in canvas and rope, and stow them under the bow seats; in case one boat is lost we will still have survival rations left in the other. Ralph has also had sense enough to bring along a bit of line and a few fishhooks—the river is lively with catfish, as we'll soon discover. We expect to spend about ten days on the river and will not see any human habitation, after Hite, until we reach the dam site a hundred and fifty miles downstream.

At last we're ready. I push my boat onto the water of an inlet and climb abroad. The floor of the boat is nothing but a single layer of rubberized canvas and sags like jelly beneath my weight. Sitting there I can feel the coolness of the water through the canvas and my blue jeans. But it floats, this toy boat, and I can find no more excuses for delay. Since Ralph has a camera and wants pictures of the launching I am obliged to go first. I paddle out of the quiet inlet and onto the brown silt-rich bosom of the Colorado.

This is my first experience with a rubber boat and I discover at once that a single canoe-type paddle is not appropriate. The shallow-drafted almost weightless boat tends to turn in circles, pivoting beneath my seat; in order to make any headway I have to shift the paddle quickly from side to side, an awkward and tiring procedure. Staying clear of the main current, drifting slowly past the shore, I paddle in circles and wait for Ralph to catch up.

He comes alongside. We lash the boats together, side by side, which makes not only for better companionship and ease of conversation but also improves the maneuverability: Ralph paddles on one side, I on the other, giving us some control over our direction.

We paddle our double craft into the current, ship paddles, lean back against the stern seats, which make good backrests and nothing much else, and smoke and talk. My anxieties have vanished and I feel instead a sense of cradlelike security, of achievement and joy, a pleasure almost equivalent to that first entrance—from the outside —into the neck of the womb.

We are indeed enjoying a very intimate relation with the river: only a layer of fabric between our bodies and the water. I let my arm dangle over the side and trail my hand in the flow. Something dreamlike and remembered, that sensation called *déjà vu*—when was I here before? A moment of groping back through the maze, following the thread of a unique emotion, and then I discover the beginning. I am fulfilling at last a dream of childhood and one as powerful as the erotic dreams of adolescence —*floating down the river*. Mark Twain, Major Powell, every man that has ever put forth on flowing water knows what I mean.

A human shout reaches our ears from the west shore. A man is waving at us from the landing of old Hite's ferry. A warning? A farewell? He shouts once more but his words are unintelligible. Cheerfully waving back, we drift past him and beyond his ken without the faintest intimation of regret. We shall not see another of the tool-making breed for a long time and we could not care less.

Misanthropy? Shakespeare could say

> Man delights not me,
> No, nor woman neither. . . .

And Raleigh, too,

> I wished I loved the human race,
> I wish I loved its silly face.

And Jeffers:

> Be in nothing so moderate
> as in love of man.

But no, this is not at all what we feel at this moment, not at all what I mean. In these hours and days of dual solitude on the river we hope to discover something quite different, to renew our affection for ourselves and the human kind in general by a temporary, legal separation from the mass. And in what other way is it possible for those not saints? And who wants to be a saint? Are saints human?

Cutting the bloody cord, that's what we feel, the delirious exhilaration of independence, a rebirth backward in time and into primeval liberty, into freedom in the most simple, literal, primitive meaning of the word, the only meaning that really counts. The freedom, for example, to commit murder and get away with it scot-free, with no other burden than the jaunty halo of conscience. I look at my old comrade Newcomb in a new light and feel a wave of love for him; I am not going to kill him and he—I trust —is not going to kill me.

(My God! I'm thinking, what incredible *shit* we put up with most of our lives—the *domestic* routine (same old wife *every* night), the stupid and useless and degrading *jobs*, the *insufferable* arrogance of elected officials, the crafty *cheating* and the *slimy* advertising of the businessmen, the tedious wars in which we kill our buddies instead of our *real* enemies back home in the capital, the foul, diseased and *hideous* cities and towns we live in, the constant *petty* tyranny of automatic washers and automobiles and TV machines and telephones—! ah *Christ!*, I'm thinking, at the same time that I'm waving goodby to that hollering idiot on the shore, what *intolerable* garbage and what utterly *useless crap* we bury ourselves in day by day, while patiently enduring at the same time the creeping strangulation of the clean white *collar* and the rich but *modest* four-in-hand garrote!)

Such are my—you wouldn't call them thoughts, would you?—such are my feelings, a mixture of revulsion and delight, as we float away on the river, leaving behind for a while all that we most heartily and joyfully detest. That's what the first taste of the wild does to a man, after having been too long penned up in the city. No wonder the Authorities are so anxious to smother the wilderness under asphalt and reservoirs. They know what they're doing; their lives depend on it, and all their rotten institutions. Play safe. Ski only in clockwise direction. Let's all have fun together.

We drift on; the current seems to accelerate a bit as the mighty river squeezes between great red walls of sandstone rising on either side to heights of a thousand feet or more, cliffs so sheer and smooth even a bird could find no perch there. One little white cloud of dubious substantiality hovers above in the strip of blue between the canyon walls. Gazing up at it I think I hear, as in a dream, a confused rumble and roar, the sound of a freight train highballing down a mountain grade. Rapids.

Actually there are not supposed to be true rapids in Glen Canyon—only "riffles." But it's been a dry winter, the river is low, the rocks high. To us these foamy waves *look* like rapids.

"White water ahead," says Ralph quietly, with a sort of complacent satisfaction, as if he had invented the phenomenon all by himself. And instead of doing anything about it he reloads his cheap pipe.

We're rounding the first major bend in the canyon. From ahead comes the sound of the rapids—toneless vibrations growing stronger, what acoustical specialists call "white noise." Like the sound of a waterfall. Supposedly a blissful and sleep-inducing impression on edgy nerves.

"I didn't know we'd hit rapids so soon," I say to Ralph. I open up my map, the only one we've brought with us, a Texaco road map of the state of Utah, and study the tributaries of the Colorado. "That must be where Trachyte Creek comes in," I explain; "if we had life jackets with us it might be a good idea to put them on now."

Actually our ignorance and carelessness are more deliberate than accidental; we are entering Glen Canyon without having learned much about it beforehand because we wish to see it as Powell and his party had seen it, not knowing what to expect, making anew the discoveries of others. If the first rapids are a surprise to us it is simply because we had never inquired if there were any on this stretch of the river.

Anyway, there's no turning back now. After the entrance, the inescapable spasm. Between narrowing walls the river rushes at increasing speed. Our little boats bounce over choppy waves toward the whitecaps that now are visible, churning to foam around glistening wet boulders strewn across our course, boulders which seem to rise and fall as we race toward them on the bounding current.

There is no longer time enough to be frightened. I have a glimpse of the willows on the shore sweeping past, the only available gauge of our velocity, before we grab the paddles, settle deep into the boats and go to work trying to keep our bows headed into the waves.

Not that it makes much difference. The spray hits our faces and closes vision, the waves come aboard, in a moment we are soaking wet and spinning through the heart of the turmoil, bouncing off one rock and into the next. A great shining boulder looms before us, unavoidable; Ralph's boat slams upon it and hangs there for a second or two until my boat, still roped to his, swings round in the spillway and pulls his free. Paddling furiously we right the boats and face the next obstacle, skin past it safely, bounce in and out of a few more troughs and suddenly find ourselves in the clear.

The waves smooth off as the river broadens through a wider channel, resuming its serene and steady flow. We've run our first rapids and are still alive. The boats are drifting along half full of water and we are drenched but the pipe in Ralph's teeth is still burning, so quickly did it all happen.

Happy, exultant, we rest for a while in the soggy boats before bailing them out. If this is the worst Glen Canyon has to offer, we agree, give us more of the same.

In a few minutes the river obliges; a second group of rapids appears, wild as the first. Forewarned and over-cautious this time, despite ourselves, we paddle too far out of the main current and end up aground in the shallows. We have to climb out of the boats and drag them over a pebble-covered bar until we again reach deep water. Hard work for game-legged Newcomb but he makes no complaint.

Back in the boats, sprawled out comfortably on our baggage, nothing lost but the road map—and there are no gas stations in Glen Canyon anyhow—we drift onward without further effort, paddles inboard and at rest. The surface of the river is wide and gleaming, slick as glass; an immaculate stillness pervades the canyon, pointed up deftly now and then by a gurgling eddy near the shore, the call of a bird.

Smoking peacefully, we watch the golden light of afternoon climb the eastern wall as the sun goes down beyond the rim to the west. An early evening breeze rustles through the willows ashore and we hear again the tinkling music of canyon wrens—like little silver bells falling across a glockenspiel—no, like wilderness lorelei—calling down to us from the rimrock, sweetest of all bird songs in the canyon country.

Other voices also speak: queer squawks and honkings from the thickets, sounds we cannot identify until we see, a little later, a great blue heron flap its wings among the lavender plumes of a tamarisk tree.

"Ralph Newcomb," I say, "do you believe in God?"

"Who?" he says.

"Who?"

"Who."

"You said it," I say.

An owl. Ravens. More canyon wrens. The splash of fish breaking the surface. Lizards palpitating on the rocks. And once we see, between us and the far shore, something sleek and dark following its nose upstream—a beaver. The same that lured the mountain men—Robidoux, Jim Bridger, Jedediah Smith—into these parts more than a century ago.

The river bears us quietly along, the canyon fills with shadow and coolness. The sky above turns a deeper darker blue as the last of the sunlight glows on the domes and turrets and elephant-backs of the Navajo sandstone above the Wingate cliffs. We begin to think about food and a camp for the night.

When a beach of white sand comes in sight, backed with a stand of green young willows, we get out the paddles and work toward it, paddling strenuously across the current. As will usually happen, we are on the wrong side of the river when we want to make a landing. And it's a wide river this time of the year. And with Ralph on the upstream side of our double boat, I have to paddle twice as hard as he does just to keep even.

Closing in on the beach, I jump out and wade ashore, towing the boats onto the sand. We tether them to a clump of willows, unload and prepare to camp. My bedroll is a little wet but everything else, well wrapped in tarpaulins, is dry, and our feelings of pleasure and satisfaction are as great as our appetite for supper.

It is a beauteous evening, calm and free. We build a small fire of dead willow branches and propitiate the gods of river and canyon with the incense of woodsmoke, an offering with which, being intangible beings, they are content; we, the worshipers of baser stuff, fry and eat the actual beans, corned beef and eggs. A crude meal, no doubt, but the best of all sauces is hunger. To us it seems a shade better than anything available at Sardi's or Delmonico's. What's more we aren't graveled for leg room.

We make the coffee with river water, dipping a canful from among the rocks and letting it set for a time until the silt settles to the bottom. For entertainment we have the murmur of the river, the drone of cicada and amphibians, the show of nighthawks plunging through the evening gulping bugs. Afterwards we sit by the fire until the fire gives out, listening, smoking, analyzing socio-economic problems:

"Look here, Newcomb," I say, "do you think it's fitting

that you and I should be here in the wilds, risking our lives amidst untold hardships, while our wives and loved ones lounge at their ease back in Albuquerque, enjoying the multifold comforts, benefits and luxuries of modern contemporary twentieth century American urban civilization?"

"Yes," he says.

I rebuild the fire and drape my sleeping bag above it on a willow bough, smoking it good and proper. When it's ready I scoop two shallow holes in the sand, one for the hipbones and one for the shoulder blades, lay out the sleeping bag and turn in. Ralph, peaceful as a hanging judge, is already sound asleep. For myself I choose to listen to the river for a while, thinking river thoughts, before joining the night and the stars.

Morning on the river: up with the dawn, before the sun, Ralph still sleeping, strange invisible birds calling and croaking from the bush, I wash last night's dishes in the muddy river. And why not? That same force which corraded a gorge five thousand feet deep through the Kaibab Plateau will also serve to scour the grease from the tin plates of the Abbey-Newcomb Expedition. The Colorado has no false pride.

Then breakfast: bacon and eggs, fried potatoes, coffee. The unknown birds continue to creak and chirrup. Some I begin to recognize—a mockingbird, killdeer, Mexican finches. Also the usual and prevalent canyon wrens and a few magpies and ravens.

Ralph awakes, stirred to life by the aroma of food, takes a bath in the river, combs and pomades his hair, his long black evil sheepherder's beard. We eat.

Afterwards as we pack and load the boats, sun coming up over the rim, we begin to feel the familiar terrible desert thirst. We drink the last of the spring water in our canteens and, still thirsty, look to the river, that sombre flow the color of burnt sienna, raw umber, *muy colorado*, too thin to plow—as the Mormons say—and too thick to drink. But we drink it; we'll drink plenty of it before this voyage is over.

The sun rises higher, fierce on our faces; the western wall blazes like hot iron. We shove off, keeping to the shady side of the canyon, and commence the second day of our journey.

Why, we ask ourselves, floating onward in effortless peace deeper into Eden, why not go on like this forever? True, there are no women here (a blessing in disguise?), no concert halls, no books, bars, galleries, theaters or playing fields, no cathedrals of learning or high towers of finance, no wars, elections, traffic jams or other amusements, none of the multinefarious delights of what Ralph calls syphilization. But on the other hand most anything else a man could desire is here in abundance: catfish in the mainstream and venison in the side canyons, cottonwoods for shade and shelter, juniper for fuel, mossy springs (not always accessible) for thirst, and the ever-changing splendor of sky, cliffs, mesas and river for the needs of the spirit.

If necessary, we agree, a man could live out his life in this place, once he had adjusted his nervous system to the awful quietude, the fearful tranquillity. The silence—meaning here not the total absence of sounds, for the river and its canyons are bright with a native music—but rather the total absence of confusion and clamor, that would be the problem. What Churchill spoke of as *"bloody peace"* —could we bear it for very long? Yet having known this, how could we ever return to the other?

"Newcomb," I say, "you're condemned. You are doomed."

"So are you," he says.

"Let's drink to that. Where's that rum we were going to bring along?"

"Stowed with the life jackets."

"And the case of beer we were going to tow instead of a dinghy?"

"We drank it all back in Albuquerque."

The thirst. I dip a can in the river under my elbow and place it on the gunwale (so to speak) of my little rubber boat, giving the mud in the water time to settle out. The river at this point is so steady and serene that the can of drinking water hardly trembles, though it's balanced on a rounded surface.

The current carries us on its back smoothly south and west toward the Gulf of California, the Sea of Cortez, but with many a wonderful meander on the way. Occasionally we lay a paddle over the side, drop the blade in the water and with the slightest, most infinitesimal of exertions turn the double boat for a view in a different direction, saving ourselves the trouble—somewhat greater—of turning our heads or craning our necks.

In this dreamlike voyage any unnecessary effort seems foolish. Even vulgar, one might say. The river itself sets the tone: utterly relaxed, completely at ease, it fulfills its mighty purpose without aim or effort. Only the slow swing of the canyon walls overhead and the illusory upstream flow of willows, tamarisk and boulders on the shore reveal and indicate the sureness of our progress to the sea.

We pass an opening in the eastern wall, the mouth of a tributary stream. Red Canyon Creek? There's no telling and it certainly doesn't matter. No rapids here; only a subtle roiling of the water, ripples corresponding to the ripples on the river's sandy bed. Beyond the side canyon the walls rise up again, slick and monolithic, in color a blend of pink, buff, yellow, orange, overlaid in part with a glaze of "desert varnish" (iron oxide) or streaked in certain places with vertical draperies of black organic stains, the residue from plant life beyond the rim and from the hanging gardens that flourish in the deep grottoes high on the walls. Some of those alcoves are like great amphitheatres, large as the Hollywood Bowl, big enough for God's own symphony orchestra.

When the sun stands noon-high between the walls we take our lunch, on board and under way, of raisins and oranges and beef jerky and the cool cloudy river water with its rich content of iron and minerals, of radium, uranium, vanadium and who knows what else. We have no fear of human pollution, for the nearest upstream town is Moab, pop. 5000, one hundred miles away. (Blessed Utah!)

In any case, when a man must be afraid to drink freely

from his country's rivers and streams that country is no longer fit to live in. Time then to move on, to find another country or—in the name of Jefferson—to make another country. "The tree of liberty is nourished by the blood of tyrants; it is its natural manure."

(Or Bakunin: "There are times when creation can be achieved only through destruction. The urge to destroy is then a creative urge.")

After lunch we paddle hard across the current again to the west side of the river, seeking shade. Shade as precious as water. Without shade, in the middle of the river, we must cower beneath our hats, hammered by sun and by the reflected heat and blaze from the mirrorlike sheen of the river, the hot red walls of the canyon. Once in the shade we can rest, expand, unsquint our eyes, and see.

All afternoon we glide onward, running a few slight rapids (slight compared to those of Cataract Canyon and Grand Canyon), smoking our tobacco, drinking the river, talking of anything and everything which comes to our heads, enjoying the delirium of bliss.

"Newcomb, for godsake where do we come from?"

"Who knows?"

"Where are we going?"

"Who cares."

"Who?"

"Who."

Words fail. I draw the rusty harmonica from my shirt pocket and play old folksongs and little tunes from the big symphonies—a thin sweet music that floats for a while like smoke in the vastness all around us before fading into the silence, becoming forever a part of the wilderness. Yielding to nostalgia, I play the Sunday-morning songs out of my boyhood: *What a friend we have in Jesus. . . . Leaning, leaning, leaning on the everlasting arms. . . .* (diatonics for the soul) and:

> We shall gather by the river,
> The beautiful the beautiful-ah riv-er . . .
> We shall gather by the river
> That flows (from?) the throne of the Lord. . . .

We make our second river camp this evening on another sandy beach near the mouth of a small creek which enters the main canyon from the northwest. Hall's Creek? Bullfrog Creek? Sometimes I regret not having brought a decent map. Not far below are what look and sound like the most ferocious of rapids, far worse than those we'd encountered on the first day. But tomorrow we'll worry.

We eat a good, simple, sandy supper of onion soup, beef and beans, tinned fruit and coffee. With the coffee we each have a pipeful of Newcomb's Mixture—half Bull Durham and half Prince Albert, the first for flavor and the second for bulk. Good cheap workingman's tobacco.

After the meal, while Ralph washes the dishes, I take the canteens and walk up the creek to get some spring water if possible. In the sand I see the prints of deer and coyote and bobcat, also a few cattle tracks, strays perhaps, fairly fresh. I find no spring within a reasonable distance and return to camp with empty canteens; there is water in the creek, of course, but we'd rather drink from the river than downstream from a Hereford cow.

Dark when I return, with only the light of Ralph's fire to guide me. As I brush away sticks and stones on the ground, making a place for my sleeping bag, I see a scorpion scuttle off, tail up and stinger ready. Newcomb and I meditate upon the red coals of the fire before turning in. Watching the sky I see shooting stars, blue-green and vivid, course across the narrow band of sky between the canyon walls. From downriver, as I fall asleep, comes the deep dull roar of the rapids, a sound which haunts the background of my dreams all night long.

We get up too late in the morning and have to cook breakfast in the awful heat of the sun. I burn the bacon and the wind blows sand in the pancake batter. But we're getting accustomed to sand—sand in our food and drink, in our teeth and eyes and whiskers, in our bedrolls and underwear. Sand becomes a part of our existence which, like breathing, we take for granted.

Boats loaded, we launch them into the river, still roped together side by side for the sake of comfort, conversation and safety. The rapids that worried my dreams turn out in daylight to be little more than a stretch of choppy waves and a few eroded boulders past which our boats slip without difficulty. If it were not so late in June, following a dry winter, the river consequently lower than usual, we would probably not notice these trivial ripples at all.

Down the river we drift in a kind of waking dream, gliding beneath the great curving cliffs with their tapestries of water stains, the golden alcoves, the hanging gardens, the seeps, the springs where no man will ever drink, the royal arches in high relief and the amphitheatres shaped like seashells. A sculptured landscape mostly bare of vegetation—earth in the nude.

We try the walls for echo values—

> HELLO. . . .
>> Hello. . . .
>>> hello. . . .

—and the sounds that come back to us, far off and fading, are so strange and lovely, transmuted by distance, that we fall into silence, enchanted.

We pass sandbars where stands of white-plumed cane and the lacy blossoms of young tamarisk wave in the breeze among driftwood logs aged to a silver finish by sun and wind and water. In the lateral canyons we sometimes see thickets of Gambel oak and occasional cottonwoods with gray elephantine trunks and bright clear-green leaves, delicately suspended, trembling in the air.

We pass too many of these marvelous side canyons, to my everlasting regret, for most of them will never again be wholly accessible to human eyes or feet. Their living marvels must remain forever unknown, to be drowned beneath the dead water of the coming reservoir, buried for centuries under mud.

Here we become aware of the chief disadvantage of our cheap little rubber boats: far too often, when we see some place that demands unhurried exploration, the strong current will carry us past before we can paddle our awkward craft to the shore. You might think we could make a landing anyway and walk back up-river on the bank but in Glen Canyon, where the sandstone walls often rise straight up out of the water, this is sometimes impossible.

Furthermore we are lazy, indolent animals, Newcomb and I, half-mesmerized by the idyllic ease of our voyage; neither of us can seriously believe that very soon the beauty we are passing through will be lost. Instinctively we expect a miracle: the dam will never be completed, they'll run out of cement or slide rules, the engineers will all be shipped to Upper Volta. Or if these fail some unknown hero with a rucksack full of dynamite strapped to his back will descend into the bowels of the dam; there he will hide his high explosives where they'll do the most good, attach blasting caps to the lot and with angelic ingenuity link the caps to the official dam wiring system in such a way that when the time comes for the grand opening ceremony, when the President and the Secretary of the Interior and the governors of the Four-Corner states are all in full regalia assembled, the button which the President pushes will ignite the loveliest explosion ever seen by man, reducing the great dam to a heap of rubble in the path of the river. The splendid new rapids thus created we will name Floyd E. Dominy Falls, in honor of the chief of the Reclamation Bureau; a more suitable memorial could hardly be devised for such an esteemed and loyal public servant.

Idle, foolish, futile daydreams. While we dream and drift on the magic river the busy little men with their gargantuan appliances are hard at work, day and night, racing against the time when the people of America might possibly awake to discover something precious and irreplaceable about to be destroyed.

> ... Nature's polluted,
> There's man in every secret corner of her
> Doing damned, wicked deeds.

The ravens mock us as we float by. Unidentifiable birds call to us from the dark depths of the willow thickets—solitary calls from the wild. We see a second beaver, again like the first swimming upstream. All of our furred and feathered and hairy-hided cousins who depend for their existence upon the river and the lower canyons—the deer, the beaver, the coyotes, the wildcats and cougars, most of

the birds and smaller animals—will soon be compelled to
find new homes. If they can. For there is no land in the
canyon country not already fully occupied, to the limit of
the range, by their own kind. There are no vacant lots in
nature.

At four or five miles per hour—much too fast—we glide
on through the golden light, the heat, the crystalline quiet.
At times, almost beneath us, the river stirs with sudden
odd uproars as the silty bed below alters in its conforma-
tions. Then comfortably readjusted, the river flows on and
the only noise, aside from that of scattered birds, is the
ripple of the water, the gurgling eddies off the sandspits,
the sound of Newcomb puffing on his old pipe.

We are deep in the wild now, deep in the lonely, sweet,
remote, primeval world, far far from anywhere familiar to
men and women. The nearest town from where we are
would be Blanding in southeast Utah, close to the Colorado line, or maybe Hanksville in south-central Utah,
north of the Henry Mountains, either place about a hundred miles away by foot and both on the far side of an
uninhabited wilderness of canyons, mesas, clay hills, slickrock domes, sand flats, pinyon and juniper forests.

Wilderness. The word itself is music.

Wilderness, wilderness. . . . We scarcely know what we
mean by the term, though the sound of it draws all whose
nerves and emotions have not yet been irreparably stunned,
deadened, numbed by the caterwauling of commerce, the
sweating scramble for profit and domination.

Why such allure in the very word? What does it really
mean? Can wilderness be defined in the words of government officialdom as simply "A minimum of not less than
5000 contiguous acres of roadless area"? This much may be
essential in attempting a definition but it is not sufficient;
something more is involved.

Suppose we say that wilderness invokes nostalgia, a justified not merely sentimental nostalgia for the lost America our forefathers knew. The word suggests the past and
the unknown, the womb of earth from which we all
emerged. It means something lost and something still pres-

ent, something remote and at the same time intimate, something buried in our blood and nerves, something beyond us and without limit. Romance—but not to be dismissed on that account. The romantic view, while not the whole of truth, is a necessary part of the whole truth.

But the love of wilderness is more than a hunger for what is always beyond reach; it is also an expression of loyalty to the earth, the earth which bore us and sustains us, the only home we shall ever know, the only paradise we ever need—if only we had the eyes to see. Original sin, the true original sin, is the blind destruction for the sake of greed of this natural paradise which lies all around us —if only we were worthy of it.

Now when I write of paradise I mean *Paradise*, not the banal Heaven of the saints. When I write "paradise" I mean not only apple trees and golden women but also scorpions and tarantulas and flies, rattlesnakes and Gila monsters, sandstorms, volcanos and earthquakes, bacteria and bear, cactus, yucca, bladderweed, ocotillo and mesquite, flash floods and quicksand, and yes—disease and death and the rotting of the flesh.

Paradise is not a garden of bliss and changeless perfection where the lions lie down like lambs (what would they eat?) and the angels and cherubim and seraphim rotate in endless idiotic circles, like clockwork, about an equally inane and ludicrous—however roseate—Unmoved Mover. (Play safe; worship only in clockwise direction; let's all have fun together.) That particular painted fantasy of a realm beyond time and space which Aristotle and the Church Fathers tried to palm off on us has met, in modern times, only neglect and indifference, passing on into the oblivion it so richly deserved, while the Paradise of which I write and wish to praise is with us yet, the here and now, the actual, tangible, dogmatically real earth on which we stand.

Some people who think of themselves as hard-headed realists would tell us that the cult of the wild is possible only in an atmosphere of comfort and safety and was therefore unknown to the pioneers who subdued half a continent with their guns and plows and barbed wire. Is this true? Consider the sentiments of Charles Marion Russell, the cowboy artist, as quoted in John Hutchens' *One Man's Montana:*

"I have been called a pioneer. In my book a pioneer is a man who comes to virgin country, traps off all the fur, kills off all the wild meat, cuts down all the trees, grazes off all the grass, plows the roots up and strings ten million miles of wire. A pioneer destroys things and calls it civilization."

Others who endured hardships and privations no less severe than those of the frontiersmen were John Muir, H. D. Thoreau, John James Audubon and the painter George Catlin, all of whom wandered on foot over much of our country and found in it something more than merely raw material for pecuniary exploitation.

A sixth example and my favorite is, of course, Major J. Wesley Powell, one-armed veteran of the Civil War, sitting in a chair lashed to the deck of the small wooden boat with which he led his brave party into the unknown canyons of the Green, Grand and Colorado rivers. From the railroad town of Green River, Wyoming, to the mouth of the Grand Canyon in what is now Lake Mead, Powell's first journey took three months. Within that time he and his men withstood a variety of unpleasant experiences, including the loss of a boat, the hard toil of lowering their boats by rope down the worst of the rapids, moldy flour and shortages of meat, extremes of heat and cold, illness, and the constant fear of the unknown, the uncertainty of success, the ever-present possibility that around the next bend of the canyon they might encounter hazards worse than any they had so far overcome. This psychological pressure eventually proved too much for three of Powell's men; near the end of the voyage these three left the expedition and tried to make their way overland back to civilization—and were all killed by Indians. Powell knew the inner gorge of the Grand Canyon as a terrible and gloomy underworld, scene of much physical and mental suffering for himself and his men, but despite this and despite all that had happened in his explorations, he would write of the canyon as a whole in panegyric accent:

"The glories and the beauties of form, color and sound unite in the Grand Canyon—forms unrivaled even by the mountains, colors that vie with sunsets, and sounds that span the diapason from tempest to tinkling raindrop, from cataract to bubbling fountain. . . .

"You cannot see the Grand Canyon in one view, as if it were a changeless spectacle from which a curtain might be lifted, but to see it you have to toil from month to month through its labyrinths. It is a region more difficult to traverse than the Alps or the Himalayas, but if strength and courage are sufficient for the task, by a year's toil a concept of sublimity can be obtained never again to be equaled on the hither side of Paradise."

No, wilderness is not a luxury but a necessity of the human spirit, and as vital to our lives as water and good bread. A civilization which destroys what little remains of the wild, the spare, the original, is cutting itself off from its origins and betraying the principle of civilization itself.

If industrial man continues to multiply his numbers and expand his operations he will succeed in his apparent intention, to seal himself off from the natural and isolate himself within a synthetic prison of his own making. He will make himself an exile from the earth and then will know at last, if he is still capable of feeling anything, the pain and agony of final loss. He will understand what the captive Zia Indians meant when they made a song out of their sickness for home:

> My home over there,
> Now I remember it;
> And when I see that mountain far away,
> Why then I weep,
> Why then I weep,
> Remembering my home.

Down the river. Our boats turn slowly in the drift, we see through a break in the canyon walls a part of the Henry Mountains retreating to the northwest, last range in the United States to be named and explored and mapped. Mount Ellsworth, one of the lower peaks, is the one we see, rising sharp and craggy against the sky, a laccolithic dome of varicolored sedimentary and igneous rock (part of the intrusion now exposed by erosion) furred over with a growth of pinyon pine, juniper and jackpine at the highest elevations. The flowers we cannot see but easily imagine will also be blooming up there in the cool—larkspur, lupine, Indian paintbrush, the Sego lily, perhaps a few columbines.

The boats continue to turn, and facing downriver now we see to the southwest, far beyond the opening in the cliffs, a kind of convulsed hump in the earth's stony crust. It is the southern end of the Waterpocket Fold, a fifty-mile-long monocline or ridge of warped sandstone, eroded along its base into triangular studs of naked rock that look, from here, like the teeth of a mowing machine. This will be our only glimpse of a weird area that is sure to be, someday, another national park complete with police, administrators, paved highways, automobile nature trails, official scenic viewpoints, designated campgrounds, Laundromats, cafeterias, Coke machines, flush toilets and admission fees. If you wish to see it as it should be seen, don't wait—there's little time. How do you get there? Well, I couldn't tell you.

A little after noon, when the surface of the river is gleaming under the sun like molten amber, we see an abandoned mining camp ahead of us on the eastern shore. We paddle hard to port and beach our craft on a steep and slippery mud bank, tethering it to a stout willow tree.

While Ralph makes himself comfortable in the shade, happy to take a siesta—he is one of those fortunates who can sleep at will or stay up talking and drinking till dawn, like Socrates, if he prefers—I go on up beyond the vegetated shore to the ledge of barren redrock on which the camp is situated.

Here I find the familiar fascinating semimelancholy debris of free enterprise: rusted tin cans, a roofless frame shack, the rags of tents and broken canvas cots, rusty shovels, a blunted old iron bullprick, rotting rat-bitten steel-toed boots, dynamite boxes, battered hard hats, two sticks of blasting powder (but no caps), sheaves of legal documents pertaining to mining claims and production agreements (rather interesting reading), a couple of withered sun-bleached topographical maps, and an astonishing heap of tattered magazines of the All-Man He-Male type—*True* (false), *Male* (a little queer), *Stag* (full of ragged does blasting Japs with machine guns), *Saga* (fairy tales), *Real* (quite phoney) and others of the *genre*, all of them badly chewed up by rodents, barely readable, with the best pictures torn out by some scoundrel. These fellows must have spent a lot of time reading; no wonder they failed to find whatever they'd been looking for—gold? God? uranium? —and had to leave.

I climb the hill behind this ghost camp, up mountainous dunes of copper-colored sand, and find the trace of a jeep trail winding off to the east into a never-never land of black buttes, salt domes and prehistoric plateaus inhabited only by mule deer and mountain lions. Perhaps this track leads to the mine; there are no diggings of any kind in the vicinity of the camp. The prospectors or miners had no doubt established their camp near the river so they'd have a reliable water supply. Everything else they needed, from boots to beans, perhaps even the jeep, must have been brought in by way of the river, for this camp is a long way from any road known to the mapmakers.

The climb gives me some comprehension of the fact that we are *down inside* the mantle of the earth. For though I stand on the summit of a considerable hill, at least a thousand feet above the river, I can see no more than ten miles in any direction. On all points the view is cut off, near or far, by the unscalable walls of buttes, mesas and plateaus far higher than the hill beneath my feet. They are ranged in bench or terrace fashion, up from the river, forming an almost horizontal skyline all around me which obstructs any sight of the mountains that I know are out there—the Henry Mountains to the northwest, the La Sal Mountains to the northeast, the Blue Mountains to the east, Navajo Mountain somewhere on the south, and Kaiparowits on the west or southwest.

In all of this vast well of space enclosed by mesa and plateau, a great irregular arena of right angles and sheer

rock in which the entire population and all the works of
—Manhattan, say—could easily be hidden, there is no
sign whatever, anywhere, of human or animal life. Nothing, not even a soaring buzzard. In the heat and stillness
nothing moves, nothing stirs. The silence is complete.

It is a strange fact that in the canyon country the closer
you get to the river which is the living artery of the entire
area, the drier, more barren, less habitable the land becomes. In this respect the desert of the Colorado is opposite to that of the Nile in Egypt or the Rio Grande in
New Mexico where, in both cases, life, men and the cities
are gathered along the shores of the rivers. Along the Colorado River there is no town from Moab in Utah to Needles in California, a distance of over a thousand miles (if
we except the two small, improvised, completely artificial
company towns connected with the building and operation
of Glen Canyon Dam and Boulder Dam).

What is true of human life is true also of plant life: except for the comparatively lush growth along the very
banks of the river and on the floors of the many narrow
side canyons, life in all forms diminishes in quantity as you
approach the Colorado. The mountains are covered with
forest; the plateaus are also forested, at the higher elevations with aspen and yellowpine and farther down with
pinyon and juniper; but as you descend through the lateral
canyons toward the great river the pinyon and juniper
yield to sagebrush and other shrubs; from that to yucca,
prickly pear and ephedra; and from that, nearing the river,
to almost nothing but scattered clumps of saltbush and
blackbrush and the fragile annuals—snakeweed, mule-ear
sunflowers, and other widely dispersed rain-dependent
growths, separated from each other by open spaces of
nothing but sand and rock.

The reason for this apparent anomaly is twofold. First,
though all of the plateau and canyon province must be
classified as an arid or semiarid region, the higher tablelands naturally receive a little more rainfall, on the average, than the lower areas. Second, the Colorado River carries its great volume of water swiftly seaward well *below*
the general level of the surrounding land, through deep

and largely impassable gorges (such as the Grand Canyon), and therefore does not and cannot water the desert through which it passes. Not until the river reaches the open country beyond the canyons is its water utilizable for agriculture and there, as we know, California and Arizona and Mexico have been fighting each other for half a century over the division of the precious liquid. (Each additional dam that is built on the Colorado, incidentally, reduces the quantity of usable water, because of unavoidable losses through evaporation and percolation into the porous sandstone containing the reservoirs.)

The sun is beginning to give me a headache. I glissade down the slopes of sand, copper-gold and coral-pink, past isolated clusters of sunflowers, scarlet penstemon and purple asters, to the shade of the willows and the life of the river. Here I take a swim and drink my fill of the cool muddy water—both at the same time.

We eat lunch, Ralph and I, and lie for another hour or two in the willow glade until the bright inferno in the sky has edged far enough westward to let the cliffs shade part of the river. Then we launch off, in the middle of the afternoon, and paddle across the current to the shady side, abandoning ourselves once more to the noiseless effortless powerful slide of the Colorado through its burnished chute of stone.

Although we are voyaging blind and ignorant, without map or compass or guide, I know (from Powell's book and hearsay) that sometime soon we should reach the mouth of the Escalante River, another small tributary. This I wish to explore for I have heard that back in its meandering depths are natural bridges and arches, cliff dwellings and hanging gardens and other spontaneous marvels.

As the sun goes down and we drift on through the smoky-blue twilight and the birdcalls I keep the Escalante in mind, one eye skinned for the likely *debouchment*. Reluctantly I allow to pass the intriguing slits and dark deep defiles which promise much but seem improbable; then we see not far ahead and on the correct, starboard shore the opening of a big canyon, full of shadows and cottonwoods. I feel at once with a thrill of certainty that here is one we must not pass. We head for shore.

But already the current is pulling us to the middle of the river and everything is farther away than it looks. We work desperately toward the riverside and the mouth of the big side canyon but we've started too late, the river sweeps us by and we're going to miss it.

This has happened to us several times before and each time, spoiled by the wonders still lying ahead, we have surrendered to the river, given up and floated on. This time, however, we resolve not to give up; we keep paddling till we hit the shore and then work our way upstream, along the bank, with the aid of the willows at the water's edge. We reach an eddy and backwater, paddle around a giant boulder and find ourselves at last safe in the quiet, warm, green floodwater of the canyon's entrance. Nearly exhausted, we rest for a while in the boats before paddling slowly into the dark canyon.

The sun has been down for an hour, the moon will not clear the rimrock for another hour. The great canyon we have entered is as dark as a cave. We move deeper inside until we see in the dimness what looks like a white beach attached precariously to the foot of a sheer wall. We make for it, land, secure the boats, find a little dead wood and start a fire.

The heat in this deep and narrow canyon seems dense, stifling, almost sickening after a day on the wide and breezy expanse of the river. We make tea but have no appetite for any supper but a tin of fruit each. After the necessary soporific smoke and a weary conversation we unroll our sleeping bags and go to bed.

I sleep uneasily, haunted by the persistent dream of rising water and the drifting away of our boats. Near midnight, the waxing half-moon overhead, I wake up to the noise of wind and splashing water. The water is lapping at the sand less than a foot from my sleeping bag. I roll out of the bag, make sure the boats are still securely tied to the willows, and am about to wake up Ralph. Hesitating, I realize that the cause of the high water is not what I'd been half-consciously fearing all along, a flash flood from the world above us, but simply a strong wind blowing waves into the canyon from the river.

The wind has freshened the air and cooled it. Naked in the moonlight, I enjoy the change, and listen for a time to the hoodoo voice of a great horned owl up on the rim somewhere. Then I go back to sleep and this time sleep well, lullabied by wind and water.

In the morning before breakfast we dump our gear loosely into the boats and paddle on up the canyon until we reach shallow water. We are now around a bend and out of sight of the river. Here I get out and tow the boats farther through the still backwaters, wading on till we come to the place where a broad shallow stream of clear water enters and merges with the dead water of the flood. This stream is about six inches deep and six feet wide, with a fast steady flow—undoubtedly the Escalante "River." The water is fresh and clean, almost cool; without bothering this time to look for cattle tracks we each take a long and satisfying drink.

Feeling much better now, our appetites returning, we make breakfast, eating the last of our bacon, the last of the eggs and the last of the canned fruit. From now on we must subsist on our dehydrated food supplies—survival rations—or on whatever we can forage from the land.

As I prepare for a day's hike up the Escalante I can hear Ralph muttering something about channel cat; I pay no attention. Bouillon cubes and raisins are good enough for me, so long as they are seasoned with plenty of sun and storm and adventure, but Newcomb, somewhat of a gourmet, has different ideas. Lacing my boots I see him attach a fragment of moldy salami to a fishhook and toss it—with a line, of course—into the deep and muddy water below the stream.

"You got a license, bud?" I demand.

For reply he clenches his right hand, extends the middle finger rigidly and thrusts it heavenward. Invoking the Deity?

I take off but before I'm out of earshot I hear a curious thumping noise. I look back and there's Newcomb beating

a giant catfish on the head with his canoe paddle, putting
it quickly out of its misery. God provides.

What little I can see of the sky between the high and
almost interlocking walls of the canyon looks cloudy, promising rain. Rain or sun it's all one to me. Burdened only
with canteen, a stick and a lunch of raisins and chipped
beef I march up the firm wet sand of the canyon floor,
reading the register: many deer, one coyote, the three-toed
track of a big bird, many killdeer or sandpipers, many lizards, the winding trail of a snake, no cattle, no horses, no
people.

All of the prints look fresh, none more than a few days
old. With good reason. The damp sand, the wet rushes
crushed riverward under a layer of silt, the dust-free polish
of pebbles and stones, the general appearance of neatness
and tidiness all indicate that the canyon has quite recently
been flushed out with a vigorous torrent.

I look at the perpendicular walls rising slick and unbroken on both sides; in case a flood should now appear,
what could I do? Nothing. I'd float with the tide back to
Newcomb and the boats, eat catfish for lunch.

The walk gets wet. The channel of the stream meanders
from one wall to the opposite and within the first mile I
have to wade it a dozen times. Hard on boots. Impossible
to outflank these meanders, for they swing hard against
and undercut the cliff first on one side and then the other.
Should have brought tennis shoes. Since I have no tennis
shoes I take off the boots and sling them over my shoulder,
proceeding barefoot. I walk lightly across shoals of quicksand and ford the river when necessary, but over the pebbled and rocky stretches the going is hard and slow.

Another half mile and I come to a "dripping spring."
This is a seep high on the canyon wall, two hundred feet
above my head, where ground water breaks out between
beds of sandstone and slides over the contours of the cliff,
nourishing the typical delicate greenery of moss, fern, columbine and monkeyflower. Below the garden the cliff
curves deeply inward, forming an overhang that would
shelter a house; at this point the water is released from the
draw of surface tension and falls free through the air in a

misty, wavy spray down to the canyon floor where I stand, as in a fine shower, filling my canteen and soaking myself and drinking all at the same time.

I go on. The clouds have disappeared, the sun is still beyond the rim. Under a wine-dark sky I walk through light reflected and re-reflected from the walls and floor of the canyon, a radiant golden light that glows on rock and stream, sand and leaf in varied hues of amber, honey, whiskey—the light that never was is here, now, in the storm-sculptured gorge of the Escalante.

That crystal water flows toward me in shimmering S-curves, looping quietly over shining pebbles, buff-colored stone and the long sleek bars and reefs of rich red sand, in which glitter grains of mica and pyrite—fool's gold. The canyon twists and turns, serpentine as its stream, and with each turn comes a dramatic and novel view of tapestried walls five hundred—a thousand?—feet high, of silvery driftwood wedged between boulders, of mysterious and inviting subcanyons to the side, within which I can see living stands of grass, cane, salt cedar, and sometimes the delicious magical green of a young cottonwood with its ten thousand exquisite leaves vibrating like spangles in the vivid air. The only sound is the whisper of the running water, the touch of my bare feet on the sand, and once or twice, out of the stillness, the clear song of a canyon wren.

Is this at last the *locus Dei?* There are enough cathedrals and temples and altars here for a Hindu pantheon of divinities. Each time I look up one of the secretive little side canyons I half expect to see not only the cottonwood tree rising over its tiny spring—the leafy god, the desert's liquid eye—but also a rainbow-colored corona of blazing light, pure spirit, pure being, pure disembodied intelligence, *about to speak my name.*

If a man's imagination were not so weak, so easily tired, if his capacity for wonder not so limited, he would abandon forever such fantasies of the supernal. He would learn to perceive in water, leaves and silence more than sufficient of the absolute and marvelous, more than enough to console him for the loss of the ancient dreams. Walking up the Escalante is like penetrating a surrealist corridor in a Tamayo dream: all is curved and rounded, the course of the mainstream and canyon as indirect as a sidewinder, winding upon itself like the intestines of a giant. The canyon floor averages about fifty feet in width but the curving walls are at least five times that high, without benches or ledges, sheer, monolithic and smooth as if carved in butter, paralleling each other in a sort of loosely jointed ball-and-socket fashion, each concavity matched by a corresponding convexity on the opposite wall. And all this inspired by the little stream that swings through the rock and the centuries—truly a perfect example of what geologists call an entrenched meander.

Others have been here before. On a mural wall I find petroglyphs—the images of bighorn sheep, snakes, mule deer, sun and raincloud symbols, men with lances. The old people, the Anasazi.

I come to a second dripping spring, water seeping from a fissure far above, falling in spray upon a massive slab of rock at the foot of the wall. On the flat surface of this tilted slab somebody, maybe a Mormon cowboy fifty years ago, maybe an Indian eight hundred years ago, has chiseled two converging grooves which catch some of the falling water and conduct it to a carved spout at the lower edge. The grooves are well worn, smooth as a pebble to the touch.

As I sit there drinking water from cupped hands, I happened to look up and see on the opposite wall, a hundred feet above the floor of the canyon, the ruins of three tiny stone houses in a shallow cave. As is the case with many cliff dwellings, the erosion of eight centuries has removed whole blocks of rock which formerly must have supported ladders and handholds, making the ghost village now inaccessible.

I am content, however, to view the remains from below. Neither a souvenir collector nor an archeologist, I have no desire to stir the ancient dust for the sake of removing from their setting a few potsherds, a few corncobs, a child's straw sandal, an arrow point, perhaps a broken skull.

What interests me is the quality of that pre-Columbian life, the feel of it, the *atmosphere*. We know enough of the homely details: the cultivation of maize, beans, melons; the hunting of rabbit and deer; the manufacture of pottery, baskets, ornaments of coral and bone; the construction of the fortlike homes—for apparently, like some twentieth century Americans, the Anasazi lived under a cloud of fear.

Fear: is that the key to their lives? What persistent and devilish enemies they must have had, or thought they had, when even here in the intricate heart of a desert labyrinth a hundred foot-miles from the nearest grassland, forest and mountains they felt constrained to make their homes, as swallows do, in niches high on the face of a cliff.

Their manner of life was constricted, conservative, cautious; perhaps only the pervading fear could keep such a community together. Where all think alike there is little danger of innovation. Every child in this quiet place would have learned, along with his language and games, the legends of old battles and massacres, flights and migrations. He would be taught that the danger of attack was always present, that in any hour of the day or night, from up or down the canyon or over the rim, the Enemy might appear—cruel, devious, hungry, terrible—perhaps in the shape of those red-horned, hollow-eyed, wide-shouldered monsters painted on the walls of Sego Canyon north of Moab.

Long ago the cliff dwellings were abandoned. Were the inhabitants actually destroyed by the enemies they had always dreaded? Or were they reduced and driven out by disease, by something as undramatic as bad sanitation, pollution of their water and air? Or could it have been, finally, simply their own fears which poisoned their lives beyond hope of recovery and drove them into exile and extinction?

As I walk on, miles beyond Ralph and the river, the canyon changes a little in character, in places growing wider, less deep, with breaks in the wall and steeply pitched ravines that seem to suggest the possibility of an exit to the world above. I make two attempts to climb out of the canyon but the first route dead-ends at the foot of another vertical cliff and the second at a deep, stagnant plunge-pool swarming with tadpoles and dragonflies. Above this pool is an overhanging drop-off down the center of which a thousand years of intermittent drainage has scooped out a pothole and then drilled clear through it, creating a long polished chute and a window in the rock. But there are many of those Moore-like formations, hundreds of them, in the canyon country.

Late in the evening, the sun already down, I find what looks like a deerpath leading up over an alluvium hill toward the southwest rim. I am tempted to take it and see where it goes but I am also hungry, tired, and a bit sorefooted; my raisins are all gone and the canyon grows dark; sadly I turn and start the long walk back.

Long before I come again to the second of the dripping springs night has covered the desert world. I sit down on a driftwood log, build a small fire with shreds of its bark, wait for moonrise. I put the boots back on; water or no water, my feet have suffered enough.

The new moon finally comes, edging above the rimrock, bright as a silver shield. Through moonlight and darkness, as the moon is revealed, then concealed, by the turning of the canyon walls, I continue the march toward camp. For company on the way I have my thoughts and the flutterings and cries of a great horned owl that chooses, for reasons of its own, to follow me for much of the distance.

The return is harder than I expected. If I didn't have the stream to follow, Ariadne's thread, it would be easy in the deceptive alternation of moonlight and shadow to take a wrong turn up one of the many side canyons, to spend the rest of the night in bewildered wandering or go to sleep on an empty stomach, covered only with my back. The repeated wading of the stream seems doubly tiring now, especially as the boots become watersoaked and layered with quicksand. I trudge onward, longing for the first sight of Ralph's campfire, hoping that each new bend in the canyon will be the last. The Escalante is no longer the free and friendly place it was during the day but totally different, strange, unknown and unknowable, faintly malevolent.

Endless, too, I'm beginning to feel, before I see at long last the glimmer of coals ahead, the embers of a fire, and in the dimness the outline of the rubber boats, a comforting sight. Ralph is sleeping when I stumble into camp but wakes up easily to show me the mess of catfish he has caught, cleaned and saved for me, wrapped in wet leaves, still cool and fresh.

It's surely after midnight but who wants to sleep? We rebuild the fire and deep-fry the fish in part of the bacon grease which Ralph has wisely been hoarding all along. I pull off my mud-caked boots, twice their original weight, sit close to the fire and eat a tremendous supper, while Newcomb fills the air with huge clouds of fragrant, philosophical pipe smoke. We discuss the day's adventures.

High above our heads the owl hoots under the lost moon. A predawn wind comes sifting and sighing through the cottonwood trees; the sound of their dry, papery leaves is like the murmur of distant water, or like the whispering of ghosts in an ancient, sacrosanct, condemned cathedral.

Late in the morning, close to noon, the sun comes glowering over the wall in a burst of fire and we are driven out of our sacks. Into the green lagoon for a bath and a swim and then Ralph baits a hook with the reliable rotten salami, I build a campfire in the shade and fill the skillet with grease, and once again we dine on channel cat—delicious fish!

After this combined breakfast and dinner we retire to the water again and deeper shade, evading the worst of the midday heat. Naked as savages, we float on our backs in the still water, squat on the cool sand under the sheltering cottonwood and smoke like sachems. We may not have brought enough food but at least we've got plenty of Bull Durham.

"Newcomb," I explain, "we've *got* to go back."

"But why?" he says. "Why?"

"Why do you grow that beard?"

"Why not?"

"Well why?"

"Well why not?"

"Well goddamnit why?"

"Well goddamnit why not?"

"Because," I explain. The role of the Explainer has become a well-established one in recent times. "Because they need us. Because civilization needs us."

"What civilization?" he says.

"You said it. That's why they need us."

"But do we need them?"

"Well," I say, "how long do you think that jar of bacon grease will last?"

That made him think. "Let's go," he says.

Sometime in the middle of the afternoon we shove our fragile boats once more into the water, climb aboard and paddle slowly out of the Escalante's womb, back to the greater world of Glen Canyon and the steady, powerful, unhurried, insouciant Colorado. It is almost like a coming home.

For the rest of the afternoon, keeping to the shady side, we drift down the splendid river, deeper and deeper and deeper into the fantastic. The sandstone walls rise higher than ever before, a thousand, two thousand feet above the water, rounding off on top as half-domes and capitols, golden and glowing in the sunlight, a deep radiant red in the shade.

Beyond those mighty forms we catch occasional glimpses of eroded remnants—tapering spires, balanced rocks on pillars, mushroom rocks, rocks shaped like hamburgers, rocks like piles of melted pies, arches, bridges, potholes, grottoes, all the infinite variety of hill and hole and hollow to which sandstone lends itself, given the necessary conditions and, as Thoreau says, a liberal allowance of time— let us say, about five thousand years? Fifty thousand? Five hundred thousand? Choose whatever sum you like.

We pass beneath *hanging* canyons, the mouths of lateral drainages which terminate above the level of the Colorado; out of these when it storms come roaring falls of thick, muddy water, of logs, trees, cows and thundering boulders, all crashing into the river hundreds of feet below, a gorgeous spectacle which we will not have the good fortune to witness.

Now and then we are offered tantalizing views, far ahead, of the blue dome of Navajo Mountain, another laccolith, a holy place, home of gods, navel of the world in the eyes of the Indians, and the shiplike prow of the high Kaiparowits Plateau.

Not all is rock: we see a redtailed hawk skimming along the cliff, once a golden eagle, and vultures soar in the distance. Closer by we hear though seldom see the wrens, finches and yellow warblers, and a few long-legged water birds.

Heart of the whole and essence of the scene is the river, the flowing river with its thin fringe of green, the vital element in what would be otherwise a glamorous but moondead landscape. The living river and the living river alone gives coherence and significance and therefore beauty to the canyon world. "I love all things which flow," said the deepest of Irishmen.

At evening we come to historic Hole in the Rock. Here we float ashore and camp for the night.

What happened here? In the year 1880, eleven years after Powell had passed this way, the Church of Jesus Christ of the Latter-Day Saints commissioned a group of the faithful, living then in south-central Utah, to establish a new settlement in the southeast corner of the state near what is now the village of Bluff.

As obedient as they were courageous, some two hundred and fifty Mormons—men, women and children, with livestock and twenty-six wagons—started east from Panguitch toward the designated place. They followed no road or trail but simply what would have seemed, on a map, to be the shortest line between the two points.

After traversing seventy miles of desert they came to the rim, the jump-off. Two thousand feet below, the Colorado River rolled across their chosen route. Instead of giving up and turning back they hammered and blasted a notch (the Hole in the Rock) down through the rim into the nearest side canyon. From there they carved and constructed a crude wagon road to the edge of the water and descended. In places the wagons had to be lowered on ropes. After fording the river these undaunted people climbed the farther side over terrain almost as difficult and continued on, week after week, through the surreal sandstone wilderness and forests of pinyon and juniper until they reached their goal. The entire expedition required about four months; the trail which they pioneered was never used a second time.

In the morning I decide to climb the old trail, up through the notch to the top of the plateau—haven't seen the outer world for a long time now. While Ralph goes fishing I start off through the willow jungle, around tangles of poison ivy and up enormous sand dunes toward the Hole. A brook trickles down the gulch below the path, a thread of water creeping from pool to pool. At the final opportunity—Last Chance Puddle—I take a hearty drink. I've left my canteen behind at the boats; Hole in the Rock, clearly visible from the river, doesn't seem far away.

The old trail climbs away from the water, switchbacking up the talus slope on the northern side of the canyon. The pitch is steep, the morning sun is blazing on my back, and the heat quickly becomes unpleasant. My sweat dries as fast as it forms—the parched air is sucking at my pores. My belly is full of water, gurgling like a wineskin, but I can almost feel it being drawn away; the knowledge that I've brought no canteen along adds poignancy to my premature thirst. I put a pebble in my mouth and keep climbing.

Above the talus I find the dugway, broad and shallow steps chipped out of the canyon wall by the first and only road-builders here, and the remains of fill and foundation —slabs and blocks of sandstone laid in place, one by one, over eighty years before. The canyon begins to narrow and pucker near the summit and the cleft is jammed with boulders big as boxcars. I squeeze among them, following the tracks of former hikers. Here at least is shade though no water. I sit down to rest, daydreaming of iced limeade, chilled tomato juice, Moorish fountains. The temperature out in the sun must be well over a hundred degrees.

Upward. Under a ledge I find the barest hint of a seep,

drops of moisture leaking from the rock and dampening the sand beneath. I am so thirsy by this time that I try digging a waterhole, but the deeper I go the drier the sand. I need water; I put some of the moist sand into my mouth, extracting what refreshment I can from it, and go on.

Up through the notch. I come out on the surface of a rolling plain of cross-bedded sandstone, the petrified dunes of the Navajo formation, and win the view I'd been hoping for. Far in the distance lie the blue ranges under hard-edged, snowy cumulus clouds: the Henry's, Elk Ridge and the Bear's Ears beyond White Canyon, 10,000-foot Navajo Mountain on the other side of the river. On the west, not so far, perhaps ten miles away, rises the Kaiparowits Plateau, also known as Fifty-Mile Mesa, another island in the sky, little-known and uninhabited, cut off on all sides but the north by its sheer, vertical walls.

I walk out onto a point from which I can look down at the river, nearly straight below. I can see the switchbacks of the trail, the fan of greenery at the outlet of the side canyon, but no sign of Newcomb or the boats, deep in the shade of the willows. From up here the sound of the river, until now a permanent part of my auditory background, is no longer perceptible, and the desert silence takes on a deeper dimension. The sound of nothingness? "In the desert," wrote Balzac, somewhere, "there is all and there is nothing. God is there and man is not."

God? Nothing moves but the heat waves, rising from the naked rock. It is somehow comforting to see, nearby, the yuccas growing from the sand and from joints in the stone. They are in full bloom today, clusters of waxy, creamy flowers on tall stalks, supported and nourished by the rosettes of daggerlike leaves that form the base of the plant. God? I think, quibbling with Balzac; in Newcomb's terms, who the hell is *He*? There is nothing here, at the moment, but me and the desert. And that's the truth. Why confuse the issue by dragging in a superfluous entity? Occam's razor. Beyond atheism, nontheism. I am not an atheist but an earthiest. Be true to the earth.

Far off, the muted kettledrums of thunder, *pianissimo*

. . . T. S. Eliot and *The Wasteland*. Certain passages in that professorial poem still appeal to me, for they remind me of Moab, Utah. In other words I like the poem for the wrong reasons—and dislike it for the right ones.

Here I am, relaxing into memories of ancient books—a surefire sign of spiritual fatigue. That screen of words, that veil of ideas, issuing from the brain like a sort of mental smog that keeps getting between a man and the world, obscuring vision. Maya. Time to go back down to the river and reality, back to Newcomb and the boats, the smell of frying catfish—there's God for you! I descend.

Evening on the river, a night of moonlight and canyon winds, sleep and the awakening. In a blue dawn under the faintest of stars we break our fast, pack our gear and launch the boats again. Farther still into the visionary world of Glen Canyon, talking somewhat less than before —for what is there to say? I think we've about said it all —we communicate less in words and more in direct denotation, the glance, the pointing hand, the subtile nuances of pipe smoke, the tilt of a wilted hat brim. Configurations are beginning to fade, distinctions shading off into blended amalgams of man and man, men and water, water and rock.

"Who is Ralph Newcomb?" I say. "Who is he?"

"Aye," he says, "and who is who? Which is which?"

"Quite," I agree.

We are merging, molecules getting mixed. Talk about intersubjectivity—we are both taking on the coloration of river and canyon, our skin as mahogany as the water on the shady side, our clothing coated with silt, our bare feet caked with mud and tough as lizard skin, our whiskers bleached as the sand—even our eyeballs, what little you can see of them between the lids, have taken on a coral-pink, the color of the dunes. And we smell, I suppose, like catfish.

We've forgotten to keep a close track of time, have no clock or calendar, and no longer know for certain exactly how many days and nights we've been on the river.

"Six, I think," he says, my doppelganger.

"No, only five."

"Five? Let's see.... No. Yes. Maybe."
"I believe."
"Seven?"
"Four?"

The time passes very slowly but not slowly enough. The canyon world becomes each hour more beautiful, the closer we come to its end. We think we have forgotten but we cannot forget—the knowledge is lodged like strontium in the marrow of our bones—that Glen Canyon has been condemned. We refuse to think about it. We dare not think about it for if we did we'd be eating our hearts, chewing our entrails, consuming ourselves in the fury of helpless rage. Of helpless *out*rage.

We pass the mouth of a large river entering the Colorado from the east—the San Juan. Somewhere not far beyond this confluence, if I recall my Powell rightly, is the opening to what he named Music Temple. We keep watch but see a dozen lovely and mysterious grottoes, all equally beguiling, pass up some, let the current rush us by others, and finally end up by choosing the wrong one. We will not have another opportunity.

"When 'Old Shady' sings us a song at night," wrote Powell in 1869, "we are pleased to find that this hollow in the rock is filled with sweet sounds. It was doubtless made for an academy of music by its storm-born architect; so we name it Music Temple."

Less than a century later his discovery will be buried under the mud of the reservoir, rendered inaccessible by those who claim they are not only "developing" but also "opening up" the canyon country. What have we lost? Here is Powell's description of the place:

"On entering we find a little grove of box-elder and cottonwood trees, and turning to the right, we find ourselves in a vast chamber carved out of rock. At the upper end there is a clear, deep pool of water, bordered with verdure. Standing by the side of this, we can see the grove at the entrance. The chamber is more than 200 feet high, 500 feet long, and 200 feet wide. Through the ceiling and on through the rock for a thousand feet above, there is a narrow, winding skylight; and this is all carved out by a little stream which runs only during the few showers that fall now and then in this arid country."

Late that evening, after sundown, Ralph and I beach our boats and make camp on a sandy spit near the outlet of a deep, narrow, labyrinthine side canyon, its name, if it has a name, unknown to us. I explore part of its length in the twilight and find another charming stream with pools of remarkable beauty—crystal-clear water in basins of rock and sand, free of weeds or mud, harboring schools of minnows. Darkness sets in before I can go very far. I go back to the campfire.

After a splendid night—clouds like clipperships racing across the starry sky, moon floating along the brink of the crag above us, wind in the tamarisk—we make a quick breakfast and I return to the exploration of the hidden passage, taking the canteens with me to fill with fresh water.

I come to where I had turned back the night before, a deep pool that fills the canyon from wall to wall. Filling the canteens, I cache them nearby, undress and wade into the water. The pool is deep, over my head. I swim across it, following a turn in the narrow canyon, here no more than ten feet wide, and emerge beyond into a curving tunnel of rock with running water on its floor.

This natural tunnel is pure rock, completely devoid of sand, soil and any trace of vegetation. The walls that tower above are so close to one another, overhanging and interlocking, that I cannot see the sky. Through a golden glow of indirect, reflected sunlight I proceed until I come to a very large grotto or chamber, somewhat like the one described by Powell, where a plunge pool and waterfall check any further advance.

Here the canyon walls are a little wider, permitting the sun, for perhaps a couple of hours during the summer day, to shine directly down into this cul-de-sac. A rivulet of clear water pours into the pool; glints and flecks of light reflected from its agitated surface dance over the dark-golden walls of the glen. Lichens are growing there, green, red, orange, and along the seep line are beds of poison ivy, scarlet monkeyflower, maidenhair fern, death camas, helleborine orchid and small pale yellow columbines. There are no trees or shrubs, for the sunlight is too brief.

The sun is gleaming on the pool, on the foam, on the transparent waterfall. I dive in, swim under the fall and take a soapless shower, lie on the rock in a patch of sunshine and gaze up at the small irregular fragment of blue which forms the sky in this place. Then I return through the tunnel to camp and companion.

Has this particular canyon been seen and named by earlier river-runners? No doubt it has, but I find no evidence to dispel the illusion that I may be the first ever to have entered here. And probably the last.

After a lunch of refried pinto beans and dehydrated apricots—a piquant combination—we climb into our double boat and float onward. Since we have missed Music Temple I am more determined than ever that we must not pass Forbidden Canyon and the trail to Rainbow Bridge, climax and culmination of any trip into Glen Canyon.

We stay close to the south and east shore of the river, despite the ferocious afternoon sun, investigating each side canyon that we come to. In one of these I accidentally start a brush fire, and am nearly cooked alive. Sheer carelessness—a gust of wind carries a flaming piece of paper into the dried-out tangle of a willow thicket; the flames spread explosively; in a minute the mouth of the canyon is choked with smoke and fire and there is nothing I can do but get out of there, quick, as the flames rush down through the jungle toward Ralph, waiting for me in the tethered boats.

He is all ready to cast off when I appear, about ten feet in front of the onrushing sheet of fire, running. I push the boats off and roll in; we paddle away as hard as we can from the fiery shore, the final wild flare of heat. With generous tact Ralph does not even ask for an explanation. You can see a photograph of what I did in Eliot Porter's beautiful book on Glen Canyon, *The Place That No One Knew.*

"Hot in there," I say, though Ralph has asked no questions.

"So I noticed."

"Had an accident."

"Is that right?"

Shakily I tamp my pipe and fumble through the pockets of my shirt. All gone.

"Here," he says. "Have a match."

The river carries us past more side canyons, each of which I inspect for signs of a trail, a clue to Rainbow Bridge. But find nothing, so far, though we know we're getting close. We can see in the canyon distance, not far ahead, the southern tip of the Kaiparowits Plateau—the landmark to guide by when seeking the way to Rainbow Bridge.

We bounce over a series of minor ripples and the river picks up speed. There is a corresponding excitement in the sky: the storm that has seemed potential for days is gathering above in definite form—wild gray scuds of vapor, anvil-headed cumuli-nimbi, rumbles of thunder coming closer.

From up ahead comes the familiar freight-train roar of white water again. A new and formidable canyon opens on the left, with a broad delta of pebbled beach, mud banks, rocks and boulders and driftwood issuing fanwise from its mouth. The boulders, carried down from the flanks of Navajo Mountain, cause the rapids which lie before us.

A little wiser now, learning from experience, we do not battle the current but rest until we are close to the rapids, then with a sudden furious effort paddle into the backwash near the shore and have no trouble making a landing in the shallows.

Ralph starts supper. I pull on boots and go exploring. I find a trail but it's a poor one, little more than a deer path, which peters out completely a mile up-canyon. There are ponds of fresh water on the canyon floor; I refill the canteens and return to the boats.

The wind by this time has risen to a magnificent howl, the sky is purple, and jags of lightning strike at Navajo Point, the remote crag two thousand feet above the river on the north side. Cold rain spatters on the hot sand of the beach, raising little puffs of dust and steam. Rock and driftwood and the flashing underside of leaves gleam with a strange, wild, shifting light from the stormy sky.

We rig the tarpaulins into a tent, preparing for rain, and

eat our supper of pancakes on which we pour a sauce of stewed raisins, in place of the syrup we haven't got. Very good. Filling, anyhow. Afterwards, tea and tobacco.

We sit outside our tent, enjoying the weather. After a week of clear skies, and the heat and glare of the relentless sun, the cool wind and the sprinkling of hard cold raindrops on our bare heads and bare bodies feel good.

The heavy rain we've been anticipating fails to come. We pile our baggage under the canvas shelter and unroll our sleeping bags in a hollow among the white dunes, under the open sky. Falling asleep, I see a handful of stars blinking through a break in the racing clouds.

A red dawn in the east, cloud banks on fire with the rising sun. I bathe in the cold river, do my laundry, and build a fire for our breakfast: dried pea soup and tea bags. The last box of raisins I have set aside for lunch. Stores seem to be getting low—from now on it'll be catfish or nothing.

Onto the river and through the whirlpools, we glide without mishap into quiet water. Our little boats are holding up well; despite all the rocks we've bounced them off and over, despite the sand and snags we've dragged them over, they have yet to sustain a puncture or spring a single leak. Aye, but the voyage is not over—shouldn't mention these things.

Within a short distance we come to another big tributary canyon on the port side or southerly shore of the river. Navajo Point, the final outcropping of the Kaiparowits Plateau, is directly overhead. This canyon too has tumbled boulders into the river, forming one more stretch of rough water. As before we take advantage of the eddies close to the rapids, swinging briefly upstream and then into the flooded mouth of the side canyon. We tie up on a mud bank and get out to investigate.

At once I spot the unmistakable signs of tourist culture —tin cans and tinfoil dumped in a fireplace, a dirty sock dangling from a bush, a worn-out tennis shoe in the bottom of a clear spring, gum wrappers, cigarette butts, and bottlecaps everywhere. This must be it, the way to Rainbow Bridge; it appears that we may have come too late. *Slobivius americanus* has been here first.

Well, no matter. We had expected this. We know with certainty that we are now only a few hours—by motorboat —from the Glen Canyon dam site. I also happen to know that the natural bridge itself is still six miles up the canyon by foot trail, a distance regarded as semiastronomical by the standard breed of mechanized tourist. His spoor will not be seen much beyond the campground.

We set up a camp of our own well beyond the motorboaters' midden, near the little stream that tumbles down the rocky canyon floor, coming from the great redrock wilderness beyond. The trail to Rainbow Bridge, passing close by, is rough, rocky, primitive. Newcomb, who has brought no boots, decides to go fishing. We divide the box of raisins and the last of the dried apricots. I stuff my share into my shirt pockets and lace up the boots, hang a canteen over my shoulder and march off.

The trail leads beside the clear-running brook and a chain of emerald pools, some of them big enough to go swimming in, with the water so transparent I can see the shadows of the schools of minnows passing over the grains of sand in the bottom of the basins. Along the canyon walls are the seeps and springs that feed the stream, each with the characteristic clinging gardens of mosses, ferns and wildflowers. Above and beyond the rimrock, blue in shadow and amber-gold in light, are alcoves, domes and royal arches, part of the sandstone flanks of Navajo Mountain.

A hot day. Delicate, wind-whipped clouds flow across the burning blue, moving in perfect unison like the fish in the pools below. I stop at one of the largest of these pools, undress and plunge in. Happily I flounder about, terrifying the minnows, and float on my back and spout cheekfuls of water at the sun.

On to the Bridge:

I come to a fork in the canyon, the main branch continuing to the right, a deep dark narrow defile opening to the left. There are no trail markers but even on the naked sandstone I can make out the passage of human feet, boot-

shod, leading into the unlikely passage on the left. And so
I follow.

Here too a stream is flowing, much smaller than the
other, through smoothly sculptured grooves, scoops and
potholes in the rock. I go by the dripping little springs that
feed it and the stream diminishes to a rill, to a trickle, to
a series of stagnant waterholes shrinking under the sun.
Frogs and toads will be croaking here, fireflies winking,
when I return.

Hot and tired I stop in the shade of an overhanging
ledge and take a drink from my canteen. Resting, I listen
to the deep dead stillness of the canyon. No wind or
breeze, no birds, no running water, no sound of any kind
but the stir of my own breathing.

Alone in the silence, I understand for a moment the
dread which many feel in the presence of primeval desert,
the unconscious fear which compels them to tame, alter or
destroy what they cannot understand, to reduce the wild
and prehuman to human dimensions. Anything rather than
confront directly the antehuman, that *other world* which
frightens not through danger or hostility but in something
far worse—its implacable indifference.

Out of the shade, into the heat. I tramp on through the
winding gorge, through the harsh brittle silence. In this
arid atmosphere sounds do not fade, echo or die softly but
are extinguished suddenly, sharply, without the slightest
hint of reverberation. The clash of rock against rock is like
a shot—abrupt, exaggerated, toneless.

I round the next bend in the canyon and all at once,
quite unexpectedly, there it is, the bridge of stone.

Quite unexpectedly, I write. Why? Certainly I had faith,
I knew the bridge would be here, against all odds. And I
knew well enough what it would look like—we've all seen
the pictures of it a hundred times. Nor am I disappointed
in that vague way we often feel, coming at last upon a
long-imagined spectacle. Rainbow Bridge seems neither
less nor greater than what I had foreseen.

My second sensation is the feeling of guilt. Newcomb.
Why did I not *insist* on his coming? Why did I not grab
him by the long strands of his savage beard and haul him

up the trail, bearing him when necessary like Christopher would across the stream, stumbling from stone to stone, and dump him finally under the bridge, leaving him there to rot or to crawl back to the river if he could? No man could have asked for a lovelier defenestration.

Through God's window into eternity.

Oh well. I climb to the foot of the east buttress and sign for Ralph and myself in the visitors' register. He is the 14,467th and I the next to enter our names in this book since the first white men came to Rainbow Bridge in 1909. Not many, for a period of more than half a century, in the age above all of publicity. But then its never been an easy journey. Until now.

The new dam, of course, will improve things. If ever filled it will back water to within sight of the Bridge, transforming what was formerly an adventure into a routine motorboat excursion. Those who see it then will not understand that half the beauty of Rainbow Bridge lay in its remoteness, its relative difficulty of access, and in the wilderness surrounding it, of which it was an integral part. When these aspects are removed the Bridge will be no more than an isolated geological oddity, an extension of that museum-like diorama to which industrial tourism tends to reduce the natural world.

All things excellent are as difficult as they are rare, said a wise man. If so, what happens to excellence when we eliminate the difficulty and the rarity? Words, words—the problem makes me thirsty. There is a spring across the canyon, another seep under a ledge below the west footing of the Bridge. I climb down and up the other side and help myself to one of the tins someone has left there, collecting water under the dripping moss.

The heat is stunning. I rest for a while in the shade, dream and sleep through the worst of the midday glare. When the sun passes beyond the rim I get up and start to return to Newcomb and our camp.

But am diverted by a faint pathway which looks as if it might lead up out of the canyon, above Rainbow Bridge. Late afternoon, the canyon filling with shadows—I should not try it. I take it anyway, climbing a talus slope and then traversing a long inclined bench that pinches out in thin air at the base of a higher cliff. Impossible to go on— but a fixed rope dangles there, hanging from some belaying point out of sight above. I test the rope, it seems to be well anchored, and with its help and a few convenient toeholds and fingerholds I work my way to the top of the pitch. From there it's a long but easy scramble to the rim of the canyon.

Now I am in the open again, out of the underworld. From up here Rainbow Bridge, a thousand feet below, is only a curving ridge of sandstone of no undue importance, a tiny object lost in the vastness and intricacy of the canyon systems which radiate from the base of Navajo Mountain. Of more interest is the view to the north, east and west, revealing the general lay of the land through which we have voyaged in our little boats.

The sun, close to the horizon, shines through the clear air beneath the cloud layers, illuminating in soft variations of rose, vermillion, umber, slate-blue, the complex features and details, defined sharply by shadow, of the Glen Canyon landscape. I can see the square-edged mesas beyond the junction of the San Juan and Colorado, the plateau-mountains of south-central Utah, and farthest away, a hundred miles or more by line of sight, the five peaks of the Henry Mountains, including Mount Ellsworth near Hite where our journey began.

Off in the east an isolated storm is boiling over the desert, a mass of lavender clouds bombarding the earth with lightning and trailing curtains of rain. The distance is so great that I cannot hear the thunder. Between here and there and me and the mountains is the canyon wilderness, the hoodoo land of spire and pillar and pinnacle where no man lives, and where the river flows, unseen, through the blue-black trenches in the rock.

Light. Space. Light and space without time, I think, for this is a country with only the slightest traces of human history. In the doctrine of the geologists with their scheme of ages, eons and epochs all is flux, as Heraclitus taught, but from the mortally human point of view the landscape of the Colorado is like a section of eternity—timeless. In all my years in the canyon country I have yet to see a rock fall, of its own volition, so to speak, aside from floods. To convince myself of the reality of change and therefore time I will sometimes push a stone over the edge of a cliff and watch it descend and wait—lighting my pipe—for the report of its impact and disintegration to return. Doing my bit to help, of course, aiding natural processes and verifying the hypotheses of geological morphology. But am not *entirely* convinced.

Men come and go, cities rise and fall, whole civilizations appear and disappear—the earth remains, slightly modified. The earth remains, and the heartbreaking beauty where there are no hearts to break. Turning Plato and Hegel on their heads I sometimes choose to think, no doubt perversely, that man is a dream, thought an illusion, and only rock is real. Rock and sun.

Under the desert sun, in that dogmatic clarity, the fables of theology and the myths of classical philosophy dissolve like mist. The air is clean, the rock cuts cruelly into flesh; shatter the rock and the odor of flint rises to your nostrils, bitter and sharp. Whirlwinds dance across the salt flats, a pillar of dust by day; the thornbush breaks into flame at night. What does it mean? It means nothing. It is as it is and has no need for meaning. The desert lies beneath and soars beyond any possible human qualification. Therefore, sublime.

The sun is touching the fretted tablelands on the west. It seems to bulge a little, to expand for a moment, and then it drops—abruptly—over the edge. I listen for a long time.

Through twilight and moonlight I climb down to the rope, down to the ledge, down to the canyon floor below Rainbow Bridge. Bats flicker through the air. Fireflies sparkle by the waterseeps and miniature toads with enormous voices clank and grunt and chant at me as I tramp past their ponds down the long trail back to the river, back to campfire and companionship and a midnight supper.

We are close to the end of our journey. In the morning Ralph and I pack our gear, load the boats, and take a last lingering look at the scene which we know we will never again see as we see it now: the great Colorado River, wild and free, surging past the base of the towering cliffs, roaring through the boulders below the mouth of Forbidden Canyon; Navajo Point and the precipice of the Kaiparowits Plateau thousands of feet above, beyond the inner walls of the canyon; and in the east ranks of storm-driven cumulus clouds piled high on one another, gold-trimmed and blazing in the dawn.

Ralph takes a photograph, puts the camera back into the waterproof pouch which he hangs across his chest, and climbs into his boat. We shove off.

This is the seventh day—or is it the ninth?—of our dreamlike voyage. Late in the afternoon, waking from a deep reverie, I observe, as we glide silently by, a pair of ravens roosting on a dead tree near the shore, watching us pass. I wonder where we are. I ask Ralph; he has no idea and cares less, cares only that the journey not yet end.

I light up the last of my tobacco, and watch the blue smoke curl and twist and vanish over the swirling brown water. We are rounding a bend in the river and I see, far ahead on the left-hand shore, something white, rigid, rectangular, out of place. Our boats drift gradually closer and we see the first billboard ever erected in Glen Canyon. Planted in rocks close to the water, the sign bears a message and it is meant for us.

ATTENTION
YOU ARE APPROACHING GLEN CANYON
DAM SITE   ALL BOATS MUST LEAVE
RIVER AT KANE CREEK LANDING ONE
MILE AHEAD ON RIGHT   ABSOLUTELY
NO BOATS ALLOWED IN
CONSTRUCTION ZONE
VIOLATORS WILL BE PROSECUTED
U.S. BUREAU OF RECLAMATION

HAVASU

ONE SUMMER I started off to visit for the first time the city of Los Angeles. I was riding with some friends from the University of New Mexico. On the way we stopped off briefly to roll an old tire into the Grand Canyon. While watching the tire bounce over tall pine trees, tear hell out of a mule train and disappear with a final grand leap into the inner gorge, I overheard the park ranger standing nearby say a few words about a place called Havasu, or Havasupai. A branch, it seemed, of the Grand Canyon.

What I heard made me think that I should see Havasu immediately, before something went wrong somewhere. My friends said they would wait. So I went down into Havasu—fourteen miles by trail—and looked things over. When I returned five weeks later I discovered that the others had gone on to Los Angeles without me.

That was fifteen years ago. And still I have not seen the fabulous city on the Pacific shore. Perhaps I never will. There's something in the prospect southwest from Barstow which makes one hesitate. Although recently, driving my own truck, I did succeed in penetrating as close as San Bernardino. But was hurled back by what appeared to be clouds of mustard gas rolling in from the west on a very broad front. Thus failed again. It may be however that Los Angeles will come to me. Will come to all of us, as it must (they say) to all men.

But Havasu. Once down in there it's hard to get out. The trail led across a stream wide, blue and deep, like the pure upper reaches of the River Jordan. Without a bridge. Dripping wet and making muddy tracks I entered the village of the Havasupai Indians where unshod ponies ambled down the only street and the children laughed, not maliciously, at the sight of the wet white man. I stayed the first night in the lodge the people keep for tourists, a rambling old bungalow with high ceilings, a screened verandah and large comfortable rooms. When the sun went down the village went dark except for kerosene lamps here and there, a few open fires, and a number of lightning bugs or fireflies which drifted aimlessly up and down Main Street, looking for trouble.

The next morning I bought a slab of bacon and six cans of beans at the village post office, rented a large comfortable horse and proceeded farther down the canyon past miniature cornfields, green pastures, swimming pools and waterfalls to the ruins of an old mining camp five miles below the village. There I lived, mostly alone except for the ghosts, for the next thirty-five days.

There was nothing wrong with the Indians. The Supai are a charming cheerful completely relaxed and easygoing bunch, all one hundred or so of them. But I had no desire to live *among* them unless clearly invited to do so, and I wasn't. Even if invited I might not have accepted. I'm not sure that I care for the idea of strangers examining my daily habits and folkways, studying my language, inspecting my costume, questioning me about my religion, classifying my artifacts, investigating my sexual rites and evaluating my chances for cultural survival.

So I lived alone.

The first thing I did was take off my pants. Naturally. Next I unloaded the horse, smacked her on the rump and sent her back to the village. I carried my food and gear into the best-preserved of the old cabins and spread my bedroll on a rusty steel cot. After that came a swim in the pool beneath a great waterfall nearby, 120 feet high, which rolled in mist and thunder over caverns and canopies of solidified travertine.

In the evening of that first day below the falls I lay down to sleep in the cabin. A dark night. The door of the cabin, unlatched, creaked slowly open, although there was no perceptible movement of the air. One firefly flickered in and circled my bacon, suspended from the roofbeam on a length of bailing wire. Slowly, without visible physical aid, the door groaned shut. And opened again. A bat came through one window and went out another, followed by a second firefly (the first scooped up by the bat) and a host of mosquitoes, which did not leave. I had no netting, of course, and the air was much too humid and hot for sleeping inside a bag.

I got up and wandered around outside for a while, slapping at mosquitoes, and thinking. From the distance came the softened roar of the waterfall, that "white noise" as soothing as hypnosis. I rolled up my sleeping bag and in the filtered light of the stars followed the trail that wound through thickets of cactus and up around ledges to the terrace above the mining camp. The mosquitoes stayed close but in lessening numbers, it seemed, as I climbed over humps of travertine toward the head of the waterfall. Near the brink of it, six feet from the drop-off and the plunge, I found a sandy cove just big enough for my bed. The racing creek as it soared free over the edge created a continuous turbulence in the air sufficient to keep away all flying insects. I slept well that night and the next day carried the cot to the place and made it my permanent bedroom for the rest of July and all of August.

What did I do during those five weeks in Eden? Nothing. I did nothing. Or nearly nothing. I caught a few rainbow trout, which grew big if not numerous in Havasu Creek. About once a week I put on my pants and walked up to the Indian village to buy bacon, canned beans and Argentine beef in the little store. That was all the Indians had in stock. To vary my diet I ordered more exotic foods by telephone from the supermarket in Grand Canyon Village and these were shipped to me by U.S. Mail, delivered twice a week on muleback down the fourteen-mile trail from Topocoba Hilltop. A little later in the season I was able to buy sweet corn, figs and peaches from the Supai. At one time for a period of three days my bowels seemed in danger of falling out, but I recovered. The Indians never came down to my part of the canyon except when guiding occasional tourists to the falls or hunting a stray horse. In late August came the Great Havasupai Sacred Peach Festival and Four-Day Marathon Friendship Dance, to which I was invited and in which I did participate. There I met Reed Watahomagie, a good man, and Chief Sinyala and a fellow named Spoonhead who took me for five dollars in a horse race. Someone had fed my mount a half-bushel of green figs just before the race—I heard later.

The Friendship Dance, which continued day and night to the rhythm of drums made of old inner tube stretched over #10 tomato cans while ancient medicine men chanted in the background, was perhaps marred but definitely not interrupted when a drunken free-for-all exploded between Spoonhead and friends and a group of visiting Hualapai Indians down from the rim. But this, I was told, happened every year. It was a traditional part of the ceremony, sanctified by custom. As Spoonhead told me afterwards, grinning around broken teeth, it's not every day you get a chance to wallop a Hualapai. Or skin a paleface, I reminded him. (Yes, the Supai are an excellent tribe, healthy, joyous and clever. Not only clever but shrewd. Not only shrewd but wise: e.g., the Bureau of Indian Affairs and the Bureau of Public Roads, like most government agencies always meddling, always fretting and itching and sweating for something to do, last year made a joint offer to blast a million-dollar road down into Havasu Canyon at no cost whatsoever to the tribe, thus opening their homeland to the riches of motorized tourism. The people of Supai or at least a majority of them voted to reject the proposal.) And the peach wine flowed freely, like the water of the river of life. When the ball was over I went home to my bunk on the verge of the waterfall and rested for two days.

On my feet again, I explored the abandoned silver mines in the canyon walls, found a few sticks of dynamite but no caps or fuses. Disappointing; but there was nothing in that area anyway that required blowing up. I climbed through the caves that led down to the foot of Mooney Falls, 200 feet high. What did I do? There was nothing that had to be done. I listened to the voices, the many voices, vague, distant but astonishingly human, of Havasu Creek. I heard the doors creak open, the doors creak shut, of the old forgotten cabins where no one with tangible substance or the property of reflecting light ever entered, ever returned. I went native and dreamed away days on the shore of the pool under the waterfall, wandered naked as Adam under the cottonwoods, inspecting my cactus gardens. The days became wild, strange, ambiguous—a sinister element pervaded the flow of time. I lived narcotic hours in which like the Taoist Chuang-tse I worried about butterflies and who was dreaming what. There was a serpent, a red racer, living in the rocks of the spring where I filled my canteens; he was always there, slipping among the stones or pausing to mesmerize me with his suggestive tongue and cloudy haunted primeval eyes. Damn his eyes. We got to know each other rather too well I think. I agonized over the girls I had known and over those I hoped were yet to come. I slipped by degrees into lunacy, me and the moon, and lost to a certain extent the power to distinguish between what was and what was not myself: looking at my hand I would see a leaf trembling on a branch. A *green* leaf. I thought of Debussy, of Keats and Blake and Andrew Marvell. I remembered Tom o'Bedlam. And all those lost and never remembered. Who would return? To be lost again? I went for walks. I went for walks. I went for walks and on one of these, the last I took in Havasu, regained everything that seemed to be ebbing away.

Most of my wandering in the desert I've done alone. Not so much from choice as from necessity—I generally prefer to go into places where no one else wants to go. I find that in contemplating the natural world my pleasure is greater if there are not too many others contemplating it with me, at the same time. However, there are special hazards in traveling alone. Your chances of dying, in case of sickness or accident, are much improved, simply because there is no one around to go for help.

Exploring a side canyon off Havasu Canyon one day, I was unable to resist the temptation to climb up out of it onto what corresponds in that region to the Tonto Bench. Late in the afternoon I realized that I would not have enough time to get back to my camp before dark, unless I could find a much shorter route than the one by which I had come. I looked for a shortcut.

Nearby was another little side canyon which appeared to lead down into Havasu Canyon. It was a steep, shadowy, extremely narrow defile with the usual meandering course and overhanging walls; from where I stood, near its head, I could not tell if the route was feasible all the way down to the floor of the main canyon. I had no rope with me—only my walking stick. But I was hungry and thirsty, as always. I started down.

For a while everything went well. The floor of the little canyon began as a bed of dry sand, scattered with rocks. Farther down a few boulders were wedged between the walls; I climbed over and under them. Then the canyon took on the slickrock character—smooth, sheer, slippery sandstone carved by erosion into a series of scoops and potholes which got bigger as I descended. In some of these basins there was a little water left over from the last flood, warm and fetid water under an oily-looking scum, condensed by prolonged evaporation to a sort of broth, rich in dead and dying organisms. My canteen was empty and I was very thirsty but I felt that I could wait.

I came to a lip on the canyon floor which overhung by twelve feet the largest so far of these stagnant pools. On each side rose the canyon walls, roughly perpendicular. There was no way to continue except by dropping into the pool. I hesitated. Beyond this point there could hardly be any returning, yet the main canyon was still not visible below. Obviously the only sensible thing to do was to turn back. I edged over the lip of stone and dropped feet first into the water.

Deeper than I expected. The warm, thick fluid came up and closed over my head as my feet touched the muck at the bottom. I had to swim to the farther side. And here I found myself on the verge of another drop-off, with one more huge bowl of green soup below.

This drop-off was about the same height as the one before, but not overhanging. It resembled a children's playground slide, concave and S-curved, only steeper, wider, with a vertical pitch in the middle. It did not lead directly into the water but ended in a series of steplike ledges above the pool. Beyond the pool lay another edge, another drop-off into an unknown depth. Again I paused, and for a much longer time. But I no longer had the option of turning around and going back. I eased myself into the chute and let go of everything—except my faithful stick.

I hit rock bottom hard, but without any physical injury. I swam the stinking pond dog-paddle style, pushing the heavy scum away from my face, and crawled out on the far side to see what my fate was going to be.

Fatal. Death by starvation, slow and tedious. For I was looking straight down an overhanging cliff to a rubble pile of broken rocks eighty feet below.

After the first wave of utter panic had passed I began to try to think. First of all I was not going to die immediately, unless another flash flood came down the gorge; there was the pond of stagnant water on hand to save me from thirst and a man can live, they say, for thirty days or more without food. My sun-bleached bones, dramatically sprawled at the bottom of the chasm, would provide the diversion of the picturesque for future wanderers—if any man ever came this way again.

My second thought was to scream for help, although I knew very well there could be no other human being within miles. I even tried it but the sound of that anxious shout, cut short in the dead air within the canyon walls, was so inhuman, so detached as it seemed from myself, that it terrified me and I didn't attempt it again.

I thought of tearing my clothes into strips and plaiting a rope. But what was I wearing?—boots, socks, a pair of old and ragged blue jeans, a flimsy T-shirt, an ancient and rotten sombrero of straw. Not a chance of weaving such a wardrobe into a rope eighty feet long, or even twenty feet long.

How about a signal fire? There was nothing to burn but my clothes; not a tree, not a shrub, not even a weed grew in this stony cul-de-sac. Even if I burned my clothing the chances of the smoke being seen by some Hualapai Indian high on the south rim were very small; and if he did see the smoke, what then? He'd shrug his shoulders, sigh, and take another pull from his Tokay bottle. Furthermore, without clothes, the sun would soon bake me to death.

There was only one thing I could do. I had a tiny notebook in my hip pocket and a stub of pencil. When these dried out I could at least record my final thoughts. I would have plenty of time to write not only my epitaph but my own elegy.

But not yet.

There were a few loose stones scattered about the edge of the pool. Taking the biggest first, I swam with it back to the foot of the slickrock chute and placed it there. One by one I brought the others and made a shaky little pile about two feet high leaning against the chute. Hopeless, of course, but there was nothing else to do. I stood on the top of the pile and stretched upward, straining my arms to their utmost limit and groped with fingers and fingernails for a hold on something firm. There was nothing. I crept

back down. I began to cry. It was easy. All alone, I didn't
have to be brave.

Through the tears I noticed my old walking stick lying
nearby. I took it and stood it on the most solid stone in
the pile, behind the two topmost stones. I took off my
boots, tied them together and hung them around my neck,
on my back. I got up on the little pile again and lifted one
leg and set my big toe on the top of the stick. This could
never work. Slowly and painfully, leaning as much of my
weight as I could against the sandstone slide, I applied
more and more pressure to the stick, pushing my body upward until I was again stretched out full length above it.
Again I felt about for a fingerhold. There was none. The
chute was smooth as polished marble.

No, not quite that smooth. This was sandstone, soft and
porous, not marble, and between it and my wet body and
wet clothing a certain friction was created. In addition,
the stick had enabled me to reach a higher section of the
S-curved chute, where the angle was more favorable. I
discovered that I could move upward, inch by inch, through
adhesion and with the help of the leveling tendency of the
curve. I gave an extra little push with my big toe—the
stones collapsed below, the stick clattered down—and
crawled rather like a snail or slug, oozing slime, up over
the rounded summit of the slide.

The next obstacle, the overhanging spout twelve feet
above a deep plunge pool, looked impossible. It *was* impossible, but with the blind faith of despair I slogged into
the water and swam underneath the drop-off and floun-
dered around for a while, scrabbling at the slippery rock
until my nerves and tiring muscles convinced my numbed
brain that *this was not the way*. I swam back to solid
ground and lay down to rest and die in comfort.

Far above I could see the sky, an irregular strip of blue
between the dark, hard-edged canyon walls that seemed to
lean toward each other as they towered above me. Across
that narrow opening a small white cloud was passing, so
lovely and precious and delicate and forever inaccessible
that it broke the heart and made me weep like a woman,

like a child. In all my life I had never seen anything so beautiful.

The walls that rose on either side of the drop-off were literally perpendicular. Eroded by weathering, however, and not by the corrasion of rushing floodwater, they had a rough surface, chipped, broken, cracked. Where the walls joined the face of the overhang they formed almost a square corner, with a number of minute crevices and inch-wide shelves on either side. It might, after all, be possible. What did I have to lose?

When I had regained some measure of nerve and steadiness I got up off my back and tried the wall beside the pond, clinging to the rock with bare toes and fingertips and inching my way crabwise toward the corner. The water-soaked, heavy boots dangling from my neck, swinging back and forth with my every movement, threw me off balance and I fell into the pool. I swam out to the bank, unslung the boots and threw them up over the drop-off, out of sight. They'd be there if I ever needed them again. Once more I attached myself to the wall, tenderly, sensitively, like a limpet, and very slowly, very cautiously, worked my way into the corner. Here I was able to climb upward, a few centimeters at a time, by bracing myself against the opposite sides and finding sufficient niches for fingers and toes. As I neared the top and the overhang became noticeable I prepared for a slip, planning to push myself away from the rock so as to fall into the center of the pool where the water was deepest. But it wasn't necessary. Somehow, with a skill and tenacity I could never have found in myself under ordinary circumstances, I managed to creep straight up that gloomy cliff and over the brink of the drop-off and into the flower of safety. My boots were floating under the surface of the little puddle above. As I poured the stinking water out of them and pulled them on and laced them up I discovered myself bawling again for the third time in three hours, the hot delicious tears of victory. And up above the clouds replied—thunder.

I emerged from that treacherous little canyon at sundown, with an enormous fire in the western sky and lightning overhead. Through sweet twilight and the sudden dazzling flare of lightning I hiked back along the Tonto Bench, bellowing the *Ode to Joy*. Long before I reached the place where I could descend safely to the main canyon and my camp, however, darkness set in, the clouds opened their bays and the rain poured down. I took shelter under a ledge in a shallow cave about three feet high—hardly room to sit up in. Others had been here before: the dusty floor of the little hole was littered with the droppings of birds, rats, jackrabbits and coyotes. There were also a few long gray pieces of scat with a curious twist at one tip— cougar? I didn't care. I had some matches with me, sealed in paraffin (the prudent explorer); I scraped together the handiest twigs and animal droppings and built a little fire and waited for the rain to stop.

It didn't stop. The rain came down for hours in alternate waves of storm and drizzle and I very soon had burnt up all the fuel within reach. No matter. I stretched out in the coyote den, pillowed my head on my arm and suffered through the long long night, wet, cold, aching, hungry, wretched, dreaming claustrophobic nightmares. It was one of the happiest nights of my life.

THE DEAD MAN AT
GRANDVIEW POINT

SOMNOLENCE—A heaviness in the air, a chill in the sunlight, an oppressive stillness in the atmosphere that hints of much but says nothing. The Balanced Rock and the pinnacles stand in petrified silence—waiting. The wildlife has withdrawn to the night, the flies and gnats have disappeared, a few birds sing, and the last of the flowers of summer—the globemallow—have died. What is it that's haunting me? At times I hear voices up the road, familiar voices ... I look; and no one is there.

Even the tourists that creep in and creep out in their lumbering, dust-covered automobiles reveal a certain weariness with desert travel, a certain longing to be elsewhere, to be where it's high, cool, breezy, fresh—mountain or seashore. And they should. Why anyone with any sense would volunteer to spend August in the furnace of the desert is a mystery to me; they must be mad, these brave tourists, as I am mad.

Each day begins clean and promising in the sweet cool clear green light of dawn. And then the sun appears, its hydrogen cauldrons brimming—so to speak—with plasmic fires, and the tyranny of its day begins.

By noon the clouds are forming around the horizon and in the afternoon, predictable as sunrise and sunset, they gather in massed formations, colliding in jags of lightning and thunderous artillery, and pile higher and higher toward the summit of the sky in vaporish mountains, dazzling under the sunlight. Afterward, perhaps, comes a little rain—that is, a violent cloudburst above some random site in the desert, flooding arroyos and washes with torrents of mud, gravel and water in equal parts, a dense mixture the color of tomato soup or blood which roars down the barren waterways to the river, leaving the land an hour later as dry as it was before. The clouds melt away, the thunder fades and the sun breaks through again, blazing with redoubled intensity upon sand and rock and scattered, introverted shrub and tree. Rainy season in the canyonlands.

These brief thundershowers are not entirely without effect: I can see these days a dull green fuzziness spreading like a mold across the distant swales of Salt Wash Valley. Near at hand are a few of the plants responsible for that coloration—the tumbleweed or Russian thistle, hairy and prickly, unpleasant both to touch and eye. At the same time the ground is being prepared for a more wholesome growth, the September resurgence of rabbitbrush, sunflower, aster, wild buckwheat and matchweed.

With evening come elaborate sunsets in every named and unnamed hue of gold, purple, crimson, green, orange and blue, spread out for fifty or a hundred miles among the floating ranks of clouds, with spokes of light radiating across the sky all the way from the western to the eastern horizon. Often the sunset is reflected not only on the mountain peaks, standing like islands in a sea of twilight, but also on ranges of clouds to the east, where the changing colors can be seen—along with flashes of silent, sudden heat lightning—long after they have faded out completely in the west.

This is the time, in these semihumid August evenings after rain, when a few nighthawks will leave their daytime hiding places to climb and circle and dive through the air, feeding on high-flying insect life invisible from the ground. Of the genus *Chordeiles*, related to the nightjar and the goatsucker (most birds have fantastic names), the nighthawks resemble in size and conformation the swallow rather than the hawk, while in their style of flight, constantly swooping and darting, they are also like bats. Now and then a nighthawk, high in the air, will fold wings and plunge earthward; the noise of the wind rushing through its feathers when the bird extends wings and pulls out of the dive is like a distant roar, a bovine bellow. And so, among its many other names, the nighthawk *Chordeiles minor* is also called a bullbat, at least in the Southwest.

They feed in the twilight between evening and night and again in that similar twilight, unknown to most Americans, between dawn and sunrise, at which times aerial insects are most abundant. In my sack on the cot out back of the trailer I am awakened many a morning by the sound of their wild cries and thrilling plunges through the air. I open my eyes and see the summer constellations, pale, dim, oddly misplaced in the sky—the Big Dipper, for example, half sunk beyond the northern horizon. At first I think it is still night but looking east I see a premonition of day in the greenish streaks of light spread out along the rim. False dawn? No, for I also see the nighthawks skating across the sky against the glow, a sure sign of the coming sunrise.

Another kind of music sometimes fills the early hours. Almost every morning for a week I have been honored by the serenade of a den of coyotes—a family perhaps—somewhere about a mile to the west of my camp. Weird, unearthly song—like the legendary wail of banshees, or more precisely, like the sounds produced by new electronic instruments such as the *cithare* and *Onde Martinote*.

Occult music is but a part of the coyotes' repertoire:

they vary the program with more conventional howls, yelps and barks when it pleases them to do so. Usually they stop their singing and retire into the rocks, out of caution, soon after the sun comes up.

I'm not going to look for their lair, for that might frighten them away, and we need coyotes, need them badly, in Arches National Monument. As does the nation as a whole, for that matter. We need coyotes more than we need, let us say, more people, of whom we have already an extravagant surplus, or more domesticated dogs, which in all fairness could and should be ground up into hamburger and used as emergency coyote food, to raise their spirits and perhaps improve the tenor of their predawn howling.

This morning I am requested via the shortwave radio to join a manhunt. Not for some suspected criminal or escaped convict but for a lost tourist whose car was found abandoned two days ago in the vicinity of Grandview Point, about fifty miles by road from my station in the Arches.

Grateful for the diversion, I throw canteens and rucksack into the government pickup and take off. I go west to the highway, south for three miles, and turn off on another dirt road leading southwest across Dead Horse Mesa toward the rendezvous. There I find the other members of the search party holding a consultation: Merle and Floyd from park headquarters, the county sheriff and one of his deputies, a relative of the missing man, and my brother Johnny who is also working for the Park Service this summer. At the side of the road is a locked and empty automobile, first noted two days earlier.

Most of the surface of this high mesa on which our man has disappeared is bare rock—there are few trails, and little sand or soft earth on which he might have left footprints. There are, however, many washes, giant potholes, basins, fissures and canyons in which a man could lose himself, or a body be hidden, for days or years.

There is also the abyss. A mile from where we stand

is the mesa's edge and a twelve-hundred-foot drop straight
down to what is called the White Rim Bench. From there
the land falls away for another fifteen hundred feet or
more to the Colorado River. If he went that way there
won't be much left worth looking for. You could put it
all in a bushel sack.

Learning from the relative—a nephew—that the missing
man is about sixty years old, an amateur photographer
who liked to walk and had never been in the Southwest
before, we assume first of all that the object of the search
is dead and that the body will be found somewhere along
the more than twenty miles of highly indented rimrock
that winds northwest and northeast from Grandview Point.

The assumption of death is made on the grounds that
an airplane search by the sheriff failed to find any sign of
the man, and that at least two days and possibly more
spent in the desert in the heat of August with only
what water (if any) he could carry is too much for a man
of sixty, unfamiliar with the terrain and the climate.

We begin the search by dividing as evenly as we can
the area to be investigated. Assigned the southernmost sec-
tor, my brother and I drive down the road another five
miles to where it dead-ends close to the farthest reach of
the mesa—Grandview Point itself. Here we share our
water supply and split up, Johnny hiking along the rim
to the northwest and I taking the opposite way.

All morning long, for the next four hours, I tramp along
the rim looking for the lost tourist. Looking for his body,
I should say—there seems little chance of finding him still
alive. I look in the shade of every juniper and overhanging ledge, likely places to find a man besieged by thirst
and sun. I look in the gullies and fissures and in the
enormous potholes drilled by wind and sand in the solid
rock—holes like wells, with perpendicular sides . . . man-
traps.

At times I step to the brink of the mesa and peer down
through that awful, dizzying vacancy to the broken slabs
piled along the foot of the wall, so far—so terribly far—
below. It is not impossible that our man might have

stumbled off the edge in the dark, or even—spellbound by that fulfillment of nothingness—eased himself over, deliberately, in broad daylight, drawn into the void by the beauty and power of his own terror . . . ?

"Gaze not too long into the abyss, lest the abyss gaze into thee."

I watch also for a gathering of vultures in the air, which would be a helpful clue. Not for *him*, of course, now perhaps beyond such cares, but for us, his hunters.

The sun burns in a lovely, perfect sky; the day is very hot. I pause when necessary beneath pinyon pine or juniper for rest and shade and for a precious drink of water. Also, I will admit, for recreation: to admire the splendor of the landscape, the perfection of the silence.

The shade is sweet and desirable, the heat very bad and early in the afternoon, out of water, I give up and return to the truck. My brother is waiting for me and by the lost expression on his face I understand at once that he has found our man.

I radio the rest of the party. Johnny and I wait in the shade of the truck. They arrive; we all wait another hour until the undertaker, who is also county coroner, comes from Moab with his white ambulance, his aluminum stretcher and his seven-foot long black rubber bag. Then Johnny leads us to the body.

The route is rough and long, across rocky gulches and sandstone terraces impassable to a motor vehicle. We walk it out. About a mile from the road we come to a ledge rising toward the rim of the mesa. Near the top of the rise is a juniper, rooted in the rock and twisted toward the sky in the classic pose of its kind in the canyon country. Beneath the little tree, in the shade, is the dead man.

Coming close we see that he lies on his back, limbs extended rigidly from a body bloated like a balloon. A large stain discolors the crotch of his trousers. The smell of decay is rich and sickening. Although the buzzards for some reason have not discovered him two other scavengers, ravens, rise heavily and awkwardly from the corpse as we approach. No canteen or water bag in sight.

The nephew makes a positive identification—I can't imagine how. But the coroner-undertaker nods, the sheriff is satisfied, and together with the deputy the three of them begin the delicate, difficult task of easing the swollen cadaver into the unzipped rubber bag.

Johnny and I retrace what we can of the dead man's course. There is no discernible trail on the slickrock but by walking around his final resting place in a big half-circle we cut sign—intersect his tracks—in a ravine a hundred yards away. There on the sandy floor we find his footprints: where he had entered the ravine, where he became panicky and retraced his way not once but twice, and where he had struggled up an alluvial bank to the ledge. From that point he could see the juniper with its promise of shade. Somehow he made his way to it, laid himself down and never got up again.

We return to where the others are waiting, gathered about the black bag on the stretcher, which the undertaker is in the act of zipping shut. The sheriff and the deputy are scrubbing their hands with sand; the undertaker wears rubber gloves.

We are not far from Grandview Point and the view from near the juniper is equally spectacular. The big jump-off is only a few steps south and beyond that edge lies another world, far away. Down below is the White Rim; deeper still is the gorge of the Colorado; off to the right is the defile of the Green River; looking past Junction Butte we can see the barren point where the two rivers join to begin the wild race through Cataract Canyon; beyond the confluence lies the wilderness of the Needles country, known to only a few cowboys and uranium prospectors; on the west side of the junction is another labyrinth of canyons, pinnacles and fins of naked stone, known to even fewer, closer than anything else in the forty-eight United States to being genuine *terra incognita*—The Maze.

Far beyond these hundreds of square miles of desiccated

tableland rise the sheer walls of further great mesas comparable in size and elevation to the one we stand on; and beyond the mesas are the mountains—the Abajos and Elk Ridge forty miles south, the La Sals and Tukuhnikivats forty miles east, the Henrys fifty miles southwest.

Except for the town of Moab, east of us, and the village of Hanksville near the Henry Mountains, and a single occupied ranch on this side of the Abajo Mountains, the area which we overlook contains no permanent human habitation. From the point of view of political geography we are standing on one of the frontiers of human culture; for the man inside the rubber sack it was land's end, the shore of the world.

Looking out on this panorama of light, space, rock and silence I am inclined to congratulate the dead man on his choice of jumping-off place; he had good taste. He had good luck—I envy him the manner of his going: to die alone, on rock under sun at the brink of the unknown, like a wolf, like a great bird, seems to me very good fortune indeed. To die in the open, under the sky, far from the insolent interference of leech and priest, before this desert vastness opening like a window onto eternity—that surely was an overwhelming stroke of rare good luck.

It would be unforgivably presumptuous to pretend to speak *for* the dead man on these matters; he may not have agreed with a word of it, not at all. On the other hand, except for those minutes of panic in the ravine when he realized that he was lost, it seems possible that in the end he yielded with good grace. We see him staggering through the fearful heat and glare, across the tilted ledge toward the juniper, the only tree in sight. We see him reach it, at great cost, and there, on the brink of nothing and everything, he lies down in the shade to rest. He would not have suffered much after that; he may have died in his sleep, dreaming of the edge of things, of flight into space, of soaring.

We are ready to go. A few flies are already circling above the dark shape on the stretcher. A few dark birds are floating on thermals far out over the chasm of the

Colorado, somewhat below the level of the mesa. It is possible from here to gaze down on the backs of soaring birds. I would like to stay for a while and watch the birds but the others are ready to go, the sun is very hot, the corpse is stinking, there is not enough shade for us all under the one small tree, and the world—the human world —is waiting for us, calling us back. For the time being.

There are eight men here, alive. More or less alive. Four pick up the stretcher and begin the march back to the road and the ambulance. The other four walk alongside to relieve when needed. We soon need relief, for the weight is greater than it looks, and the rock, sand, brush and cactus make walking with a load difficult. The sun is pitiless, the smell is worse, and the flies are worst of all, buzzing in swarms around the putrid mass in the rubber sack.

The dead man's nephew, excused from this duty, walks far ahead out of earshot. We are free as we go stumbling and sweating along to say exactly what we please, without fear of offending.

"Heavy son of a bitch. . . ."

"All blown up like he is, you'd think he'd float like a balloon."

"Let's just hope he don't explode."

"He won't. We let the gas out."

"What about lunch?" somebody asks; "I'm hungry."

"Eat this."

"Why'd the bastard have to go so far from the road?"

"There's something leaking out that zipper."

"Never mind, let's try to get in step here," the sheriff says. "Goddamnit, Floyd, you got big feet."

"Are we going in the right direction?"

"I wonder if the old fart would walk part way if we let him out of that bag?"

"He won't even say thank you for the ride."

"Well I hope this learned him a lesson, goddamn him. I guess he'll stay put after this. . . ."

Thus we meditate upon the stranger's death. Since he was unknown to any of us we joke about his fate, as is only natural and wholesome under the circumstances. If he'd meant anything to us maybe we could mourn. If we had loved him we would sing, dance, drink, build a stupendous bonfire, find women, make love—for under the shadow of death what can be wiser than love, to make love, to make children?—and celebrate his transfiguration from flesh to fantasy in a style proper and fitting, with fun for all at the funeral.

But—we knew thee not, old man. And there is, I suspect, another feeling alive in each of us as we lug these rotting guts across the desert: satisfaction.

Each man's death diminishes me? Not necessarily. Given this man's age, the inevitability and suitability of his death, and the essential nature of life on earth, there is in each of us the unspeakable conviction that we are well rid of him. His departure makes room for the living. Away with the old, in with the new. He is gone—we remain, others come. The plow of mortality drives through the stubble, turns over rocks and sod and weeds to cover the old, the worn-out, the husks, shells, empty seedpods and sapless roots, clearing the field for the next crop. A ruthless, brutal process—but clean and beautiful.

A part of our nature rebels against this truth and against that other part which would accept it. A second truth of equal weight contradicts the first, proclaiming through art, religion, philosophy, science and even war that human life, in some way not easily definable, is significant and unique and supreme beyond all the limits of reason and nature. And this second truth we can deny only at the cost of denying our humanity.

We finally reach the road, which I had begun to fear we would never see—the death march seemed everlasting —and shove stretcher and burden into the undertaker's ambulance, a white Cadillac glittering with chrome and powdered with the red dust of Utah. He slams shut the doors, the undertaker does, shakes a few hands and drives off, followed by the nephew driving the dead man's car.

The air is clean and sweet again. We can breathe. We rest for a while in the shade of the other cars, passing around water bags, smoking, talking a little. Someone tells a bad joke, and the party breaks up. We all go back the thirty-five miles to the highway and from there by separate ways to our separate places, my brother south to Blanding, myself to the Arches.

Evening now, a later day. How much later? I'm not quite sure, I can't say, I've been out here in the heart of light and silence for so long that the numbers on a calendar have lost their meaning for me. All that I can be certain of at this moment is that the sun is down, for there is Venus again, planet of beauty and joy, glowing bright and clear in the western sky, low on the horizon, brilliant and steady and serene.

The season is late—late summer on the high desert. The thunderstorms have been less frequent lately, the tumbleweeds are taking on the reddish tinge of their maturity, and the various grasses—bluestem, fescue, Indian ricegrass, grama grass—which flourished after the summer rains have ripened to a tawny brown; in the slanting light of morning and evening the far-off fields in Salt Valley, where these grasses are most abundant, shine like golden velvet.

The nighthawks, sparse in numbers earlier, have gone away completely. I haven't seen one for a week. But not all the birds have left me.

Southwest, toward Grandview Point and The Maze, I can see V-shaped black wings in the lonely sky, soaring higher and higher against a yellow sunset. I think of the dead man under the juniper on the edge of the world, seeing him as the vulture would have seen him, far below and from a great distance. And I see myself through those cruel eyes.

I feel myself sinking into the landscape, fixed in place like a stone, like a tree, a small motionless shape of vague outline, desert-colored, and with the wings of imagination look down at myself through the eyes of the bird, watching a human figure that becomes smaller, smaller in the receding landscape as the bird rises into the evening—a man at a table near a twinkling campfire, surrounded by a rolling wasteland of stone and dune and sandstone monuments, the wasteland surrounded by dark canyons and the course of rivers and mountain ranges on a vast plateau stretching across Colorado, Utah, New Mexico and Arizona, and beyond this plateau more deserts and greater mountains, the Rockies in dusk, the Sierra Nevadas shining in their late afternoon, and farther and farther yet, the darkened East, the gleaming Pacific, the curving margins of the great earth itself, and beyond earth that ultimate world of sun and stars whose bounds we cannot discover.

TUKUHNIKIVATS,
THE ISLAND IN
THE DESERT

Late in August the lure of the mountains becomes irresistible. Seared by the everlasting sunfire, I want to see running water again, embrace a pine tree, cut my initials in the bark of an aspen, get bit by a mosquito, see a mountain bluebird, find a big blue columbine, get lost in the firs, hike above timberline, sunbathe on snow and eat some ice, climb the rocks and stand in the wind at the top of the world on the peak of Tukuhnikivats.

On a Monday evening before my two days off I load bedroll, rucksack, climbing boots and grub box into the pickup and drive away, turning my back on the entrance station and housetrailer and ramada, the lone juniper and all the hoodoo rocks. Take care of yourselves as best you can, I'm thinking—your slave is off to the high country. Cousin buzzard, keep an eye peeled for trouble.

Over the rocky wagon road—that trail of dust and sand and washouts which I love, which the tourists hate so deeply—I go jouncing, banging, clattering in the old Chevvy, scaring the daylights out of the lizards and beetles trying to cross the road.

Stepping harder on the gas I speed over the sand flats at 65 mph, trailing a funnel of dust about a mile and a half long. Washout ahead: playing the brakes lightly, fishtailing over the sand ripples, I gear down into second, into low and when I hit the new gulch slam the brakes hard and shift into compound low—creeper gear—to negotiate the rocks and logs strewn over the roadway. A hundred yards down the wash I can see the culvert, displaced by the flood and half-buried in quicksand—ought to anchor that thing. Into low, into second, up to the surface of a long ledge of sandstone dotted here and there with stunted junipers and the iridescent silver-blue sage; from there in high at highest feasible velocity—thirty mph —through a slalom course of boulders, trees and tight curves to the bank of Courthouse Wash, where a sliver of metallic-looking water snakes from pool to pool over the gravel, quicksand and mud. On the shores of the wash are reeds and rushes all bowed downstream under the weight of silt. In low gear at full throttle I gun the truck across the wash, anxious not to get bogged down, and roar up over the rocks and ruts on the far side. Easy enough: from here it's only a mile of dust, potholes and dunes of blowsand to the paved highway, which I reach without difficulty.

I look at my watch. I've driven the eight miles from park entrance to highway in only seventeen minutes or at an average rate of nearly thirty miles an hour. Very good, considering the obstacles. Why the tourists complain so much about this road I cannot understand: every foot of it offers some kind of challenge to nerve and skill and the drive as a whole is nothing less than a small adventure for man and machine. With brilliant scenery all the way, coming or going—what more could they want?

Well, damn the lot of them, I think, rolling down the broad asphalt trail to Moab at a safe and sane eighty-five, not forgetting to keep one eye skinned for a sign of Fred Burkett the local highway patrolman, whose favorite hiding place north of town was behind a Chamber of Commerce billboard welcoming tourists to "Moab, Uranium Capital of the World,"—was until I leveled the billboard to the ground one night with a bucksaw which I had borrowed for the job from the United States National Park Service, Department of the Interior (Help Keep America Beautiful)—good thing Fred wasn't there at the time; his new Plymouth Interceptor would've got badly wrinkled—assuming he was alseep as usual.

Yes, I say, let them all SQUEEZE TO RIGHT FORM SINGLE LANE REMOVE SUNGLASSES TURN ON LIGHTS REDUCE SPEED OBEY SIGNALS MERGING TRAFFIC AHEAD as they supinely gas themselves dead (passive nonresistance) tunneling into Hoboken Manhattan Jersey City Brooklyn New Haven Boston Baltimore Oakland Berkeley San Francisco Washington Seattle Chicago Pittsburgh L.A. San Diego etc. Atlanta Birmingham Miami etc. etc. Denver Phoenix Sacramento Salt Lake Tulsa OK City etc. etc. etc. Houston etc. & Hell. . . . But not here please. Not at my own Arches Natural Money-Mint National Park.

I drive swiftly on thinking the unthinkable, past Arches headquarters where I glimpse the superintendent mowing his front lawn, and across the bridge over the Colorado River, rich and red as beet soup with a load of Moenkopi mud flushed by yesterday's deluge out of Onion Creek Canyon. Poison water—selenium, arsenic, radon in solution. Into Moab and the bright lights, the jostling throng of kids, cowboys, miners, young bronzed hoods with sideburns and the sleeves removed from their shirts, through the blaring traffic and under the nervous neon—ATOMIC CAFE!—to the liquor store. Just in time; they close at seven here. A bottle of *Liebfraumilch* and then to the market for meat, fruit. Gasoline for my machine.

Getting late: the sun is down beyond Back-of-the-Rocks, beyond the escarpment of Dead Horse Point. A soft pink mist of light, the alpenglow, lies on the mountains above timberline. I hurry on, south from Moab, off the highway on the gravel road past the new airport, past the turnoff to old Roy's place and up into the foothills. Getting dark: I switch on the lights and keep moving. I know exactly where I want to camp tonight and will keep driving till I get there.

Up to the top of Wilson's Mesa and eastward and upward through the pygmy forest of juniper and pinyon pine. Pale phantom deer leap across the road through the beams of my lights—a four-point buck and one, two, three does. Climbing steadily in second gear I leave the pinyon-juniper zone and enter the scrub-oak jungles, the manzanita, sumac and dogbane; higher still appear stands of jackpine and yellowpine, common though not abundant in the La Sal range.

I turn off the main dirt road and take one narrower, rougher, with a high grass-grown center, drive through a meadow where the golden eyes of more deer gleam in my headlights, and enter groves of quaking aspen, tall straight slim trees with bark as white as that of birches, easy to cut with a knife, much in favor among sheepherders, hunters, lovers.

A bunch of cattle in the road. Too dull-witted to get out of the way, they trot along in front of the truck for a quarter of a mile before I can pass them. The road gets tougher, resembling a cobblestone alley—but here every cobble is loose and no two the same size or shape. When I come to a very steep pitch the rear wheels spin, the motor stalls. I get out and load rocks into the back of the bed, adding weight and traction enough to climb the grade.

In compound low, engine overheating, radiator at boiling point, I keep going, looking for a certain dim trail off to the right into the aspens; it comes, I turn off the road and drive through an opening in a derelict rail fence, brush beneath leafy boughs and emerge in a small grassy glade surrounded on all sides but one by solid ranks of aspens. Here I stop, turn off the lights, let the motor idle for a minute and then shut it off.

After the droning mechanical grind of the long pull up

the mountain the silence of the forest seems startling, deafening, most welcome. I get out, stretch, relieve myself. The air is chill and I put on a jacket.

As my ears and nerves recover from the long oppression of the drive I can hear the flutter of aspen leaves above my head and the ripple of running water not far away. In the light of the stars I walk through tall, dewy grass past a stone fireplace which I remember well, for I am the one who built it, to the edge of a brook.

The water is gushing over roots, splashing among stones. It mills in a pool at my feet and races on into the darkness. On the surface of the pool I see fragmented stars, glints of light on the whirling water. Cupping my hands I take a drink. Fresh from melting snowbanks on the peak above, the water is cold as ice. My hands tingle, burning with cold.

I find some dry sticks, build a little fire in the fireplace, uncork the wine. Excellent. Waiting for the fire to settle down to exactly where I want it, I spread a tarp on the ground close to the fire and place my bedroll on it for a cushion, sitting like a tailor. I'll not unroll the sleeping bag until I'm ready to sleep; I want to save that desert warmth stored up inside it.

The fire is right. I set a light grill over the flames and on the grill roll out a big thin tough beefsteak, which happens to be the kind of beefsteak I prefer. I reach for the bottle.

Very quietly and selfishly, all by my lonesome, I cook and drink and eat my supper, smoke a cigar for dessert, finish the wine. The stars look kindly down. Drunk as a Navajo I pull off my boots and crawl into the snug warm down-filled womblike mummy bag. The night is cold, perhaps freezing—should I drain the radiator? To hell with it. High on the lap of Tukuhnikivats the King, wrapped in the sack in my home away from home, I close my eyes and go to sleep.

In the sweet chill of the dawn I wake up, hearing the ratchetlike screech of a squirrel. I open my eyes and see first a tall stem of grass bending over my face, weighed

down by a drop of dew that glistens like a pearl on its
tip. Beyond the grass the pale trunks of the aspens stand
in serried formation, thick as corn, blue-white and ghostly,
their leafy crowns in perpetual motion. The trees are in
shadow but above the forest shafts of sunlight fan out
across the blue. Deep in the sky rises the bald peak of
Tukuhnikivats, sunlit. Time to get up there.

I wash my face in the icy stream, shocking myself wide
awake. Make a fire, put water on to boil for tea, lay thick
slices of bacon tenderly across the grill. While the bacon
broils above the coals I crack eggs in a skillet—five eggs—
add slices of green chile and scramble. Hunger stirs within
me like a great music. Turning the bacon with a fork, I
watch the light deepen on the mountain, am watched in
turn by a bluejay, a redheaded woodpecker, the gray
squirrel. In the bark of the nearest aspen, deeply inscribed,
are the initials "C.E.M.," without a date. I squat close
to the fire, lean half over it inhaling aspen smoke, trying
to keep warm, and eat my breakfast.

After the meal I pack fruit, nuts, cheese and raisins into
the rucksack, take my cherrywood stick and start up the
mountain. I follow the little stream, keeping close to its
course up through the clear green shade of the aspens.
Though resembling the birch, the quaking aspen like the
cottonwood is a member of the willow family, and reveals
its kinship by the delicate suspension of the leaves. Like
that of the cottonwood, the foliage of the aspen responds
to the slightest movement of air—even a blow on the
trunk with my stick makes the leafy assembly vibrate like
bangles. In autumn the leaves turn a bright, uniform yellow, glorifying entire mountainsides with bands and
slashes of gold.

I hear and see a few birds—woodpecker, flicker, bluejay, phainopepla—but no sign of any animal life except
squirrel and deer. According to reputation there are still a
few mountain lions in the Sierra La Sal, ranging through
from time to time, and possibly even bear, but it's not
my kind of luck today to find their tracks. But if the
animals are few the flowers are plentiful, expecially in the

open glades and along the brook, where I find clusters of larkspur, blue flax and Sego lilies.

The larkspur is of the species called Subalpine or Barbey (*Delphinium barbeyi*), with a thick stem, deep blue petals, and a toxic content of delphinine. Too much larkspur and the flower-eating cow or sheep turns belly up, legs in the air, dead as a log and crawling with maggots.

Equally beautiful and not so potent is the blue flax with its pale sky-blue petals veined in violet, and the Sego lily or Mariposa lily, state flower of Utah. *Calochortus nuttalli* . . . "beautiful herb." Each deep cup-shaped bloom sparkles with morning dew. The Sego lily grows from an onionlike bulb and if I were hungry or the flower more abundant I'd dig one up and try the thing for flavor. Instead I content myself with a stem of grass.

Climbing higher, I enter by degrees into the Hudsonian life zone, leaving behind the Canadian with its aspen and Douglas fir, and find myself in the dark cool depths of the silver fir and spruce forest. The shade grows darker, the silence deeper; gracing the air is the subtle fragrance of sun-warmed, oozing resin. There is no trail and the many dead and fallen trees make progress difficult. I leave the stream and work my way directly up the mountainside toward the light of timberline.

As I ascend the trees become smaller and at the edge of the woods, on the margin of the scree that leads to the summit, the trees are little more than shrubs, gnarled, twisted and stormblasted, with matlike tangles of Englemann spruce growing over the rock. I stop to orient myself and to look for the best route to the top.

I stand on broken rock, slabs of granite veined with feldspar and quartz, colored with patches of green and auburn lichens. I am on the north face of Tukuhnikivats; blocking the view to the east and northeast are Mounts Peale and Mellanthin but north and west and southwest the world is open and I can see the knobs and domes of the Arches, the gray-blue Roan Cliffs beyond, the town and valley of Moab 7000 feet below, the looming headlands of Hatch Point, Dead Horse Point and Grandview

Point, and farther away, farthest of all, wonderfully remote, the Orange Cliffs, Land's End and The Maze, an
exhilarating vastness bathed in morning light, room enough
for a lifetime of exploration.

I look up to the peak. Timberline at this latitude is in
the neighborhood of 11,000 feet; therefore I have about
2000 vertical feet to climb. There is no trail to the summit
and from where I stand no ridge of solid rock to make the
climb easier. Nothing but the immense talus slopes of
loose, jumbled, broken slabs, a few islands of tundra, and
up the middle a long couloir partly filled with snow. I
start toward that.

Munching raisins, I climb and scramble over the rocks,
which sometimes seesaw under my weight or start sliding, adding the hazards of surprise, twisted knee, sprained
ankle or crushed foot to the general interest of the ascent.
Aside from the awkward footing the climb is simple
enough, requiring no special equipment except heart and
legs. In the technical sense of the mountaineer not a *climb*
at all but only a *scramble*. Not that such distinctions
matter to me; the easier the better so far as I'm concerned.
I am more interested in the pikas squealing under the
rocks, in the subalpine buttercups on the grassy patches,
in the furtive elusive gray spiders that dance over the
slabs before me than in engineering exercises with nylon
rope, carabiners, brakebars, pitons, slings, crampons, star
drills and expansion bolts. For the present, anyway.

I can hear the pikas all around me signaling each other
with their whistles but never catch a glimpse of one. They
stay in their tunnels and lairs under the rock, listening to
the strange two-legged monster stumbling over their
homes. Pika: a harelike mammal, a lagomorph, having two
pairs of upper incisors, one set behind the other—why?
The better to gnaw the tough roots of the scrubby tundra
plants.

When I reach one of the islandlike areas of solid rock
in the midst of the scree I lie down for a while to catch
my breath and examine at close range, six inches, the
buttercups, the Sticky Polemonium, the moss campion

(lovely name) and the miniature alpine violets with their flowers no bigger than the head of a thumbtack. I also hope to find the flower called Rocky Mountain Pussytoes, a favorite of mine for no better reason than the name.

Here are the buttercups, alpine or subalpine, with their hairy sepals, divided leaves, shiny yellow petals: hold one close to your nose, the old wives say, and if your nose reflects the yellow you are a butter-lover. I have no mirror with me except a knifeblade and do not perform the experiment. In any case the game was not meant for the solitary but for two alone—lad and lass, man and maid.

Sticky Polemonium has an engaging sound. It is a tiny tubular purplish flower with orange anthers, clusters of them on fuzzy stalks about ten inches high; *Polemonium viscosum*, alias Sky Pilot, for it often lives at 13,000 feet or more. As for the moss campion I am lying on it; it makes a pleasant cushioning on the rock and the small pink flowers will not be damaged by my temporary sojourn here.

It won't do to pause for long on a mountain climb. The longer you rest the harder it is to get up and go on. The steady oxlike plod is best. I rise from the flowerbed and continue, moving up from rock to shaky rock, sliding, slipping, sometimes losing ground but gaining in the long run. The long field of snow looks good and I make straight for it, hoping the snow will be firm enough to climb, soft enough to kick toeholds in.

I am also eager for a drink of water; the keen chill air of the upper world whets my thirst and I'm carrying no water in my pack. I am already close enough to the snowfield to hear the muted roar, as of an underground waterfall, of the melted snow rushing downward through the piled slabs over which I struggle.

Coming near the edge of the snowfield I find running water close to the surface, visible among the rocks. I stop to drink. The water is bitterly, brilliantly cold, with particles of glacial grit—utterly delicious.

A few more steps and I reach the snowfield, which extends for a thousand feet, bell-curved, up through the couloir toward the summit. It looks like it might go. I advance upon it slowly and carefully, kicking out footholds as I climb. The snow is firm, solid, as expected, and at first it seems easier to go this way. But the kicking of niches becomes tiring; an ice axe would be handy now. Also one false step, one slip, and I'll be back down at my starting point in seconds. Somewhat regretfully I decide to leave the snow and traverse over to the rocks, continuing the climb up those unstable fragments.

It seems odd that the mountainside should be covered with this loose debris but so it is with Tukuhnikivats; nearly symmetrical, like a volcano, it has weathered evenly on all sides, unlike its neighbor Mount Peale for instance, which can be reached over spurs and ridges of solid base rock. Which is also for that matter a little bit higher, according to the surveyors.

Then why climb Tukuhnikivats? Because I prefer to. Because no one else will if I don't—and *somebody has to do it*. Because it is the most dramatic in form of the La Sals, the most conspicuous and beautiful as seen from my terrace in the Arches. Because, finally, I like the name. Tukuhnikivats—in the language of the Utes "where the sun lingers."

The mountain resists me. Slowly, laboriously I struggle upward, clambering over the tricky slabs. Halfway up, the mountain hits me with a sudden storm. First the wind and a sinister clot of gray scud crawling over the peak; then a rain of sleet followed by hailstones that bombard me like a cascade of marbles. I have put on my jacket, pulled my hat tight on my skull—I keep on climbing. What else can I do? There's no shelter and little comfort in simply standing still and suffering.

In a few minutes the storm melts away, the clouds break, the sun comes out to warm my body and melt the hailstones that are piled like mothballs in every cranny among the rocks. As the weather improves so does the terrain. The scree gives way to outcroppings of solid country rock which I climb to reach the firm, grass-covered dome of the peak. A cairn of stones over the brassheaded benchmark of the Geodetic Survey marks the highest point and there I sit to eat my lunch, shielded from the wind by the cairn and drenched in warmth from a sun that has never seemed so close, so dazzling, in such a dark and violet sky.

The sun in fact has changed color. Seen from the desert it is a golden glare and sometimes, on the horizon or during a sandstorm, red as blood. But from here, at 13,000 feet above sea level, the sun is a white star, a white fire fierce as radium, burning in a sky of deeper, darker blue.

Peeling an orange I survey the larger globe below. All around the peaks of the Sierra La Sal lies the desert, a sea of burnt rock, arid tablelands, barren and desolate canyons. The canyon country is revealed from this magnificent height as on a map and I can imagine, if not read, the names on the land. The folk poetry of the pioneers:

Desolation Canyon, Labyrinth Canyon, Stillwater Canyon, Dark Canyon, Happy Canyon, Cohabitation Canyon, Nigger Bill Canyon, Recapture Canyon;

Mollie's Nipple, The Bishop's Prick, Queen Anne's Bottom;

Dirty Devil River, Onion Creek, Last Chance Creek, Salvation Creek, Moonlight Wash, Grand Gulch;

Cigarette Spring, Stinking Spring, Hog Spring, Squaw Spring, Frenchman's Spring, Matrimony Spring, Arsenic Spring;

Woodenshoe Butte, Windowblind Peak, Looking Glass Rock, Lizard Rock, Elephant Hill, Turk's Head, Candlestick Spire, Cleopatra's Chair, Jacob's Ladder, Copper Globe, Black Box;

Waterpocket Fold, Sinbad Valley, Beef Basin, Fable Valley, Ruin Park, Devil's Pocket, Robbers' Roost, Goblin Valley, Soda Springs Basin, Potato Bottom Basin, Cyclone Lane, Buckhorn Flat, Surprise Valley, The Big Draw, Professor Valley, Kodachrome Flats, Calamity Mesa, Upheaval Dome;

Poison Strip, Yellowcat, Hidden Splendor, Happy Jack, Rattlesnake, Mi Vida (all uranium mines);

Ernie's Country, Pete's Mesa, Zeke's Hole, Pappy's Pasture;

Wolf Hole and Poverty Knoll;

Pucker Pass (where the canyon puckers up) and Hooray Pass (hooray we made it);

Tavaputs, Kaiparowits, Toroweap, Owachomo, Hovenweap, Dinnehotso, Hoskinnini, Dot Klish, Betatakin, Keet Seel, Tes-Nos-Pas, Kayenta, Agathla, Tukuhnikivats;

Grand Mesa, Thunder Mesa, Wild Horse Mesa, Horsethief Point, Dead Horse Point, Grandview Point, Land's End;

Capitol Reef, San Rafael Swell, Dandy Crossing (a dandy place to cross the river), Hell's Backbone, Big Rock Candy Mountain, Book Cliffs;

Hondoo Arch, Angel Arch, Druid Arch, Delicate Arch; The Needles, The Standing Rocks, The Maze;

Dugout Ranch, Lonesome Beaver Camp, Paria, Bundyville, Hanksville, Bluff, Mexican Hat, Mexican Water, Bitter Springs, Kanab; Bedrock and Paradox;

Moab (cf. Kings II:iii, *The Holy Bible*).

The wind stops, completely, as I finish my lunch. I strip and lie back in the sun, high on Tukuhnikivats, with nothing between me and the universe but my thoughts. Deliberately I compose my mind, quieting the febrile buzzing of the cells and circuits, and strive to open my consciousness directly, nakedly to the cosmos. Under the influence of cosmic rays I try for cosmic intuitions—and end up earthbound as always, with a vision not of the universal but of a small and mortal particular, unique and disparate . . . her smile, her eyes in firelight, her touch.

Well, let it be. You'll find no deep thinkers at 13,000 feet anyway. The wind comes up again, I get to my feet and dance along the cornice of a snowbank that hangs above the void. Down there in the forest, somewhere, is my camp, my old truck, my fireplace—home. I look for a quick and easy way to return.

The climb up from timberline had taken about two

hours. Looking down at the graceful curve of the thousand-foot snowfield it seems to me that the descent should not require more than five minutes. I put on my clothes, shoulder the rucksack and work down over the rock to the couloir and the upper end of the slide.

It looks too steep. Experimentally I push a slab onto the snow and let it go. It drops away rapidly, picking up speed and throwing a spray of snow into the air, turns on edge and rolls and bounds like a clumsy wheel all the way to the bottom, shattering on the rocks below. A certain length of time passes before I hear the sound of the explosion.

What I need is a braking device. An ice axe now would be the thing; I could squat on my heels and glissade down the snowfield in good form, controlling direction and velocity by dragging the blade in the snow.

I launch a second big stone and watch it go down, sliding then skimming over the hard snow, faster and faster until, like the first, it catches on something, turns on its edge and bounces like a wheel the rest of the way down. I see it now; the point is to stay flat. The pitch of the snowfield is less steep toward the bottom; it should be possible to slow down or stop before smashing into the rocks at the lower edge.

I choose a third flat rock and drag it to the margin of the snowfield. Facing downhill with my heels braced in the snow, I straddle the rock, grasp and elevate its forward edge with both hands (my stick tucked under my arm) and sit down firmly, taking a deep breath.

Nothing happens. My feet are still dug in and seem unwilling to obey my command to rise—instinct more powerful than reason. I urge them again; grudgingly they come up. Look at it this way, fellows—nobody lives forever. The descent begins.

Too late for arguments now and as usual not enough time for panic. We're sledding down the mountain at a sensational clip, accelerating according to formula. I brake my speed with my boot heels as best I can but can't see a thing because of the gush of snow flying in

my face. Halfway down I lose the slab I'm riding and go
on for a piece without it. The rock follows hard upon me,
almost at my neck. I manage to recapture it and climb
partway back on but before I can get comfortable again I
see an outcrop of immovable granite, which I hadn't noticed before, rising in our path. I abandon the slab, roll
to the side, and go skidding past the obstacle by an adequate margin. Things are out of control at this point but
fortunately the snowfield begins to level off. I get my
boots in front of my body, dig in, and coast to a stop a few
feet short of the broken rocks at the bottom of the couloir. As I sit there resting another loose object thunders by
on my left, perhaps the same rock or part of it that I had
started down with. A moment later comes my walking
stick.

Everything seems to be in good shape except my hands,
which are bruised and numb, and the heels and soles of
my boots, which are hanging to the uppers by a few
threads and a couple of bent nails. I hammer them back
together with a stone and continue my descent the hard
way, crawling over the rubble until I reach the scrub
spruce and the fringe of the forest.

The ascent of Tukuhnikivats has taken me half the
day, the descent from summit to timberline less than half
an hour. I have plenty of time before sundown for another
hike. But the boots are in a bad way, soles flapping like
loose tongues at every step, my frozen toes sticking out,
the heels twisted out of line. I limp back to camp to
exchange them for something else.

On the way, in an area where spruce and fir mingle with
quaking aspen, in a cool shady well-watered place, I discover a blue columbine, rarest and loveliest of mountain
flowers. This one is growing alone—perhaps the deer have
eaten the others—there must have been others—and wears
therefore the special beauty of all wild and lonely things.
Silently I dedicate the flower to a girl I know and in
honor both of her and the columbine open my knife and
carve something appropriate in the soft white bark of the
nearest aspen. Fifty years from now my inscription will

still be there, enlarged to twice its present size by the growth of the tree. May the love I feel at this moment for columbine, girl, tree, symbol, grass, mountain, sky and sun also stay, also grow, never die.

Back to camp. My feet are wet and cold. I build a fire and toast my bare feet lightly in the flames until sensation is restored. The glade is quiet except for the whisper of aspen leaves and running water, the air warm in the late afternoon sunlight. There is no wind here, though I can see by the streamers of cloud off the peaks that it is still blowing up above. I put on dry socks and moccasins, and cook my supper: refried pinto beans with chile and a number of eggs, a potato baked in tinfoil. I am very hungry. Tea and cigar for the final course.

The quiet forest. There are few birds in the high woods, less wildlife it seems than down below in the sunbaked desert. Probably because at this altitude the summer is so brief—"much too beautiful to last"—and the winter long.

One bird, however, is singing, if you could call it singing. The song is so laconic and melancholic that it very nearly takes all the joy out of my smoke. I don't know what kind of bird it is, if it is a bird, but the song goes like this, repeated over and over, *lentissimo*:

When I've had enough of this sentiment (there is a bird called the Townsend Solitaire) I get up and walk away, out to the dirt road beyond the old rail fence and up the road to a wide meadow from which I can watch the sun go down over the western world. Mesa, canyon and plateau, the pacific desert lies in whiskey-colored light and lilac dusk, a sea of silence. Clouds edged with fire sail on the clear horizon.

Somebody's goddamned cows, Scobie's perhaps or Mc-Kee's, I can't see the brand, gape at me from the lower side of the meadow. I wave my arm and stick at them and they bolt suddenly for the trees, like deer. I walk among thistles and coarse dying goldenrod (signs of overgrazing) and a kind of sunflower called Five-Nerve Helianthella, knock a few heads off—helping to spread the seed—and ponder the meaning of my solitude. Reaching no conclusions.

Tomorrow morning, *Deo volente*, I plan a walk to the summit of the pass between Tukuhnikivats and Mount Tomaski. There is a little lake not far over the saddle, a tarn really, a mountain pond bordered in marsh marigold and yarrow, with water black and glassy as obsidian. Bottomless? Certainly. There are some old friends living there whom I haven't seen for a long time.

Afterwards . . . back to Moab. Back to the juniper, the red sand, and the fanatic rocks. Into September, the final month.

EPISODES AND VISIONS

Ranger, where is Arches National Monument?
I don't know, mister. But I can tell you where it was.

LABOR DAY. Flux and influx, the final visitation of the season, they come in herds, like buffalo, down from The City. A veil of dust floats above the sneaky snaky old road from here to the highway, drifting gently downwind to settle upon the blades of the yucca, the mustard-yellow rabbitbrush, the petals of the asters and autumn sunflowers, the umbrella-shaped clumps of blooming wild buckwheat.

What can I tell them? Sealed in their metallic shells like molluscs on wheels, how can I pry the people free? The auto as tin can, the park ranger as opener. Look here, I want to say, for godsake folks get out of them there machines, take off those fucking sunglasses and unpeel both eyeballs, look around; throw away those goddamned idiotic cameras! For chrissake folks what is this life if full of care we have no time to stand and stare? eh? Take off your shoes for a while, unzip your fly, piss hearty, dig your toes in the hot sand, feel that raw and rugged earth, split a couple of big toenails, draw blood! Why not? Jesus Christ, lady, roll that window down! You can't see the desert if you can't smell it. Dusty? Of course it's dusty—this is Utah! But it's good dust, good red Utahn dust, rich in iron, rich in irony. Turn that motor off. Get out of that piece of iron and stretch your varicose veins, take off your brassiere and get some hot sun on your old wrinkled dugs! You sir, squinting at the map with your radiator boiling over and your fuel pump vapor-locked, crawl out of that shiny hunk of GM junk and take a walk—yes, leave the old lady and those squawling brats behind for a while, turn your back on them and take a long quiet walk straight into the canyons, get lost for a while, come back when you damn well feel like it, it'll do you and her and them a world of good. Give the kids a break too, let them out of the car, let them go scrambling over the rocks hunting for rattlesnakes and scorpions and anthills—yes sir, let them out, turn them loose; how dare you imprison little children in your goddamned upholstered horseless hearse? Yes sir, yes madam, I entreat you, get out of those motorized wheelchairs, get off your foam rubber backsides, stand up straight like men! like women! like human beings! and walk—walk—WALK upon our sweet and blessed land!

"Where's the Coke machine?"

"Sorry lady, we have no Coke machine out here. Would you like a drink of water?" (She's not sure.)

"Say ranger, that's a godawful road you got in here, when the hell they going to pave it?" (They gather round, listening.)

"The day before I leave." (I say it with a smile, they laugh.)

"Well how the hell do we get out of here?"

"You just got here, sir."

"I know but how do we get out?"

"Same way you came in. It's a dead-end road."

"So we see the same scenery twice?"

"It looks better going out."

"Oh ranger, do you live in that little housetrailer down there?"

"Yes madam, part of the time. Mostly I live out of it."

"Are you married?"

"Not seriously."

"You must get awfully lonesome way out here."

"No, I have good company."

"Your wife?"

"No, myself." (They laugh; they all think I'm kidding.)

"Well what do you do for amusement?"

"Talk with the tourists." (General laughter.)

"Don't you even have a TV?"

"TV? Listen lady . . . if I saw a TV out here I'd get out my cannon and shoot it like I would a mad dog, right in the eye."

"Goodness! Why do you say that?"

"What's the principle of the TV, madam?"

"Goodness, I don't know."

"The vacuum tube, madam. And do you know what happens if you stick your head in a vacuum tube?"

"If you stick your head . . . ?"

"I'll tell you: *you get your brains sucked out.*" (Laughter!)

"Hey ole buddy, how far from here to Lubbock?"

"Where's Lubbock, sir?"

"Texas, ole buddy. Lubbock, Texas."

"Well sir, I don't know exactly how far that is but I'd guess it's not nearly far enough."

"Any dangerous animals out here, ranger?"

"Just tourists." (Laughter; tell the truth, they never believe you.)

"Where you keep these here Arches anyway?"

"What arches? All I see around here are fallen arches."

"Does it ever rain in this country, ranger?"

"I don't know, madam, I've only been here eleven years."

"Well you said yesterday it wasn't going to rain and it did rain."

"Did I? Well, that shows you can't ever trust the weather."

"You work out hear all year round?"

"No sir, just for the summer."

"What do you do in the winter?"

"I rest."

"How much do you get paid for this kind of work?"

"Too much. But I give part of it back April 15th."

And then, after a brief and deadly dull lecture on the geology of the Arches, I send them on to the campgrounds and picnic grounds—"Be sure to let me know if you get lost"—relieved, happy and laughing. It's a great country: you can say whatever you like so long as it is strictly true—nobody will ever take you seriously.

In the evening, about suppertime, feeling somewhat guilty and contrite—for they are, most of them, really good people and not actually as simple-minded as they pretend to encourage me to pretend us all to be—I visit them again around the fires and picnic tables, help them eat their pickles and drink their beer, and make perhaps a trace of contact by revealing that I, too, like most of them, come from that lost village back in the hills, am also exiled, a displaced person, an internal emigrant in this new America of concrete and iron which none of us can quite understand or accept or wholly love. I may also, if I am lucky, find one or two or three with whom I can share a little more—those rumors from the underground where whatever hope we still have must be found.

Among the visitors on this last big weekend are many Moabites and other native Utahns: the Mormons, the Latter-Day Saints. Some of my liberalized friends regard the LDS with disdain; they see in the Church only a bastion of sectarian foolishness and political reaction and in its adherents a voting bloc of Know-Nothings, racially prejudiced, religiously bigoted, opposed alike to the graduated income tax, the United Nations, urban renewal, foreign aid, legislative reapportionment, public welfare, Medicare and even free lunches for schoolchildren—actually or potentially a rabble of John Birchers.

What can you expect, they ask, of a sect which gave Utah a governor like J. Bracken Lee and Eisenhower a secretary of agriculture like Ezra T. Benson? Which denies full church membership to Negroes because they are believed to be the outcast sons of Ham? Whose patron saint was an angel called Moroni? Whose founding father Joseph Smith claimed to have carried about under his arms solid gold tablets which, if they were the size he said they were (no one else ever saw them), would have weighed about half a ton? (Gold a very heavy metal, specific gravity 19.3.) Whose official newspaper *The Deseret News* solemnly proclaims on its masthead "We believe that the Constitution of the United States was Divinely Inspired" but fails to explain why the Almighty changed His mind on the Eighteenth Amendment?

One can grant the accuracy of these charges without conceding that the Mormon religion is any more whimsical on points of doctrine than most other sects—the Baptists, for example, with their insistence on total immersion as a prerequisite to the salvation of the soul: All Christians must be totally immersed. (In what or for how long not being clearly specified.) Or the Jews, with their prepuce-collecting Yahweh, who created light on the first day and several days later, apparently as an afterthought, created the sun: "Six days He labored; on the seventh He was arrested." Or the Roman Catholics, with their dogmatic assertion of the physical Assumption of the Virgin Mary—launching her on a flat trajectory into outer space, like a shot off a shovel, without even a crash helmet or a pressure suit. Or the Hindus, with their sanctified ritual for nasal emunction: only one nostril may be discharged at a time, etc. Or the small-town atheist for that matter, with his Little Blue Books and sneering jokes against ancient and venerable institutions.

Leaving aside the comical aspects of their creed, one can argue that the Mormons in practice achieved a way of life in which there was much to admire, much worth saving. In addition to their pioneering migrations, full of unusual heroism and examples of fortitude (e.g., Brigham Young and his seventeen wives), the Mormons deserve respect for settling the most rugged, difficult as well as spectacular, terrain in the West. What was unusual, however, was their communitarian approach to the problems of settlement in an inhospitable environment. Their emphasis on mutual aid, cooperation and sharing was not unknown among other American communities—and indeed such qualities are vital to survival in a frontier situation—but the Mormons went about it in a far more deliberate, conscious manner, with more successful results. For example, in settling a given area they did not scatter themselves abroad over the landscape in isolated farms and ranches, each man for himself and the devil take the hindmost, but rather built small, rational, beautiful and durable towns in which all could live together, centered about the Church, which served not only as a religious center but also as a social and political focal point for the community (in this respect harking back to the model of New England). Irrigation systems were then built with the cooperative labor of all, the irrigable land divided fairly among the member families, and the back country—canyon and mesa—left open to all who might wish to engage in cattle raising, as well as farming. And nearly all did. (This formed the "open range" until the advent of large-scale fencing and the Taylor Grazing Act closed it off to all but an established few.) Each community, through the Church, also set up what we may call a public welfare service to provide sufficient and generous aid to those brought down by accident, illness, bad luck or other misfortune. In sum, the Mormons built coherent, self-sustaining communities with a vigorous common life in which all could participate, free of any great disparities in wealth, small enough to make each member important. There was even room for the dissenter and nonconformist—every town had a few jack-

Mormons, those who smoked tobacco, drank tea or coffee or hard liquor, and perhaps even joined the Democratic Party.

Subsequently swamped by the new American mode, by industrialism, commercialism, urbanism, rugged and ragged individualism, the old Mormon communities are now disappearing. But in such small towns as Moab, Kanab, Boulder and Escalante we can still see the handsome homes of hand-carved sandstone blocks, the quiet streets lined with irrigation ditches and giant cottonwoods, the gardens and irrigated pastures, the children riding their horses, which remind us on the downhill side of the twentieth century of what life must have been like back in the nineteenth. On its gentle side, that is.

As for the people themselves, at least those whom I have come to know in and around Moab, they are generally very conservative in their political opinions, yes, and old-fashioned in their morality, but despite this or because of it have the usual virtues of country people: are friendly, hospitable, honest, self-reliant and self-confident. Not very interesting, perhaps, but good to know, good to have as friends and neighbors. Capable of taking care of themselves, and with the means to do it, it is not surprising that they question the justice of being taxed by the Federal Government in order to help support the teeming proletariat (literally and etymologically "the re-producers") of cities which to some of these independent people seem as remote and foreign as Calcutta or Cairo.

All of this is now under change, of course, and in the accelerating process of urbanization the Mormons of Utah are already discovering their interdependence with the rest of the nation and with the world. Certainly in Salt Lake City itself there is no lack of intriguing social problems—air pollution, traffic jams, angry adolescents, babies born from sinlock and all the rest of it—and very soon the Latter-Day Saints will be forced to confront directly the symptoms of discontent and desperation with which most Americans are now familiar: from LDS to LSD. Even unto the Land of Moab.

In the meanwhile the desert people persist in some of

their quaint and antiquated ways. Leslie McKee's wife, a sweet and kindly woman and a pillar of the Church, tells me that she has unilaterally *bound* my soul to hers, in accordance with the teaching of her faith, which has provided this unusual technique for the salvation of souls which otherwise would obviously be lost and shoveled into Hell. This *binding* means, if I understand her rightly, that when she goes to Heaven my soul likewise will be dragged along like the tail of a kite, with or without my consent. And suppose she goes to Hell? She assures me that this cannot happen, that she has already been saved and the place reserved—for both of us. But I am not entirely set at ease; something might go wrong. Furthermore she is a generation older than I—what about the time factor? Is my soul to be prematurely and summarily unhoused in its prime, if as seems likely her demise precedes mine by some twenty or thirty years? On this point she is uncomfortably vague. Perhaps it is all a sinister scheme to rid the world of the pagan Gentile without incurring suspicion.

However, it's too late now. Like it or not I am on my way:

> We're marching to Zion,
> To beautiful beautiful Zion,
> We're marching upward to Zion,
> The beautiful city of love.

It does not, after all, sound unpromising. God knows I have little to lose. But . . . let's not hurry. What's the rush?

Fresh snow on Tukuhnikivats and the other high peaks. They gleam like—like alabaster towers—under the noon sun and glow at evening in a soft, subtle shade of rosy pink, like mighty cones of strawberry ice cream. Very attractive. I prefer the desert.

Why? Because—there's something about the desert. Not much of an answer. There are mountain men, there are men of the sea, and there are desert rats. I am a desert rat. But why? And why, in precisely what way, is the desert more alluring, more baffling, more fascinating than either the mountains or the oceans?

The majority of the world's great spirits, from Homer to Melville and Conrad, have felt the call of the sea and responded to its power and mystery, its rhythm, antiquity and apparent changelessness. And the mountains, at least since Rousseau (anticipated by Petrarch) and that great expansion of human consciousness called the Romantic Movement, which opened up for men a whole new world of truth, have been explored and celebrated, strenuously if not adequately, by swarms of poets, novelists, scientists and frost-bitten inarticulate ("because it's there") mountain climbers. The desert, however, has been relatively neglected.

Not entirely, of course. There was T. E. Lawrence who liked the desert because, as he said, "it is clean," and another mad Englishman, C. M. Doughty—*Travels in Arabia Deserta*—who almost never came back. A few Americans have tried to understand the desert: Mary Austin in her book *Land of Little Rain*, John C. Van Dyke in an unjustly forgotten book *The Desert*, Joseph Wood Krutch with *The Voice of the Desert*, the contemporary novelists Paul Bowles and William Eastlake in part of their work (but only in an incidental way), and such obscure figures as the lad Everett Ruess, author of *On Desert Trails*, who disappeared at the age of twenty-six into the canyon country of southern Utah, never to return. This happened back in the late Thirties; his burros were found, part of his gear, but the young man himself, never. For all we know he is still down in there somewhere, living on prickly pear and wild onions, communing with the gods of river, canyon and cliff. Also deserving of mention, in this mere preliminary sketch of a desert bibliography, are the historical studies by Wallace Stegner—*Beyond the 100th Meridian* and *Mormon Country*—and of course the classic *Exploration of the Colorado River and Its Canyons* by Powell.

None of the works I have named attack directly the problem to which I wish to address myself here: what is the peculiar quality or character of the desert that distinguishes it, in spiritual appeal, from other forms of landscape? In trying to isolate this peculiarity, if it exists at all and is not simply an illusion, we must beware of a danger well known to explorers of both the micro- and the macrocosmic—that of confusing the thing observed with the mind of the observer, of constructing not a picture of external reality but simply a mirror of the thinker. Can this danger be avoided without falling into an opposite but related error, that of separating too deeply the observer and the thing observed, subject and object, and again falsifying our view of the world? There is no way out of these difficulties—you might as well try running Cataract Canyon without hitting a rock. Best to launch forth boldly, with or without life jackets, keep your matches dry and pray for the best.

The restless sea, the towering mountains, the silent desert—what do they have in common? and what are the essential differences? Grandeur, color, spaciousness, the power of the ancient and elemental, that which lies beyond the ability of man to wholly grasp or utilize, these qualities all three share. In each there is the sense of something ultimate, with mountains exemplifying the brute force of natural processes, the sea concealing the richness, complexity and fecundity of life beneath a surface of huge monotony, and the desert—what does the desert say?

The desert says nothing. Completely passive, acted upon but never acting, the desert lies there like the bare skeleton of Being, spare, sparse, austere, utterly worthless, inviting not love but contemplation. In its simplicity and order it suggests the classical, except that the desert is a realm beyond the human and in the classicist view only the human is regarded as significant or even recognized as real.

Despite its clarity and simplicity, however, the desert wears at the same time, paradoxically, a veil of mystery. Motionless and silent it evokes in us an elusive hint of something unknown, unknowable, about to be revealed. Since the desert does not act it seems to be waiting—but waiting for what?

In sailing the ocean we reach the other shore and find, as we should have expected, everything much the same on either side. During the voyage we see only the unvarying expanse of heaving green or gray, and an empty sky, and not very much of either—the horizon at sea is only twelve miles away. In other words the journey is the central thing, the expectation of what is to come; the ocean itself is merely a medium of travel. (Only a trip by air or space is more abstract, more synthetic, from the passenger's point of view. When and if our astronauts are actually launched off to the moon or Mars through the cold black and white of space they will, I predict, be expertly drugged beforehand—how else could they endure the coffinlike confinement, the static surroundings, of such a venture?) The most appealing part of the sea, in fact, is its meeting with the land; it is the *seashore* which men love and not the ocean itself. (We are not writing here of the seafarer's trade, or of the underwater world.)

In climbing a mountain, if we persevere, we reach the summit; we get, you might say, to the point. Once on the mountaintop there is nothing to do but come down again; the weather up there is usually too hostile for delay; the situation is not suitable for reflection and meditation. Descending the mountain we enter by degrees into a friendlier, more comfortable, more human environment— forest, rushing streams, sunny meadows—and soon hear the cowbells, see the villages and roads, all that is familiar and reassuring.

The desert is different. Not so hostile as the snowy peaks, nor so broad and bland as the ocean's surface, it lies open —given adequate preparation—to leisurely exploration, to extended periods of habitation. Yet it can hardly be called a humane environment; what little human life there is will be clustered about the oases, natural or man-made. The desert waits outside, desolate and still and strange, unfamiliar and often grotesque in its forms and colors, inhabited by rare, furtive creatures of incredible hardiness and cunning, sparingly colonized by weird mutants from the plant kingdom, most of them as spiny, thorny, stunted and twisted as they are tenacious.

There is something about the desert that the human sensibility cannot assimilate, or has not so far been able to assimilate. Perhaps that is why it has scarcely been approached in poetry or fiction, music or painting; every region of the United States except the arid West has produced distinguished artists or has been represented in works of art which have agreed-upon general significance. Only the hacks rush in where genius hesitates to tread, and the baffling reality is lost behind the dust clouds thrown up by herds of Zane Greys and Louis L'Amours, by the anonymous painters of sugar-sweet landscapes and Roman-Indian portraits that clutter up certain galleries, and by those tough old humorous retired cowladies whose memoirs are so lovingly reprinted by the regional university presses—*No Life for a Lady, No High Adobe, No Time for Tea, No Sin in the Saddle,* etc. Behind the dust, meanwhile, under the vulture-haunted sky, the desert waits—mesa, butte, canyon, reef, sink, escarpment, pinnacle, maze, dry lake, sand dune and barren mountain—untouched by the human mind.

Even after years of intimate contact and search this quality of strangeness in the desert remains undiminished. Transparent and intangible as sunlight, yet always and everywhere present, it lures a man on and on, from the red-walled canyons to the smoke-blue ranges beyond, in a futile but fascinating quest for the great, unimaginable treasure which the desert seems to promise. Once caught by this golden lure you become a prospector for life, condemned, doomed, exalted. One begins to understand why Everett Ruess kept going deeper and deeper into the canyon country, until one day he lost the thread of the labyrinth; why the oldtime prospectors, when they did find the common sort of gold, gambled, drank and whored it away as quickly as possible and returned to the burnt hills and the search. The search for what? They could not have said; neither can I; and would have muttered something about silver, gold, copper—anything as a pretext. And how could they hope to find this treasure which has no name and has never been seen? Hard to say —and yet, when they found it, they could not fail to recognize it. Ask Everett Ruess.

Where is the heart of the desert? I used to think that somewhere in the American Southwest, impossible to say exactly where, all of these wonders which intrigue the spirit would converge upon a climax—and resolution. Perhaps in the vicinity of Weaver's Needle in the Superstition Range; in the Funeral Mountains above Death Valley; in the Smoke Creek Desert of Nevada; among the astonishing monoliths of Monument Valley; in the depths of Grand Canyon; somewhere along the White Rim under Grandview Point; in the heart of the Land of Standing Rocks. Not so. I am convinced now that the desert has no heart, that it presents a riddle which has no answer, and that the riddle itself is an illusion created by some limitation or exaggeration of the displaced human consciousness.

This at least is what I tell myself when I fix my attention on what is rational, sensible and realistic, believing that I have overcome at last that gallant infirmity of the soul called romance—that illness, that disease, the insidious malignancy which must be chopped out of the heart once and for all, ground up, cooked, burnt to ashes . . . consumed. And for so long as I stay away from the desert, keep to the mountains or the sea or the city, it is possible to think myself cured: Not easy: one whiff of juniper smoke, a few careless words, one reckless and foolish poem —*The Wasteland*, for instance—and I become as restive, irritable, brooding and dangerous as a wolf in a cage.

In answer to the original question, then, I find myself in the end returning to the beginning, and can only say, as I said in the first place: There is *something* about the desert. . . . There is something there which the mountains, no matter how grand and beautiful, lack; which the sea, no matter how shining and vast and old, does not have.

Minor points on the same issue: I like horses. There is
no place for horses on the ocean; and in the mountains
you will learn that mules, generally speaking, are more
useful. Also, of course, the people: though rare as radium
you find, if you can find them, a superior breed in the
deserts—consider the Bedouin, the Kazaks and Kurds, the
Mongols, the Apaches, the Kalahari, the Aborigines of
Australia. Mountain people tend to get goiters, become
inbred and degenerate and no one for a long time has lived
in the sea. As for those others, the wretched inhabitants of
city and plain, can we even think of them, to be perfectly
candid, as members of the same race?

Revealing my desert thoughts to a visitor one evening,
I was accused of being against civilization, against science,
against humanity. Naturally I was flattered and at the
same time surprised, hurt, a little shocked. He repeated
the charge. But how, I replied, being myself a member
of humanity (albeit involuntarily, without prior consultation), could I be against humanity without being against
myself, whom I love—though not very much; how can I
be against science, when I gratefully admire, as much as
any man, Thales, Democritus, Aristarchus, Faustus, Para-
celsus, Copernicus, Galileo, Kepler, Newton, Darwin and
Einstein; and finally, how could I be against civilization
when all which I most willingly defend and venerate—
including the love of wilderness—is comprehended by the
term?

We were not communicating very well. All night long
we thrashed the matter out, burning up half a pinyon
pine in the process, transforming its mass into energy,
warmth, light, and toward morning worked out a rough
agreement. With his help I discovered that I was not opposed to mankind but only to man-centeredness, anthropo-
centricity, the opinion that the world exists solely for the
sake of man; not to science, which means simply knowledge, but to science misapplied, to the worship of technique and technology, and to that perversion of science
properly called scientism; and not to civilization but to
culture.

As an example of scientism he suggested the current superstition that science has lengthened the human life-span. One might as well argue that science, meaning technology, has actually reduced the average man's life expectancy to about fifteen minutes—the time it takes an ICBM to cover the distance between the U.S.S.R. and the U.S.A. The superstition, my visitor pointed out, is based on a piece of trickery, statistical sleight-of-hand: e.g., in a primitive culture without modern medical techniques, perhaps half of all the babies born die within the first year of infancy; the remainder survive and live for the normal, usual seventy years; taking the total born and dividing by the number of full-lived survivors, the statistician announces that the average life expectancy at birth for the members of this hypothetical society is thirty-five years. Confusing life expectancy with life-span, the gullible begin to believe that medical science has accomplished a miracle—lengthened human life! And persist in believing it, even though the Old Testament, written more than three thousand years ago, refers to "three score and ten" as being the typical number of years alloted to mortal man. The heroes, naturally, lived far longer, and not in that condition of medicated survival found in a modern hospital where the patient, technically still alive, cannot easily be distinguished from the various machines to which he is connected. But this is now familiar stuff, common knowledge—why kick around a dead horse? Far more interesting is the distinction to be made between civilization and culture.

Culture, we agreed, means the way of life of any given human society considered as a whole. It is an anthropological term referring always to specific, identifiable societies localized in history and place, and includes all aspects of such organizations—their economy, their art, their religion. The U.S.A., for example, is not a civilization but a culture, as is the U.S.S.R., and both are essentially *industrial* cultures, the former in the mode of monopoly capitalism, the latter in the mode of state socialism; if they seem to be competing against each other it is not because they are different but because they are basically so much alike; and the more they compete the more alike they become: MERGING TRAFFIC AHEAD.

Civilization on the other hand, while undoubtedly a product of various historical cultures, and as a category one which overlaps what we label culture, is by no means identical with culture. Cultures can exist with little or no trace of civilizations; and usually do; but civilization while dependent upon culture for its sustenance, as the mind depends upon the body, is a semi-independent entity, precious and fragile, drawn through history by the finest threads of art and idea, a process or series of events without formal structure or clear location in time and space. It is the conscious forefront of evolution, the brotherhood of great souls and the comradeship of intellect, a *corpus mysticum.* The Invisible Republic open to all who wish to participate, a democratic aristocracy based not on power or institutions but on isolated men—Lao-Tse, Chuang-Tse, Guatama, Diogenes, Euripides, Socrates, Jesus, Wat Tyler and Jack Cade, Paine and Jefferson, Blake and Burns and Beethoven, John Brown and Henry Thoreau, Whitman, Tolstoy, Emerson, Mark Twain, Rabelais and Villon, Spinoza, Voltaire, Spartacus, Nietzsche and Thomas Mann, Lucretius and Pope John XXIII, and ten thousand other poets, revolutionaries and independent spirits, both famous and forgotten, alive and dead, whose heroism gives to human life on earth its adventure, glory and significance.

To make the distinction unmistakably clear:

Civilization is the vital force in human history; culture is that inert mass of institutions and organizations which accumulate around and tend to drag down the advance of life;

Civilization is Giordano Bruno facing death by fire; culture is the Cardinal Bellarmino, after ten years of inquisition, sending Bruno to the stake in the Campo di Fiori;

Civilization is Sartre; culture Cocteau;

Civilization is mutual aid and self-defense; culture is the

judge, the lawbook and the forces of Law & Ordure;

Civilization is uprising, insurrection, revolution; culture is the war of state against state, or of machines against people, as in Hungary and Vietnam;

Civilization is tolerance, detachment and humor, or passion, anger, revenge; culture is the entrance examination, the gas chamber, the doctoral dissertation and the electric chair;

Civilization is the Ukrainian peasant Nestor Makhno fighting the Germans, then the Reds, then the Whites, then the Reds again; culture is Stalin and the Fatherland;

Civilization is Jesus turning water into wine; culture is Christ walking on the waves;

Civilization is a youth with a Molotov cocktail in his hand; culture is the Soviet tank or the L.A. cop that guns him down;

Civilization is the wild river; culture, 592,000 tons of cement;

Civilization flows; culture thickens and coagulates, like tired, sick, stifled blood.

In the morning my visitor, whose name I didn't quite catch, crawled into his sack and went to sleep. I had to go to work. I went back to see him in the evening but he was gone, leaving behind only a forged signature in the registration book which wouldn't have fooled anybody—J. Prometheus Birdsong. He won't be back.

But don't get discouraged, comrades—Christ failed too.

Now here comes another clown with a scheme for the utopian national park: Central Park National Park, Disneyland National Park. Look here, he says, what's the matter with you fellows?—let's get cracking with this dump. Your road is bad; pave it. Better yet, build a paved road to every corner of the park; better yet, pave the whole damned place so any damn fool can drive anything anywhere—is this a democracy or ain't it? Next, charge a good stiff admission fee; you can't let people in free; that leads to socialism and regimentation. Next, get rid of all these homely rangers in their Smokey the Bear suits. Hire a crew of pretty girls, call them rangerettes, let them sell the tickets and give the campfire talks. And advertise, for godsake, advertise! How do you expect to get people in here if you don't advertise? Next, these here Arches—light them up. Floodlight them, turn on colored, revolving lights—jazz it up, man, it's dead. Light up the whole place, all night long, get on a 24-hour shift, keep them coming, keep them moving, you got two hundred million people out there waiting to see your product—is this a free country or what the hell is it? Next your campgrounds, you gotta do something about your campgrounds, they're a mess. People can't tell where to park their cars or which spot is whose—you gotta paint lines, numbers, mark out the campsites nice and neat. And they're still building fires on the ground, with wood! Very messy, filthy, wasteful. Set up little grills on stilts, sell charcoal briquettes, better yet hook up with the gas line, install jets and burners. Better yet do away with the campgrounds altogether, they only cause delay and congestion and administrative problems—these people want to see America, they're not going to see it sitting around a goddamned campfire; take their money, give them the show, send them on their way—that's the way to run a business. . . .

I exaggerate. Slightly. Was he real or only a bad dream? Am I awake or sleeping? Will Tuesday never come? No wonder they call it Labor Day.

The holiday is over and a strange sweet stillness, better than any music, soars above the Arches. Gratefully I empty the overflowing garbage cans, read the soggy old newspapers—we believe that the Constitution of the United States has finally expired—collect the scattered beer cans and soda pop cans and burn them, along with the garbage, in the dump. (Hastens oxidation.)

The magpies and jays squawk among the pinyon pines, which are heavy-laden with clusters of light-green, rosin-sticky, fresh, fat cones—we'll have a good crop of pine nuts this year. A variety of asters are blooming along the road and among the dunes; with yellow centers and vivid purple petals, the flowers stand out against their background of rock and coral-red sand with what I can only describe as an existential assertion of life; they are almost audible. Heidegger was wrong, as usual; man is *not* the only living thing that *exists*. He might well have taken a tip from a fellow countryman: *Wovon man nicht spraechen Kann, darueber muss man schweigen.*

Also the chamisa, bright and stinking as rancid butter; and the mule-eared sunflowers, enjoying a great autumnal renascence; and the wild buckwheat, the matchweed, the yellow borage, and on the mountain slopes a league away, the preliminary golden dying of the aspens. Like a fire ignited in the spring, smoldering through the terrible summer, my desert world flares up briefly and brilliantly before the coming of cold and snow, the ashy winter, for the last time this season.

Even the night has changed. Over a late campfire, kept going now for heat as well as liturgical requirements, I see new constellations dominating the sky. Instead of Draco, Lyra, Sagittarius and vast Scorpio, a different group is moving in and taking over:

Cassiopeia, the big "W," symbolizing—what? Who? In the year 1572 a temporary star appeared near this constellation bright enough to be seen in full sunshine, throwing all the Christians of Europe into uproar. With good reason; they had much to be fearful of, the swine. Only seventeen years earlier they had burned alive Bishops Ridley and Latimer at Oxenford; a year later Archbishop Cranmer and 277 other religious leaders were also burned, also in Merrie England; only twelve years earlier they had hanged twelve hundred Huguenots at Amboise; ten years earlier an unrecorded number were massacred at Vassy, followed by more religious wars culminating in the St. Bartholomew's Massacre of August 24, 1572. Something about trans-substantiation, con-substantiation and whether or not infants are damned at birth or not until later. *Gloria in Excelsis Deo.* . . . Now the high priests of nuclear physics dispute about the number of electrons that can rotate on the point of a pin—where will this lead? But their disputes are peaceful; only the bystanders get burned nowadays.

Not far from Cassiopeia is Pegasus, for the Greeks a winged horse, to the Phoenicians the emblem of a ship. According to some astronomers the major stars of this constellation are approaching us at an inconceivable speed. According to other astronomers, however, these same stars are receding from us at an inconceivable speed. Opinions on the matter are revised, exchanged, forgotten and revived with comforting regularity, just as in the other "hard" or exact sciences.

Linked to Pegasus by one star is Andromeda, the chained lady, low in the eastern sky. Within this constellation, visible to the naked eye, is a great nebula, the first to be discovered. Seen through my 7 by 50 binoculars it is a splendid sight—a cloud of glory.

And there is the Water Carrier, the Sea Goat, the Ram, the Whale and last, least and most obscure Musca the Fly, about half-way between Aries and the Pleiades, hard to see, scorned by the astrologers, neglected by all but me, a tiny group so far away that they may be already extinct, dead, extinguished, reminding us only by these last dim signals of their former existence.

So much for the stars. Why, a man could lose his mind in those incomprehensible distances. Is there intelligent life on other worlds? Ask rather, is there intelligent life on earth? There are mysteries enough right here in America, in Utah, in the canyons.

Had a letter today. Bob Waterman is coming from Aspen with his beard, his Land Rover and one hundred and fifty feet of new nylon rope. We are finally going to have a look into The Maze.

TERRA INCOGNITA:
INTO THE MAZE

"Do we really need all that rope?" I ask Waterman, as he proudly and smugly coils his new nylon and stows it into his pack, along with slings, carabiners, brakebars and other hardware. "Who's going to carry it?"

"I'll carry it," he says cheerfully, through a magnificent, sandy beard; "you can carry the water."

But before we can explore The Maze we have to find out how to get to it. There's only one man in Moab who claims to have been there, a garage mechanic named Bundy, so we pay him a visit. Squatting on his heels, he draws us a map in the sand. Gas up at Green River, he says—it'll be your last chance. Take about twenty gallons extra. Go south twenty-five miles toward Hanksville. About a mile past Temple Junction you'll see a little dirt road heading east. Take it. Keep going about thirty-five,

forty miles till you get to an old cabin. That's French
Spring. Better fill your water cans there; might be your
last chance. Then south a few miles toward Land's End
brings you out to the head of Flint Trail. Look it over
careful before you try to go down. If you make it head
north six miles past Elaterite Butte to Big Water Spring
—should be water there, though this time of year you can't
always be certain. Keep bearing north and east. Seven
miles past Big Water Spring you come to The Maze overlook and that's the end of the trail. From there on you
could use wings.

We follow his instructions carefully and they turn out
to be as correct as they are precise. We camp the first
night in the Green River Desert, just a few miles off the
Hanksville road, rise early and head east, into the dawn,
through the desert toward the hidden river. Behind us the
pale fangs of the San Rafael Reef gleam in the early sunlight; above them stands Temple Mountain—uranium
country, poison springs country, headwaters of the Dirty
Devil. Around us the Green River Desert rolls away to the
north, south and east, an absolutely treeless plain, not
even a juniper in sight, nothing but sand, blackbrush,
prickly pear, a few sunflowers. Directly eastward we can
see the blue and hazy La Sal Mountains, only sixty miles
away by line of sight but twice that far by road, with
nothing whatever to suggest the fantastic, complex and
impassable gulf that falls between here and there. The
Colorado River and its tributary the Green, with their
vast canyons and labyrinth of drainages, lie below the
level of the plateau on which we are approaching them,
"under the ledge," as they say in Moab.

The scenery improves as we bounce onward over the
winding, dusty road: reddish sand dunes appear, dense
growths of sunflowers cradled in their leeward crescents.
More and more sunflowers, whole fields of them, acres
and acres of gold—perhaps we should call this the Sunflower Desert. We see a few baldface cows, pass a corral
and windmill, meet a rancher coming out in his pickup
truck. Nobody lives in this area but it is utilized neverthe-

less; the rancher we saw probably has his home in Hanksville or the little town of Green River.

Halfway to the river and the land begins to rise, gradually, much like the approach to Grand Canyon from the south. What we are going to see is comparable, in fact, to the Grand Canyon—I write this with reluctance —in scale and grandeur, though not so clearly stratified or brilliantly colored. As the land rises the vegetation becomes richer, for the desert almost luxuriant: junipers appear, first as isolated individuals and then in stands, pinyon pines loaded with cones and vivid colonies of sunflowers, chamisa, golden beeweed, scarlet penstemon, skyrocket gilia (as we near 7000 feet), purple asters and a kind of yellow flax. Many of the junipers—the females —are covered with showers of light-blue berries, that hard bitter fruit with the flavor of gin. Between the flowered patches and the clumps of trees are meadows thick with gramagrass and shining Indian ricegrass—and not a cow, horse, deer or buffalo anywhere. *For God's sake, Bob,* I'm thinking, *let's stop this machine, get out there and eat some grass!* But he grinds on in singleminded second gear, bound for Land's End, and glory.

Flocks of pinyon jays fly off, sparrows dart before us, a redtailed hawk soars overhead. We climb higher, the land begins to break away: we head a fork of Happy Canyon, pass close to the box head of Millard Canyon. A fork in the road, with one branch old, rocky and seldom used, the other freshly bulldozed through the woods. No signs. We stop, consult our maps, and take the older road; the new one has probably been made by some oil exploration outfit.

Again the road brings us close to the brink of Millard Canyon and here we see something like a little shrine mounted on a post. We stop. The wooden box contains a register book for visitors, brand-new, with less than a dozen entries, put here by the BLM—Bureau of Land Management. "Keep the tourists out," some tourist from Salt Lake City has written. As fellow tourists we heartily agree.

On the French Spring, where we find two steel granaries and the old cabin, open and empty. On the wall inside is a large water-stained photograph in color of a naked woman. The cowboy's agony. We can't find the spring but don't look very hard, since all of our water cans are still full.

We drive south down a neck of the plateau between canyons dropping away, vertically, on either side. Through openings in the dwarf forest of pinyon and juniper we catch glimpses of hazy depths, spires, buttes, orange cliffs. A second fork presents itself in the road and again we take the one to the left, the older one less traveled by, and come all at once to the big jump and the head of the Flint Trail. We stop, get out to reconnoiter.

The Flint Trail is actually a jeep track, switchbacking down a talus slope, the only break in the sheer wall of the plateau for a hundred sinuous miles. Originally a horse trail, it was enlarged to jeep size by the uranium hunters, who found nothing down below worth bringing up in trucks, and abandoned it. Now, after the recent rains, which were also responsible for the amazing growth of grass and flowers we have seen, we find the trail marvelously eroded, stripped of all vestiges of soil, trenched and gullied down to bare rock, in places more like a stairway than a road. Even if we can get the Land Rover down this thing, how can we ever get it back up again?

But it doesn't occur to either of us to back away from the attempt. We are determined to get into The Maze. Waterman has great confidence in his machine; and furthermore, as with anything enormously attractive, we are obsessed only with getting *in*; we can worry later about getting out.

Munching pinyon nuts fresh from the trees nearby, we fill the fuel tank and cache the empty jerrycan, also a full one, in the bushes. Pine nuts are delicious, sweeter than hazelnuts but difficult to eat; you have to crack the shells in your teeth and then, because they are smaller than peanut kernels, you have to separate the meat from the shell with your tongue. If one had to spend a winter in

Frenchy's cabin, let us say, with nothing to eat but pinyon nuts, it is an interesting question whether or not you could eat them fast enough to keep from starving to death. Have to ask the Indians about this.

Glad to get out of the Land Rover and away from the gasoline fumes, I lead the way on foot down the Flint Trail, moving what rocks I can out of the path. Waterman follows with the vehicle in first gear, low range and four-wheel drive, creeping and lurching downward from rock to rock, in and out of the gutters, at a speed too slow to register on the speedometer. The descent is four miles long, in vertical distance about two thousand feet. In places the trail is so narrow that he has to scrape against the inside wall to get through. The curves are banked the wrong way, sliding toward the outer edge, and the turns at the end of each switchback are so tight that we must jockey the Land Rover back and forth to get it around them. But all goes well and in an hour we arrive at the bottom.

Here we pause for a while to rest and to inspect the fragments of low-grade, blackish petrified wood scattered about the base of a butte. To the northeast we can see a little of The Maze, a vermiculate area of pink and white rock beyond and below the ledge we are now on, and on this side of it a number of standing monoliths— Candlestick Spire, Lizard Rock and others unnamed.

Close to the river now, down in the true desert again, the heat begins to come through; we peel off our shirts before going on. Thirteen miles more to the end of the road. We proceed, following the dim tracks through a barren region of slab and sand thinly populated with scattered junipers and the usual scrubby growth of prickly pear, yucca and the alive but lifeless-looking blackbrush. The trail leads up and down hills, in and out of washes and along the spines of ridges, requiring four-wheel drive most of the way.

After what seems like another hour we see ahead the welcome sight of cottonwoods, leaves of green and gold shimmering down in a draw. We take a side track toward them and discover the remains of an ancient corral, old firepits, and a dozen tiny rivulets of water issuing from a thicket of tamarisk and willow on the canyon wall. This should be Big Water Spring. Although we still have plenty of water in the Land Rover we are mighty glad to see it.

In the shade of the big trees, whose leaves tinkle musically, like gold foil, above our heads, we eat lunch and fill our bellies with the cool sweet water, and lie on our backs and sleep and dream. A few flies, the fluttering leaves, the trickle of water give a fine edge and scoring to the deep background of—silence? No—of stillness, peace.

I think of music, and of a musical analogy to what seems to me the unique spirit of desert places. Suppose for example that we can find a certain resemblance between the music of Bach and the sea; the music of Debussy and a forest glade; the music of Beethoven and (of course) great mountains; then who has written of the desert?

Mozart? Hardly the outdoor type, that fellow—much too elegant, symmetrical, formally perfect. Vivaldi, Corelli, Monteverdi?—cathedral interiors only—fluid architecture. Jazz? The best of jazz for all its virtues cannot escape the limitations of its origin: it is *indoor* music, city music, distilled from the melancholy nightclubs and the marijuana smoke of dim, sad, nighttime rooms: a joyless sound, for all its nervous energy.

In the desert I am reminded of something quite different—the bleak, thin-textured work of men like Berg, Schoenberg, Ernst Krenek, Webern and the American, Elliott Carter. Quite by accident, no doubt, although both Schoenberg and Krenek lived part of their lives in the Southwest, their music comes closer than any other I know to representing the apartness, the otherness, the strangeness of the desert. Like certain aspects of this music, the desert is also a-tonal, cruel, clear, inhuman, neither romantic nor classical, motionless and emotionless, at one and the same time—another paradox—both agonized and deeply still.

Like death? Perhaps. And perhaps that is why life nowhere appears so brave, so bright, so full of oracle and miracle as in the desert.

Waterman has another problem. As with Newcomb down in Glen Canyon—what is this thing with beards?—he doesn't want to go back. Or says he doesn't. Doesn't want to go back to Aspen. Where the draft board waits for him, Robert Waterman. It seems that the U.S. Government—what country is that?—has got another war going somewhere, I forget exactly where, on another continent as usual, and they want Waterman to go over there and fight for them. For *IT*, I mean—when did a government ever consist of human beings? And Waterman doesn't want to go, he's afraid he might get killed.

As any true patriot would, I urge him to hide down here under the ledge. Even offer to bring him supplies at regular times, and the news, and anything else he might need. He is tempted—but then remembers his girl. There's a girl back in Denver. I'll bring her too, I tell him. He decides to think it over.

In the meantime we refill the water bag, get back in the Land Rover and drive on. Seven more miles rough as a cob around the crumbling base of Elaterite Butte, some hesitation and backtracking among alternate jeep trails, all of them dead ends, and we finally come out near sundown on the brink of things, nothing beyond but nothingness—a veil, blue with remoteness—and below the edge the northerly portion of The Maze.

We can see deep narrow canyons down in there branching out in all directions, and sandy floors with clumps of trees—oaks? cottonwoods? Dividing one canyon from the next are high thin partitions of nude sandstone, smoothly sculptured and elaborately serpentine, colored in horizontal bands of gray, buff, rose and maroon. The melted ice-cream effect again—Neapolitan ice cream. On top of one of the walls stand four gigantic monoliths, dark red, angular and square-cornered, capped with remnants of the same hard white rock on which we have brought the Land Rover to a stop. Below these monuments and beyond them the innumerable canyons extend into the base of Elaterite Mesa (which underlies Elaterite Butte) and into the south and southeast for as far as we can see. It is like a labyrinth indeed—a labyrinth with the roof removed.

Very interesting. But first things first. Food. We build a little juniper fire and cook our supper. High wind blowing now—drives the sparks from our fire over the rim, into the velvet abyss. We smoke good cheap cigars and watch the colors slowly change and fade upon the canyon walls, the four great monuments, the spires and buttes and mesas beyond.

What shall we name those four unnamed formations standing erect above this end of The Maze? From our vantage point they are the most striking landmarks in the middle ground of the scene before us. We discuss the matter. In a far-fetched way they resemble tombstones, or altars, or chimney stacks, or stone tablets set on end. The waning moon rises in the east, lagging far behind the vanished sun. Altars of the Moon? That sounds grand and dramatic—but then why not Tablets of the Sun, equally so? How about Tombs of Ishtar? Gilgamesh? Vishnu? Shiva the Destroyer?

Why call them anything at all? asks Waterman; why not let them alone? And to that suggestion I instantly agree; of course—why name them? Vanity, vanity, nothing but vanity: the itch for naming things is almost as bad as the itch for possessing things. Let them and leave them alone—they'll survive for a few more thousand years, more or less, without any glorification from us.

But at once another disturbing thought comes to mind: if we don't name them somebody else surely will. Then, says Waterman in effect, let the shame be on their heads. True, I agree, and yet—and yet Rilke said that things don't truly exist until the poet gives them names. Who was Rilke? he asks. Rainer Maria Rilke, I explain, was a German poet who lived off countesses. I thought so, he says; that explains it. Yes, I agree once more, maybe it does; still—we might properly consider the question strictly on its merits. If any, says Waterman. It has some, I insist.

Through naming comes knowing; we grasp an object, mentally, by giving it a name—hension, prehension, apprehension. And thus through language create a whole world, corresponding to the other world out there. Or we trust that it corresponds. Or perhaps, like a German poet, we cease to care, becoming more concerned with the naming than with the things named; the former becomes more real than the latter. And so in the end the world is lost again. No, the world remains—those unique, particular, incorrigibly individual junipers and sandstone monoliths —and it is we who are lost. Again. Round and round, through the endless labyrinth of thought—the maze.

Amazing, says Waterman, going to sleep.

The old moon, like a worn and ancient coin, is still hanging in the west when I awake. All night long the wind has been blowing, haunting my dreams with intimations of disaster, and in the east above the rim and mountains are salmon-colored clouds whipped into long, sleek, fishlike shapes by the wind. Portents: Red skies at morning, sailors take warning. Northeast the sky is vaguely overcast, a pallid gray.

As I start a fire and prepare breakfast the wind stops, suddenly, and the tremendous silence flows back, sealing the canyon country beneath a transparent dome of timelessness. The sun comes up, a resounding fire, the great golden gong of the dawn: Waterman stirs feebly in his bag.

After breakfast we get ready for the descent into The Maze, the first so far as we know since the Indians left seven centuries before—if they were here at all. Once again Waterman checks the beautiful rope, all one hundred and fifty feet of it, and his other climbing equipment, while I divide and pack our rations for the day: raisins, shelled nuts, hard chocolate, cheese, dried beef, oranges and water.

The drop-off over the white rim is too far for our rope but about a mile to the east we find a break in the caprock where we can descend to the dark-red stratum below. We are still nearly a thousand feet above the actual floor of The Maze. We traverse the red ledge in a westerly direction and find some notches through which we can climb down to the bulging, rounded, buff-colored rock of the Cutler formation, principal material of The Maze and of the similar Needles area on the east side of the river.

Here we find ourselves rimmed-up, five hundred feet or so above the canyon floor. After further exploring we find a good spot for a rappel, with a pinyon pine to serve as belay. The only trouble is that it is impossible to see from here whether or not there is a feasible route the rest of the way down. If further descent turns out to be impossible, then whoever goes down the rope first is going to be in a tough situation. The wall at this point is somewhat overhanging, requiring a free rappel of forty to fifty feet—easy enough going down but cruel hard work to get back up. I don't know about Waterman but am certain that I could never climb that far up a rope myself. Of course there are various techniques for doing it but none of them is easy. I invite Waterman to go first, he invites me, and we waste about ten minutes in the Alphonse-Gaston routine.

He loses patience first, as I felt sure he would, gets into a sling, hooks up his carabiners, runs the doubled rope around a brake bar, backs over the edge and slides out of sight. I crawl along a narrow shelf to one side and watch him free himself from the rope and disappear below among the crevices and boulders. Presently he comes back and tells me to come on down, he has found a way clear to the bottom.

So it's my turn to dangle in mid-air. I've never made a free rappel before and am a little nervous about it. As I lean back over the edge I can't help but look down and the sight of Waterman far below looking up at me is frankly kind of sickening.

"What are you waiting for?" he wants to know.

"Are you sure this rope is strong enough?"

"It held me, didn't it?"

"Yes, but I weigh more than you do."

"Well, give it a try anyway."

A very humorous fellow. But there's no honorable way out of this for me. After another minute of equivocation and technical inquiries, I lean back farther, keeping my eyes on the rope, and go down. Nothing to it. Half an hour later we're down on the sandy floor of the canyon and inside The Maze. We've brought the rope with us, of course, and therefore will have to find a different route up to the rim, if there is one. But that problem can be deferred for a while. If necessary we've got enough food for two days.

The air is hot, clear, dry and our canteens nearly empty; we've taken three hours in the descent. The first thing we've got to do is find water. We start walking down the canyon. If we keep going we will reach the Green River, about ten miles away according to our map, just above its confluence with the Colorado. There may, of course, be obstacles; we don't know.

Within half a mile, however, we find cottonwoods and shoals of damp, firm sand on the canyon floor. I dig a hole as big around as my fist and elbow-deep and come to wet gravel; a few more inches and I find water.

There is a stand of wild cane nearby. I cut two stalks, a fat one and a thin one, and punch the pith out of the joints of the bigger one by using the smaller as a ramrod. Happy now, greatly relieved, I recall for Waterman's edification a few appropriate lines from Burns:

> Green grow the rashes, O!
> Green grow the rashes, O!
> The lasses they have cozy bores,
> The widows all have gashes, O!

Now we've got a siphon, two feet long. I offer it to the thirsty Waterman, he sticks it in the hole and drinks heartily. When he is finished I take it, blow out the sand, and also drink. The water is warm, smelly, but potable and quite refreshing. Feeling much better we sit in the shade of the trees and eat some lunch. I cut a few holes at odd intervals in the drinking straw, creating a sort of crude recorder, and play a few tunes in a barbarous scale never heard before this side of the Atlas Mountains. I

stop, Waterman comes back and lies down for a siesta. I
go exploring.

At one place on the canyon wall I find three arches
or natural bridges, one above another, all three spanning
the same drainage chute. Going farther up-canyon I
come to a fork, the first of many branches in the canyon
system. The main or wider canyon turns to the left, revealing vistas of alluvium flats covered with sagebrush,
more cottonwoods, more and more branching canyons
with deep alcoves high in the walls, likely sites for Indian ruins. But I keep to the right, under the rim of the
overlook where we had camped the night before, and scan
the walls for a possible route to the top.

I come after a time to a lovely pool in a basin of sand,
fed by a trickle of water flowing down the canyon's rocky
floor. I drink again, fill my canteen and go on. This canyon, like all the others, forks again and again; I keep to
the right-hand branch each time and finally arrive at a
dead end, a box, with unscalable walls rising three, four,
five hundred feet straight up toward the hot blue sky. I
go back to the pool and take a dip in the water.

Lying on my back on the smooth sandstone beside the
pool I notice a fingerlike ridge that juts into the canyon
from the base of the main wall under the plateau above.
If we can climb the ridge to the maroon bench above the
Cutler, we might be able to traverse laterally to the opening in the white rim through which we had originally
descended. From here it looks as if it might go.

I'm just starting up to investigate the ridge when Waterman appears, tracking me up the canyon floor. He joins
me, we climb the ridge together and discover that it does
indeed go all the way to the red ledge. There are a couple
of tricky pitches with rotten rock and fingerholds of exquisite delicacy but most of the way is easy. We return
to the bottom of The Maze to get out packs and the rope,
and to do a little more exploring, if possible.

It is now late in the afternoon. We don't have much
time left before sundown. Our sleeping bags are up on the
rim in the Land Rover and we have nothing to eat but

nuts and raisins. We decide it best to climb out of The
Maze before dark and save further exploration for tomorrow. We go back to the pool and the base of the
ridge. On the way Waterman points out to me the petroglyph of a snake, which I had missed. The Indians had
been here. But nobody else, so far as we can tell. Nowhere have we seen a trace of the white man or of his
horse or cow—or helicopter. But then we have seen only a
tiny corner of The Maze, maybe no more than one per-
cent of it. The heart of it remains unknown.

We climb the ridge, scale the bluffs, and traverse without difficulty the sloping red bench for a mile to the
east, where we find the notch that leads to the top through
the white rimrock. As we proceed we mark our route with
pointer stones; this will be known hereafter, for a thousand years, as the Abbey-Waterman Trail. Maybe. More
likely the BLM or the Park Service will bypass our trail
with an electrical chair lift for crippled tourists.

We reach the rim a little before sundown and after a
quick supper—for it's cold and windy up here—go early
to bed. Above the Orange Cliffs a dismal sunset of bloody
sun and gray overcast lingers for a long time on the horizon while the wind howls across our prostrate forms all
night long.

In the morning the wind is still blowing, it's much
colder, and the entire sky is dark with storm clouds threat-
ening rain or possibly, judging by the chill in the air, even
snow. It would not be the first time that a blizzard hit
the high plateaus in mid-September. I try to wake up Waterman: snow, I tell him, it's going to snow. He only curls
up tighter in the sack; he doesn't want to go home.

I build a big roaring fire, hang the coffee pot in the
flames, dump a pound of bacon into the skillet and stir
briskly with a fork. The fierce wind fans the fire and
chases sparks, coals, and shreds of juniper bark over the
edge of the cliff, ten feet away. A dried-up tumbleweed
comes over the rise from the north, dances past and sails
into space above The Maze. Ecstasy—and danger: we'll

never get the Land Rover up those switchbacks if it storms. A few drops of rain sprinkle the sandstone at my feet and patter gently on Waterman in his bag. He makes no move. Breakfast, I tell him; let's eat! He comes to life.

As we eat we discuss the situation. We each have another day to spare but no more; I have to return to the Arches, he has to register for the fall term at Colorado University, far over on the eastern slope. If we get caught down in here by the storm it may be a number of days before we can get out. And we don't have much food left. Of course in an emergency we could always descend again into The Maze, hike down the river, build a raft, float fifty miles down to Hite, and hitchhike a ride from there back to civilization, if anyone happened to be going that way. We agree, regretfully, to start back at once.

It takes us only a few minutes to roll up our sacks and pile our gear into the vehicle; a light rain sizzling in the fire encourages our movements. Soon we are grinding back along the trail, four-wheel drive all the way to Big Water Spring through the grand and beautiful desolation of the middle bench country—above the inner canyons, under the ledge—where nothing grows but the sword-bladed yucca, the scattered clumps of blackbrush and occasional stunted junipers. Next time I come this way, I think (and may it be soon!) I'm going to bring a boxful of Christmas tree decorations—silver-blue tinsel, red candles, peppermint canes, silver bells, golden stars and frosted baubles—and I'm going to pick out the loneliest, most forlorn of those little junipers and dress it in splendor, gay and glittering, and leave it there shining in the wilderness for a season or two, until the winds and the sun and the birds strip it bare again.

We reach the foot of the Flint Trail. The storm is building up, the wind colder and harder than ever, but luckily for us the heavy rain has not yet come down. Waterman shifts into low range; I get out and walk along behind to assist on the turns. There is no trouble: getting up proves to be no harder than coming down, through we do find it necessary to add a little water to the radiator when we arrive on top.

7000 feet up now; we put on jackets and hoods as a fine sleet drives down from the sky and turns the dust into mud. While Waterman pours more gasoline into the tank I load my pockets with pinyon nuts—might need them yet. We go on, past the old cabin at French Spring and through the woods and past the flowery meadows now gray beneath a mist of snow and rain. We stop at the BLM shrine to record our visit.

"First descent into The Maze," writes Waterman in the book, though we cannot be absolutely certain of this. And I write, "For God's sake leave this country alone—Abbey." To which Waterman adds "For Abbey's sake leave this country alone—God." The air is thick with a million fluttering snowflakes; we hurry on through the forty miles of desert, reach the paved road without getting stuck and get back in Moab at dark, just in time for cocktails and dinner, while a great storm, first and biggest of the autumn season, blankets the high country with snow from Denver to Salt Lake City.

BEDROCK AND PARADOX

THE TOURISTS have gone home. Most of them. A few still rumble in and ramble around in their sand-pitted dust-choked iron dinosaurs but the great majority, answering a mystical summons, have returned to the smoky jungles and swamps of what we call, in wistful hope, American civilization. I can see them now in all their millions jamming the freeways, glutting the streets, horns bellowing like wounded steers, hunting for a place to park. They have left me alone here in the wilderness, at the center of things, where all that is most significant takes place. (Sunset and moonrise, moaning winds and stillness, cloud transformations, the metamorphosis of sunlight, yellowing leaf and the indolent, soaring vulture. . . .)

Who am I to pity the degradation and misery of my fellow citizens? I, too, must leave the canyon country, if only for a season, and rejoin for the winter that miscegenated mesalliance of human and rodent called the rat race (*Rattus urbanus*). Today is my last day at the Arches; tonight I take a plane for Denver and from there a jet flight to New York. Of course I have my reasons which reason knows nothing about; reason is and ought to be, as Hume said, the slave of the passions. He foresaw the whole thing.

The old pickup truck will stay here. I've already jacked it up on blocks in a friend's backyard, drained the radiator and engine block and covered the hood with a tarp to keep out the rain and dust.

Everything is packed, all my camping gear stored away, even my whiskers shaved off. Bald-faced as a bank clerk, I stood in front of a mirror this morning and tried on my only white shirt, recently starched. Like putting on chain mail. I even knotted a tie around my neck and tightened it in the proper style—adjusting the garrote for fit. A grim business, returning to civilization. But duty calls. Yes, I hate it so much that I'm spending the best part of a paycheck on airplane tickets.

Balance, that's the secret. Moderate extremism. The best of both worlds. Unlike Thoreau who insisted on one world at a time I am attempting to make the best of two. After six months in the desert I am volunteering for a winter of front-line combat duty—caseworker, public warfare department—in the howling streets of Megalomania, U S.A. Mostly for the sake of private and selfish concerns truly, but also for reasons of a more general nature. After twenty-six weeks of sunlight and stars, wind and sky and golden sand, I want to hear once more the crackle of clamshells on the floor of the bar in the Clam Broth House in Hoboken. I long for a view of the jolly, rosy faces on 42nd Street and the cheerful throngs on the sidewalks of Atlantic Avenue. Enough of Land's End, Dead Horse Point, Tukuhnikivats and other high resolves; I want to see somebody jump out of a window or off a roof. I grow weary of nobody's company but my own —let me hear the wit and wisdom of the subway crowds again, the cabdriver's shrewd aphorisms, the genial chuckle of a Jersey City cop, the happy laughter of Greater New York's one million illegitimate children.

If I'm serious, and I am, the desert has driven me crazy. Not that I mind. We get some strange ones out here. Last night for example came a fellow in suspenders and short leather britches who spoke English with a Bavarian accent. A toolmaker in a Porsche on vacation from Munich, he carried a case of Lowenbrau under the hood of his car where the motor should have been. He spotted my campfire burning out back of the housetrailer and invited himself over, along with his beer. I was glad enough to see him. He turned out to be a typical comical Nazi, his feelings still wounded by the fact that the United States had fought against instead of with Hitler; Americans, he said, are very much like Germans and should with them the dirty Russians together fight. Courteously I declined the intended honor of the comparison: not yet, I said, not quite. We argued all night long. I defended the Americans—no one else was available—while he explained to me the positive aspects of anti-Semitism. Thus two monologues converged, near dawn, upon a murder. I could have opened his skull with a bottle of his own Lowenbrau, and was powerfully tempted. Maybe I would have done it, too, but fatigue set in, and besides I didn't have the heart—after all he hadn't seen the Arches yet or even the Grand Canyon. When he finally departed my best wishes went with him: may his fan belt snap, his tires develop blisters, his fuel pump succumb to chronic vapor lock—may he never come back.

October. Rabbitbrush in full bloom. The tumbleweeds on the move (that longing to be elsewhere, elsewhere), thousands of them rolling across the plains before the wind. Something like a yellow rash has broken out upon the mountainsides—the aspen forests in their autumn splendor. Sunsets each evening that test a man's credulity —great gory improvisations in scarlet and gold that remind me of nothing so much as God's own celestial pizza pies. Followed inevitably by the night with its razzle-dazzle of stars in silver, emerald and sapphire blue, the same old routine.

For tonight I prophesy a snowstorm. I feel it in the cold stillness of the air, the strange uncertainty of the sun, the unbroken mass of aluminum-gray clouds that hang all day above the north and east, an enormous lid soon to be shoved into place above the canyons and plateaus. The *immanence* of snow.

In the government truck I make a final tour of the park. East past the Balanced Rock to Double Arch and the Windows; back again and north east to Turnbow Cabin and up the trail to Delicate Arch; back again and northwest beyond the Fiery Furnace into the Devil's Garden, where I walk for the last time this year out the trail past Tunnel Arch, Pine Tree Arch, Landscape Arch, Partition Arch, Navajo Arch, and Wall Arch, all the way out to Double-O Arch at the end of the path. My own, my children, mine by right of possession, possession by right of love, by divine right, I now surrender them all to the winds of winter and the snow and the starving deer and the pinyon jays and the emptiness and the silence unbroken by even a thought.

In deep stillness, in a somber solemn light, these beings stand, these fins of sandstone hollowed out by time, the juniper trees so shaggy, tough and beautiful, the dead or dying pinyon pines, the little shrubs of rabbitbrush and blackbrush, the dried-up stalks of asters and sunflowers gone to seed, the black-rooted silver-blue sage. How difficult to imagine this place without a human presence; how necessary. I am almost prepared to believe that this sweet virginal primitive land will be grateful for my departure and the absence of the tourists, will breathe metaphorically a collective sigh of relief—like a whisper of wind—when we are all and finally gone and the place and its creations can return to their ancient procedures unobserved and undisturbed by the busy, anxious, brooding consciousness of man.

Grateful for our departure? One more expression of human vanity. The finest quality of this stone, these plants and animals, this desert landscape is the indifference manifest to our presence, our absence, our coming, our staying or our going. Whether we live or die is a matter of absolutely no concern whatsoever to the desert. Let men in their madness blast every city on earth into black rubble and envelope the entire planet in a cloud of lethal gas—the canyons and hills, the springs and rocks will still be here, the sunlight will filter through, water will form and warmth shall be upon the land and after sufficient time, no matter how long, somewhere, living things will emerge and join and stand once again, this time perhaps to take a different and better course. I have seen the place called Trinity, in New Mexico, where our wise men exploded the first atomic bomb and the heat of the blast fused sand into a greenish glass—already the grass has returned, and the cactus and the mesquite. On this bedrock of animal faith I take my stand, close by the old road that leads eventually out of the valley of paradox.

Yes. Feet on earth. Knock on wood. Touch stone. Good luck to all.

Throughout the afternoon the mountains are wrapped in a storm of clouds, a furious battleground. Tukuhnikivats has gone under, drowning in wild vapors, and a blue light covers the desert. In coat and hat and scarf and gloves and long underwear, freezing, I linger on my terrace near the ramada, which is now being unroofed branch by branch in the winds, the red flag whipped to shreds, the windbells jangling like a Chinese fire alarm. All of my old cedar posts and juniper logs have gone into one last magnificent bonfire, flaring like a transparent rose on the open rock, my signal to the world—unheeded. No matter, it's all one to me and the red dust of Utah. Five hundred and sixty tumbleweeds roll toward the horizon, herded by the wind; may they, too, never come back. All things are in motion, all is in process, nothing abides, nothing will ever change in this eternal moment. I'll be back before I'm fairly out of sight. Time to go.

The trailerhouse is cleaned out, locked up, water lines

drained, gas disconnected, windows shut tight, power plant under canvas. My own belongings are packed in the truck. The red bandana, the bells? I'll leave them here in place to wave and jingle all through the winter, unseen and unheard, more power to the both of them.

All is ready for departure and I see by my watch I've already put in ten minutes of free overtime for the government. I had hoped to see the mountains in full glory, all covered with fresh snow, before leaving, but it looks as if the storm will last all night. I had wished also to see the red rock of our 33,000-acre garden, the arches and buttes and pinnacles and balanced boulders, all lit up in evening light but the sun too is buried in clouds.

The fire is dying, the sparks scattering over the sand and stone—there is nothing to do but go. Now that all is finally ready I am overtaken by the insane compulsion to be gone, to be elsewhere, to go, to go. Abruptly I cancel plans for a ceremonial farewell to the hoodoo rocks and the lone juniper with its dead claw snagging the wind—I had planned a frivolous music—and turn away and hurry to the truck, get in, slam the door, drive off.

When I reach park headquarters near Moab I telephone the airport and learn that nobody is flying from here to Denver tonight; the storm has ruled out all flights in the area. A new ranger, Bob Ferris, offers to drive me up to the town of Thompson where I can catch a Western & Rio Grande night train to Denver. I accept and following a good dinner by his gracious wife, we load my baggage into his car and drive to the railway, thirty miles north.

No end of blessings from heaven and earth. As we climb up out of the Moab valley and reach the high tableland stretching northward, traces of snow flying across the road, the sun emerges clear of the overcast, burning free on the very edge of the horizon. For a few minutes the whole region from the canyon of the Colorado to the Book Cliffs—crag, mesa, turret, dome, canyon wall, plain, swale and dune—glows with a vivid amber light against the darkness on the east. At the same time I see a mountain peak rising clear of the clouds, old Tukuhnikivats fierce as the Matterhorn, snowy as Everest, invincible.

"Ferris, stop this car. Let's go back."

But he only steps harder on the gas. "No," he says, "you've got a train to catch." He sees me craning my neck to stare backward. "Don't worry," he adds, "it'll all still be here next spring."

The sun goes down, I face the road again, we light up our after-dinner cigars. Keeping the flame alive. The car races forward through a world dissolving into snow and night.

Yes, I agree, that's a good thought and it better be so. Or by God there might be trouble. The desert will still be here in the spring. And then comes another thought. When I return will it be the same? Will I be the same? Will anything ever be quite the same again? If I return.

About the Author

Born and raised on a farm in Pennsylvania, Edward Abbey has lived since 1947 in the Southwest. He is the author of THE MONKEY WRENCH GANG, BLACK SUN, SLICKROCK, APPALACHIA, CACTUS COUNTRY, DESERT SOLITAIRE, FIRE ON THE MOUNTAIN, THE BRAVE COWBOY and other books.